GAY ESSENTIALS

GAY ESSENTIALS
FACTS FOR YOUR QUEER BRAIN

DAVID BIANCO

alyson books
los angeles | new york

MANUFACTURED IN THE UNITED STATES OF AMERICA
COVER DESIGN BY CHRISTOPHER HARRITY

THIS TRADE PAPERBACK ORIGINAL IS PUBLISHED BY ALYSON PUBLICATIONS,
P.O. BOX 4371, LOS ANGELES, CA 90078-4371.
DISTRIBUTION IN THE UNITED KINGDOM BY TURNAROUND PUBLISHER SERVICES LTD.,
UNIT 3 OLYMPIA TRADING ESTATE, COBURG ROAD, WOOD GREEN,
LONDON N22 6TZ ENGLAND

FIRST EDITION: OCTOBER 1999

99 00 01 02 03 **a** 10 9 8 7 6 5 4 3 2 1

ISBN 1-55583-508-2

LIBRARY OF CONGRESS CATALOGING-IN-PUBLICATION DATA
    BIANCO, DAVID, 1970–
       GAY ESSENTIALS : FACTS FOR YOUR QUEER BRAIN / DAVID BIANCO.
       ISBN 1-55583-508-2
       1. HOMOSEXUALITY—HISTORY. 2. GAY MEN—HISTORY. 3. GAYS—HISTORY.
    4. LESBIANS—HISTORY. I. TITLE.
    HQ76.25.B53 1999
    306.76'6'09—DC21   99-36465 CIP

Table of Contents

Introduction

Most people didn't learn much gay and lesbian history in high school and college. Yet for gays and lesbians and people who care about them, knowledge of the gay and lesbian past is indispensable. Understanding the struggles and successes of gays and lesbians in the past can provide role models, serve as a crystal ball, and remind members of an often diffuse and divided group that they are anything but alone.

This book aims to offer glimpses into the gay and lesbian past that shed light on the present and fill in parts of the narrative that most histories of America and the world leave out.

I have not attempted, however, to write a comprehensive history of homosexuality. That is a project that has yet to be done well and will require decades of painstaking work by researchers and archivists before a historian can hope to do a reasonable job of synthesizing it all. Instead, I have selected 101 topics I find interesting and compiled them to create a lively, broad introduction to lesbian and gay history. The choices are admittedly arbitrary, and much has necessarily been left out. I'd like to offer some thoughts as to how I selected the topics that form this book.

Biography has a prominent role in this book. Included here are many of the usual suspects of gay and lesbian history (Sappho, Walt Whitman, Gertrude Stein, Barney Frank). I've also taken pains to include people who play an important role in gay history or serve as examples of broader forces in the history of sexuality who have thus far been largely excluded from the canon of gay and lesbian history (Leopold and Loeb, Janet Flanner, Margaret Mead).

Other subjects discussed herein deal not with individual biographies but with broad trends that have shaped gay and lesbian life. You'll read about the lesbian pulp novels and gay men's physique magazines of the 1950s and how they helped shape the consciousness of a generation of Americans coming to terms with their homosexuality. Many readers will be surprised to discover that contemporary gay phenomena like bathhouses and the word *queer* actually have long histories. And the gay and lesbian slant on such broad historical phenomena as McCarthyism and the Vietnam War are described in detail.

But perhaps my favorite pieces describe episodes from the gay and lesbian past that illustrate the dreams, struggles, and triumphs of gays and lesbians. I've enjoyed researching and writing about the gay men who wanted to "colonize" an entire county in California, the lesbians who commandeered a women's conference wearing LAVENDER MENACE T-shirts, and Karen Thompson's struggle for the right to care for her disabled lover.

Most of the pieces in this book are about gays and lesbians in the United States, but there are important excursions into Canada, Britain, Germany, Cuba, and Japan. A broad cross section of ethnicities, sexual orientations, gender identities, and political persuasions are also represented.

With the exception of about a dozen pieces that break new ground (especially the Alpine County Project, Naiad Press, the history of the pink triangle, and the gay letters to Reagan), very little of this book is based on primary research. Instead, I have relied on the investigation and analysis of dozens of journalists, historians, and other scholars. I hope my writing can make some of what they have discovered and explained more accessible, but interested readers also are encouraged to look at the work of such talented individuals as Allan Bérubé, George Chauncey, John D'Emilio, Martin Duberman, Lillian Faderman,

Jonathan Ned Katz, Elizabeth Kennedy and Madeline Davis, Esther Newton, Vito Russo, and Randy Shilts.

Most of this book initially appeared as part of my syndicated column, *Past Out*, which has appeared in more than 90 gay and lesbian publications in 47 states and four countries since the beginning of 1996. I'd like to thank the many people involved in making the column so successful, including dozens of editors and publishers too numerous to name here.

The Past Out Editorial Board (Aaron Bianco, Carl Bianco, Barbara Bianco, Jeff Bianco, Jen Pollack Bianco, Joann Bianco, Tom Chatt, Andrew Collins, Rabbi Elliott Dorff, Victoria Stagg Elliott, Steve Friess, Howard Goldberg, Bob Goldfarb, Bob Hamilton, Gerard Koskovich, Courtney Lane, Simon LeVay, Steve McCarroll, Martin Meeker, Rich Migliore, Joe Minsky, Craig Rimmerman, Eric Rosenthal, Tom Swift, Robin Wehl, Michael Weingrad, Rodney Wilson, and Hastings Wyman) was instrumental in giving feedback on much of what became this book. I am grateful for their help. Thank you to Professor Aron Rodrigue for guidance during my research on the pink-triangle piece and to Professor George Chauncey for his helpful comments on the "history of queer" piece. Thanks also to the International Gay and Lesbian Archives, the Gay and Lesbian Historical Society of Northern California, the Ronald Reagan Library, and the June Mazer Collection for making their materials accessible to me. And of course, thanks to Scott Brassart and the folks at Alyson for making this book possible.

I'd especially like to thank fellow historian Paula Martinac, who was outstanding and instrumental in helping me prepare a number of the pieces contained here. She has my deepest gratitude.

—David Bianco
DaveBianco@aol.com

1. Who was Sappho?

The very term *lesbian* refers to the most famous resident of the Greek isle of Lesbos: Sappho, who lived in the seventh century before the common era, was a celebrated poet whose sexuality has been the source of controversy for more than two millennia.

It is difficult to speak with much historical certainty about events and personalities that occurred more than 2,500 years ago, especially when written sources are scarce. In the case of Sappho, less than 10% of her poetry has survived, and much of what we have is fragmentary. Nonetheless, Sappho's literary reputation has garnered much attention, and some biographical details are fairly clear.

Sappho was born to an aristocratic family in the town of Eressos on the southwest coast of Lesbos. Her mother was a Lesbian, her father was a Lesbian, and she had three Lesbian brothers. She may have been in charge of a girls' school, and she wrote nine books of lyric poetry. Her poetic genius was such that a few centuries after her death, Plato wrote, "Some say the Muses are nine, but how carelessly! Look at the tenth, Sappho from Lesbos."

Most of the surviving poetic fragments from Sappho's repertoire have come from Greek and Roman authors who quote her—from a few words to several lines—in their own works. In addition, some fragments of papyrus and a shard of pottery with lines from her poetry have been found in Egypt. Because her surviving works are so fragmentary—and because

sung Greek poetry doesn't translate easily into written English—it is difficult to convey the power Sappho's corpus had
over the ancients. Nonetheless, her works continue to fasci-
nate modern readers, especially those interested in her expres-
sions of affection for other women.

The closest we have to a surviving complete Sapphic poem
is her "Hymn to Aphrodite," in which she celebrates her affectionate relationship with the goddess of love. In the song
Aphrodite asks Sappho which woman is currently causing her
heartache and reassures the poet that "if she won't love you,
she soon will."

In another song, Sappho expresses her jealousy for a man
who is able to talk calmly with a beautiful woman. In contrast,
for Sappho:

> the instant I look upon you,
> I cannot anymore speak one word,
> But in silence my tongue is broken,
> a fine fire at once runs under my skin,
> with my eyes I see not one thing,
> my ears buzz,
> Cold sweat covers me,
> trembling seizes my whole body,
> I am more moist than grass;
> I seem to be little short of dying...

Although the lesbian desire in the above fragment is un-
mistakable, many interpreters have argued that the poem actually signifies Sappho's celebration of one of her students'
heterosexual engagements.

The heterosexualization of Sappho has often had comic or

ironic results. In his book *Lesbian Love: Old and New*, published in the United States in 1966, Walter Braun argued, "In fact Sappho was a heterosexual, who in her attitude toward girls under her care can be compared with the attitude Socrates took to the boys he had to educate." Well, sort of.

Many writers have pointed to ancient sources that claim Sappho had a husband named Kerkylas, from the island of Andros. But the Greek word *kerkos* (tail) is common slang for penis, and *andro* means male. Claiming that a prominent woman-loving woman had a husband named, essentially, "Dick from Manville" is at best dubious evidence of her heterosexuality.

While many scholars have tried to interpret away Sappho's erotic attraction for women, others have tried to destroy her work altogether. One reason so few of her poems have survived is that much of her work was burned by Christian zealots in late antiquity.

Despite such persecution, Sappho's work and reputation have had a major influence on modern lesbian identity. Obviously the terms *sapphic* and *lesbian* owe their origin to the Greek poet, but her influence is far greater. Many 20th-century lesbian poets, such as Amy Lowell and May Sarton, refer directly to Sappho in their work. A seminal text in the lesbian-feminist movement of the early 1970s was entitled *Sappho Was a Right-On Woman*. And for the last 25 years, a British organization named Sappho has organized social, political, and literary activities for lesbians.

2. How gay was the Renaissance?

The Renaissance (Western history roughly between 1400 and 1650) was a time of exploration and great artistic endeavor in Europe, marked by a revival of interest in classical civilizations. A closer look at that age suggests that the Renaissance was also an era buzzing with homosexual activity.

Scholars have found considerable evidence of same-sex relations between adult men and between men and boys in Renaissance Europe, and much of this evidence comes from church and court records. Sodomy was both a religious and a criminal offense, subject to severe punishment by church and state. As part of Henry VIII's religious reformation, in 1533 the English government took over from the church the prosecution of "sodomites," making anal intercourse ("buggery") a felony punishable by hanging. Ireland followed suit in 1634. In the mid-16th century, Geneva instituted several gruesome punishments for sodomy, including beheading and drowning. Under a 15th-century Florentine body called Uffiziali di Notte (Officers of the Night), designed to sniff out and prosecute homosexuals, the great artist and inventor Leonardo da Vinci was twice charged with sodomy and twice exonerated for lack of evidence.

Many men of the Renaissance, especially those of the upper class, would probably be called bisexual today. According to custom, noblemen married and procreated to carry on their titles, but they kept young pages and attendants on the side as sexual play things—a model taken from classical times. In the all-male world of the clergy, intergenerational same-sex relations were also common. Two popes, Paul II and Julius II, were both notorious for seducing young men. (The latter was a benefactor of Michelangelo, who is said to have had same-sex attractions, though he doesn't seem to have acted on them.) In the artisan class, homosexual relations often occurred between craftsmen and their apprentices, and historians have also found evidence of sexual relationships between adult working-class men.

The theater was another all-male province; young men and boys played all the female roles. As a consequence, same-sex relations between older and younger actors abounded, and acting became a dishonorable profession. In his play *Poetaster*, Ben Jonson noted the horror a father experienced when he realized his son was going to be an actor: "What? Shall I have my son...an ingle ["boy favorite"] for players?"

In addition, two canonical English playwrights of the Renaissance period, William Shakespeare and Christopher Marlowe, are often claimed today as gay. While there is no evidence to answer the question of whether Shakespeare had sex with men, 126 of his 154 sonnets rhapsodize about the beauty of an unnamed young man and were published only after his death. A number of his plays either had homoerotic content (for example, *Troilus and Cressida*) or employed gender-bending comedy (*Twelfth Night*).

Marlowe, Shakespeare's contemporary, wrote the homoerotic play *Edward II*, in which he sympathetically chronicled the love of King Edward for his favorite, Gaveston. Edward's tragedy was the clash of his need to fulfill his role as king and husband and his powerful love for another man. In his personal life as well as his writings, Marlowe left clues about his sexuality: "All they that love not Tobacco and Boies [are] fooles," he reputedly said.

Same-sex relations between women during the Renaissance are much harder to pin down. Women had few outside social contacts and were dependent on men for economic survival. Also, few women (except nuns) were literate, so women could not document their experiences. In a highly sex-segregated society, it seems likely that intimate attachments between women would have formed, and the lives of some famous women point to this possibility. Queen Christina of Sweden, for example, was romantically attached to one of her ladies-in-waiting and abdicated rather than marry a man. Juana Inès de la Cruz, a Mexican noblewoman, became a nun to get an education and to avoid marriage. As Sor Juana, she reputedly had a passionate friendship with the wife of the viceroy of Mexico.

Some male writers discussed lesbian sex in their work, most likely to titillate other men. In doing so they inadvertently left records that sex between women was not unheard of. The 16th-century writer Pierre de Bourdeille, *Seigneur de Brantôme*, waxed poetic about lovemaking between women, which he labeled "*donna con donna.*" For him as for other men, lesbian sex was merely prelude or preparation for the real thing— male-female intercourse.

The work of one female writer of the Renaissance, Katherine Phillips, has survived. Phillips is sometimes called the English Sappho. Her poems were published posthumously in the 1660s, and over half of them addressed her love for specific women. Phillips called her relationships "innocent" romantic friendships, but the comparison of her love for women with the love of a bridegroom suggests something deeper.

Men and women of the Renaissance cannot be called gay or lesbian by today's definitions. Homosexuality was an act or a behavior, rather than an identity or culture. Still, literary and historical research shows that same-sex relations were an established fact in Europe hundreds of years before the word *homosexual* was coined.

3. When were the first sodomy laws passed in America?

In the United States sodomy is primarily defined as oral or anal sex between two men or two women. More than a third of the states still have sodomy laws on their books, and the Supreme Court upheld those laws in its antigay decision *Bowers* v. *Hardwick* (1986). But the original colonial sodomy laws, passed in the 1600s, had a much broader view of what constituted sodomy.

American sodomy laws derived from the English so-called buggery law, passed by parliament in 1533 in the reign of Henry VIII. Until that year the Catholic Church had been responsible for judging and meting out punishment for sodomy, which was considered a mortal sin. Under the English Reformation, the king declared himself head of the church in England, cutting off the authority of the pope. Buggery (a popular word derived from the French *bougres,* meaning heretical) became a criminal offense punishable in the courts by hanging. Even clergy were subject to criminal prosecution for the offense.

In the so-called New World, the settlement at Jamestown, Va., was founded in 1607 by the London Company as a British military and trading post. During its first years, Jamestown had few clergy members or women, both of which were seen as "civilizing" influences. Though British law was implicitly in force, in May of 1610 the governor of Virginia, Sir Thomas Gates, instituted martial law to keep the young male colonists more firmly in line. Virginia's Articles, Laws, and Orders, Divine, Politique, and Martial covered a long list of both secular and religious infractions punishable by "pain of death": theft, blasphemy, adultery, rape, illegal trade with Indians, and "the detestable sins of Sodomie." (It was plural because it included male-male and male-female anal and oral sex as well as bestiality.) The new code sought to instill a sense of order on what was seen as a wild, unruly group in need of "severe discipline...sharp laws...a hard life, and much labor." Martial law remained in effect for eight years, until more women and families began to arrive from England as settlers.

There were, however, no recorded executions for sodomy until 1624. The first person to be executed in Virginia was Richard Cornish, a ship's captain accused of sexually assaulting his indentured servant, William Cowse. The charge, as chronicled in the minutes of the Virginia court, sounds today like a case of sexual harassment: Cornish wanted to have sex with Cowse, who refused and then was given extra work. On the basis of the testimony of another crew member who overheard Cornish proposition Cowse, Cornish was tried and hanged. Two men who publicly objected to Cornish's execution as unjust received punishments of their own—standing on the pillory and having their ears cut off.

As the number of colonial settlements grew in the 1600s, each instituted its own local code of laws, and each listed sodomy as a capital offense. The New England colonies in particular, which were founded by strict religious separatists, punished sodomy harshly because they considered it a crime against marriage and the family—a charge that echoes in today's debates over homosexuality. But the concept of family was different 300 years ago; the family was, in fact, the major economic unit of production of that agricultural society. Early New Englanders faced brutal, unfamiliar weather conditions, crop failures, starvation, disease, high infant mortality, and common death in childbirth. Procreation was the key to the economic survival of the colonies. In this survivalist atmosphere sodomy—both same-sex and opposite-sex—and masturbation "tended to the frustrating of the ordinance of marriage and the hindering of the generation of mankind," as John Winthrop declared in the 1646 sodomy trial of a man in Guilford, Conn. "Spilling" or "spending" male "seed" in any kind of nonprocreative activity was considered a sinful waste because it put the future of the colonies in jeopardy.

Gay historians have found approximately 20 recorded cases from 1624 to 1740 of sodomy charges being brought against male colonists, four of which resulted in the death penalty. Because lesbian sexual activity didn't involve "seed spilling," it was apparently viewed more leniently. In one case in Plymouth of "lewd behavior...upon a bed" between two women, both women were merely given a warning. Only the New Haven colony authorized death for "filthiness" between women, judging lesbian sex acts as contrary to "the natural use of women"—that is, childbearing. There are, however, no recorded instances of the punishment being carried out.

After the American Revolution separation of church and state became one of the founding principles of the new republic. Punishment for sodomy was gradually reduced to jail time and loss of property. Still, until 1961 all 50 states had some form of sodomy law. Today most of the states with these antiquated laws on their books are in the South. Though rarely enforced, these statutes are used when convenient against lesbians and gay men, especially in child custody cases.

4. Were there any gay heroes in the American Revolution?

For decades American gays and lesbians have researched and publicized evidence of the homosexuality of famous gays and lesbians in the past, including figures from the American Revolution. Just like African-Americans pointing to the role of Crispus Attucks during the Boston Massacre and American Jews glorifying Haym Solomon's contributions to financing the Continental Army, American gays and lesbians have searched for gay heroes in our nation's founding drama. Finding fellow travelers who played a role in the genesis of the country is a way of asserting a community's ownership of part of American history and its continuing right to exist in America. (A similar process takes place within the gay and lesbian community when drag queens or people of color who feel marginalized assert that they were responsible for the Stonewall rebellion.)

Of course, claiming that gays contributed to the American Revolution is quite different from demonstrating that specific famous Revolutionaries had same-sex relationships or identities that we would recognize as gay. Indeed, there is scant evidence of Americans before the late-19th century whose identities embraced same-sex sexuality. Nonetheless, here are three men who have been put forward as gay heroes of the American Revolution:

- Alexander Hamilton. Jonathan Ned Katz's *Gay American History*, published in the bicentennial year of 1976, contains several letters from the future first secretary of the treasury to fellow Revolutionary soldier John Laurens. The letters are filled with passion and innuendo, such as when he ended a 1779 letter with, "I have gratified my feelings, by lengthening out the only kind of intercourse now in my power with my friend."

- Baron Friedrich Von Steuben. Randy Shilts's 1993 book *Conduct Unbecoming* makes a strong case that Von Steuben—a Prussian military hero whom Benjamin Franklin recruited to help train the Continental Army—was gay. Steuben left Europe under accusations of "having taken familiarities with young boys." He arrived at Valley Forge, where he led Continental soldiers in uniform drills and military exercises—and became close friends with both Hamilton and Laurens. He was eventually promoted to division commander right before the war was finally won at Yorktown.

- George Washington. Though his view is accepted by few scholars, in his 1993 article "George Washington's Gay Mess: Was the Father of Our Country a Queen?" University of Massachusetts Professor Charley Shively argued in the affirmative. Shively's assumptions and methods are unconventional; he asserts, "Assume everyone is homosexual until proven otherwise." His article (which was printed without footnotes) nonetheless does a yeoman's job of questioning the assumptions of traditional historians that all famous people are straight unless evidence of repeated same-sex intercourse can be proven beyond a reasonable doubt. Shively's portrait of Washington is one of a prissy queen "who spent hours fussing over his uniform, his hairdo, his sword and other military paraphernalia." He surrounded himself with handsome and brave young soldiers and evinced little interest in women, including his wife Martha, with whom he bore no children.

How much evidence does it take to prove that a George Washington or an Alexander Hamilton was gay? And if they were gay, does it matter? Scholars struggle with questions like these all the time. Certainly, knowing that important people in the past were gay can help boost the self-esteem of gays and lesbians, especially youth. But rather than rewriting "straight" biographies of American heroes to make them "gay" biographies, a more promising project (albeit more ambitious) would be to look at the biographies of all famous Americans of the past with an understanding of the complex nature of human sexuality—and the impotence of labels like *straight* or *gay* as applied to people who never encountered any such categories.

5. Were "passing" women lesbians?

Throughout American history there were a number of women who cross-dressed in order to pass as men in society. Lesbians today usually claim these "passing" women as their dyke foremothers. While it's true that some of these women sought to conceal same-gender relationships, others who passed in the past were probably closer to what we would now call transgendered.

The earliest recorded instance of an American woman passing as a man was during the Revolutionary War. Deborah Sampson was born and raised in Massachusetts and spent her youth working first as a domestic servant and then as a schoolteacher. In 1782, near the end of the American Revolution, Sampson disguised herself as a man and enlisted in the Continental Army under the name Robert Shurtleff. As a soldier in the Massachusetts Regiment, Sampson fought with distinction in several battles and was wounded near Tarrytown, N.Y. While hospitalized, Sampson's secret was discovered, and she was quietly given an honorable discharge on October 25, 1783.

Though her cross-dressing probably started for reasons of employment opportunity and personal freedom, Sampson romanced several women during her passing period, which suggests that she had same-gender erotic desires that her cross-dressing allowed her to act on. Eventually, though, Sampson married a man and had three children. In a biography of Sampson written in 1797, the author emphatically denied popular rumors that Sampson "refuses her husband the rites of the marriage bed."

Other women who sought economic independence by passing were at the same time trying to hide existing relationships with women. In the first years of the 20th century, Cora Anderson, a Native American woman, lived and studied nursing in Chicago with her companion, Mary White. Anderson and White soon discovered the difficulties of trying to support themselves in a society where women earned very little money and had to contend with the sexual demands of their employers. As Anderson later put it, "Steady work in my profession...depended upon the giving of myself."

To avoid sexual harassment Anderson metamorphosed into Ralph Kerwinieo and as a man was able to move around freely and find work easily. The couple began living as Mr. and Mrs. in Cleveland, where Kerwinieo first worked as a hotel bellboy and later in manufacturing jobs, earning enough so that White could stay home. However, Kerwinieo apparently developed a roving eye and after 13 years abandoned White for another woman, Dorothy Klenowski, whom Kerwinieo legally married. For revenge White revealed Kerwinieo's secret to authorities, and Kerwinieo was charged with "disorderly conduct" for impersonating a man. Kerwinieo denied any sexual relations with Klenowski, but the denial was probably out of self-protection, to avoid a morals charge.

About the same time in Oregon, Alberta Lucille Hart was a rare case—a female medical student. In addition to her unorthodox career choice, she also had what she considered a "phobia" about men and sought treatment from a psychologist in Portland. The personal history she related to the doctor (as chronicled in Jonathan Ned Katz's *Gay American History*) sounds to modern readers very much like a young butch lesbian battling her sexual longings. The psychologist, however, perceived Hart's erotic desires and her career aspirations as masculine ambitions that were unnatural to women. Following contemporary ideas about lesbians as a "third sex," the psychologist recommended that Hart have a hysterectomy and pose as a man. Hart took the doctor's advice, even though she had never had the desire to be a man. She lived from the 1920s until 1962 as Dr. Alan Hart, a leading physician in the field of tuberculosis detection. Hart eventually married a woman, and the fact that "all parties to the deal were fully cognizant of all the facts involved," as the psychologist cagily put it, seems to indicate a lesbian relationship.

In another famous case, in 1930s Oklahoma City, musician Dorothy Tipton found herself unable to get a job in the male-dominated world of bands and nightclubs. Wrapping her chest tightly, donning men's clothing, and lowering her voice, Dorothy transformed herself into Billy and immediately got a job with a band. Over the next 30 years, Billy Tipton enjoyed a successful career, becoming the leader of his own band. His female lovers later claimed that they had not known Tipton was biologically female because he never took his clothes off in front of them and he apparently concealed a dildo in his underwear. "The first time we danced," one of his lovers recalled, "I noticed he seemed to have a permanent hard-on." Tipton was probably transgendered, since he identified as a "normal person" (to use his words) and not as a lesbian.

In terms of sexual identity, then, each passing woman was unique and should not automatically be considered lesbian. The reasons for passing were complex, from a desire to fulfill same-sex attractions to an affinity for the accouterments of manhood, such as pants or pipes. However, the one common reason that women passed for men was economic—the inability as women to get the jobs they wanted. "The world is made by man—for man alone," Cora Anderson/Ralph Kerwinieo said in defense of passing. "Do you blame me for wanting to be a man?"

6. Who was Walt Whitman?

Walt Whitman, the preeminent 19th-century American poet, is sometimes called the "good gray poet" because as an older man he sported a flowing white beard and hair. But we might also dub him the "good *gay* poet," since his homoerotic poems were early celebrations of love between men and his intimate relationships were all with men and boys.

Whitman was born in 1819 near Huntington, N.Y., a town on Long Island. His family moved a lot during Whitman's childhood as his father, who was beset by financial problems, tried his hand at everything from farming to construction. Whitman left school at age 11 to help support his family by apprenticing to a newspaper printer.

When he was 17 the mostly self-taught Whitman began a brief career as a teacher, taking several short-term positions in towns around Huntington. Though most sources are vague about why he left teaching four years later, one recent biographer, David Reynolds, found evidence that Whitman may have made advances toward his male students and been driven out of the profession.

Whitman discovered a second, more lasting career in journalism, and in 1838 founded a weekly newspaper, *The Long Islander,* which is still in circulation 160 years later and boasts "Founded by Walt Whitman" on its masthead. For the next few decades, Whitman held editorial positions at seven different newspapers, mostly in New York City but also in New Orleans, and he always wrote as an outspoken advocate of social, economic, and political reform.

But it was his poetry that secured him a place in American history. His first collection, *Leaves of Grass,* was published in 1855 as a slim volume of 90 pages, which he set into type at a Brooklyn print shop. Always a perfectionist, Whitman revised and republished the book eight times during his life. The 1860 edition is the most significant for gay readers because it contains the original "Calamus" cycle of poems, which extol male camaraderie, or "adhesiveness," as Whitman called it. "I believe," he wrote in one of these poems, "the main purport of America is to found a new ideal of manly love...."

While many of the Calamus poems use vague words like "brotherly," "the man I love," and "comrade," it's hard to mistake the meaning behind some of the more erotic ones. In "Loafe With Me Upon the Grass," Whitman reminisced about:

> ...how we once lay, such a transparent summer morning;
>> How you settled your head athwart my hips, and gently turned over upon me...

Other poems are filled with same-sex longing as well, as in "Once I Passed Through a Populous City," written about his sojourn in New Orleans:

> I remember only the man who wandered with me, there for love of me,
>> Day by day and night by night, we were together....

At the time that Whitman wrote these poems, homosexuality as an identity and a sexual orientation did not quite exist. It wasn't until the late 1800s that doctors and psychiatrists became interested in same-sex desire and began to theorize about it as an "inversion" of proper, man-woman desire. What once passed in Whitman's poems as nonsexual, brotherly devotion thus became a sexual abnormality several decades after the poems were written. In subsequent editions of *Leaves of Grass*, Whitman repeatedly changed pronouns from "he" to "she." The "man who wandered with me" in his New Orleans poem became, in a revised version, "a woman I casually met there who detain'd me for love of me." Whitman invented a heterosexual history for himself, complete with six illegitimate children, though there is absolutely no evidence to support his claims.

In fact, the evidence all points to Whitman's intimacy with men and boys. Peter Doyle, a former Confederate soldier whom Whitman met while living and working in Washington, D.C., during and after the Civil War, is perhaps the best known of his "camarados," as he referred to his companions. "Our affection is quite an affair, quite romantic," Whitman wrote home. Forty years later Doyle remembered their chance meeting on a streetcar as love at first sight: "We were familiar at once—I put my hand on his knee—we understood."

In his final years, incapacitated by a stroke, Whitman relied on first a teenage, live-in "special friend," Bill Duckett, and then a personal secretary, Horace Traubel. He held court at his row house in Camden, N.J., greeting such well-known admirers as Oscar Wilde and Edward Carpenter. Though Whitman continued until his death to be evasive about his sexuality, more openly gay poets like Carpenter, who were inspired by Whitman's homoeroticism, had few doubts about the older man's sexual leanings. "Walt Whitman," Carpenter wrote, "was before all a lover of the Male. His thought turned toward men first and foremost, and it is no good disguising that fact."

7. Who was Karl Heinrich Ulrichs?

The currently popular idea that homosexuality is innate and that gay people are therefore entitled to full civil rights didn't get its start with today's search for a "gay gene." More than 130 years ago, Karl Heinrich Ulrichs, a German lawyer and journalist, began searching for the reasons why he felt "different" since childhood. Ulrichs postulated a biological theory of homosexuality and devised a system of classifying individuals who had previously been labeled "sodomites" or "pederasts."

Born near Kirchdorf, Germany, in 1825, Ulrichs knew he was different from other boys at a young age, when he experienced ridicule from his classmates for his effeminacy. He fell in love for the first time at age 10, with a fellow student at the local boys' school. As a teenager, Ulrichs began writing secret love poems to other boys, and he continued to compose passionate poetry for men throughout his life. His first gay sexual experience seems to have occurred when he was 25.

Trained as a lawyer, Ulrichs worked for a number of years as an assistant city attorney in Hanover. An "incident" in 1854, which he never elaborated on but that was probably related to his homosexuality, made him leave public service and take up journalism. Ulrichs wrote widely on topics such as law, politics, and language.

Privately, Ulrichs intellectualized his experience of "difference" for many years. Then the 1862 arrest on a morals charge of a prominent lawyer named Schweitzer outraged Ulrichs and spurred him to put his thoughts into a letter to his sister and other family members—probably the first coming-out letter in history.

Ulrichs told his family about his "feminine spirit," and they encouraged him to try to change. He also outlined for them the system of sexual classification he had formulated from both ancient mythology and the new science of embryology. According to Ulrichs, human embryos had a common "germ" of sexuality; they were physically the same until the 12th week of development. At that time the genitals of some changed and became male, while others stayed the same and were female. A number of those who became physically male, however, remained female in spirit. These individuals were "Urnings" or "Uranians." Ulrichs saw them as the spiritual descendants of the Greek goddess Aphrodite, daughter of Uranus. Those who were "truly male," both physically and spiritually, Ulrichs called "Dionings," the descendants of a second Aphrodite, the child of Zeus and Dione. In this rather crude way, Ulrichs created the categories of homosexual and heterosexual, though he used different terms.

Over the next few years, Ulrichs elaborated on his system in a series of self-published pamphlets collectively titled "Researches on the Riddle of Love Between Men." The first five appeared under the pseudonym Numa Numantius, but the remaining pamphlets bore his own name. Though he eventually devised a name for lesbians ("Urningin"), Ulrichs was primarily concerned with finding an explanation for male (i.e., his own) same-sex desires. As he wrote to his family, "To justify myself, and to do it completely, is now nothing less than my life's work."

Since Urnings were born, not made, Ulrichs considered it cruel and unfair to prosecute them. He submitted a resolution to the Congress of German Jurists in the hope of changing existing laws against Urnings. But the Congress never responded, and Ulrichs raised money from fellow Urnings to attend the jurists' annual conference in Munich and present his statement. On August 29, 1867, in front of 500 lawyers, Ulrichs called for equality under the law for Urnings. His statement met with cries of "Stop! Stop!" until the commotion forced him to step from the podium before finishing. Since his interest in Urnings was deemed a sure sign that he was one himself, Ulrichs's speech was both a historic coming out and the first public endorsement of homosexual rights.

Ulrichs's writings brought him into contact with many other Urnings, and he expressed his intention to form an "Urning union." But the plan fell through when he became disillusioned about legal reform in Germany and emigrated to Italy in 1870. His ideas, however, had enormous influence on others and fostered the development of a range of scientific theories about and names for those with same-sex desires. In May, 1868, Károly Mária Kertbeny, a doctor, coined the terms *homosexual* and *heterosexual.* In two pamphlets published the following year, Kertbeny, who was heterosexual, supported Ulrichs's position that the state should not meddle in consensual sexual behavior.

Sadly and ironically, Ulrichs's ideas were misused by other scientists. In 1886 neurologist Richard von Krafft-Ebing, to whom Ulrichs had sent his pamphlets in hope of finding a supporter, published his theory of homosexual psychopathy—that homosexuals were born mentally ill but could be "cured." This idea persisted in psychiatry until the 1970s and is still believed by some religious conservatives.

On a brighter note Ulrichs's writings also sparked the gay rights movement in Germany. In 1897 two years after Ulrichs's death, Magnus Hirschfeld, who had read Ulrichs's work, founded the first gay rights organization in the world. The following year he published a collection of Ulrichs's pamphlets. Ulrichs's revolutionary idea that "there is no such thing as an unnatural love" lives on today in the modern gay rights movement.

8. How did San Francisco become so gay?

Americans who know little else about homosexuality know that San Francisco has a lot of gays; one ice-cream shop in the Midwest sells a shake called "the San Francisco"—it's filled with fruits. Some of this reputation is overblown; San Francisco has plenty of straight people, of course. But the political power and unusual visibility of San Francisco's gay and lesbian community is no myth and deserves explanation.

The Gold Rush of the late 1840s and 1850s turned a small town into an important city, and most of the newcomers to San Francisco were single men seeking their fortunes. These men lived together, drank together—even danced together. While the gender imbalance was not permanent, some variation of an all-male social world has existed in San Francisco since the mid-19th century. We also have evidence of lesbian prostitutes and women who passed as men in this period.

By the 20th century the city had gained enough of a reputation for homosexuality and other vices that the massive 1906 earthquake was blamed by many ministers on the moral excesses of what they called "Sodom by the Sea." This reputation, however, was not due to an open, politically active gay and lesbian community; rather, gay life in early 20th-century San Francisco consisted mostly of private parties, furtive encounters, and discreet relationships.

The Second World War represented a sea change in San Francisco's gay and lesbian life. Most Pacific-bound sailors and soldiers came through San Francisco, many of them eager to sow their wild oats before risking their lives against Japan. Opportunities abounded, from prostitutes to girlie bars. For soldiers seeking same-sex company, there were a growing number of bars and lounges—the Black Cat, the Silver Dollar, the Subway—in which they could meet civilians who might offer a place to spend the night.

During and after the war, the military discharged thousands of gay men and lesbians, often sending humiliated soldiers and sailors back to the mainland through San Francisco. Many of these personnel were too ashamed or uncomfortable to face their families and hometowns with a "blue" (antigay) discharge, so they stayed in the port city, which often held fond memories of pre-war flings.

In the postwar period San Francisco saw an increase in both gay bars and gay bards as beat poets such as Allen Ginsberg drew attention to the relative florescence of gay life in San Francisco. Equally significant was the founding of social and political organizations. In 1953 the Mattachine Society came to San Francisco, followed two years later by the founding chapter of the Daughters of Bilitis, America's first lesbian social and political organization. Many of those organizing for social change were veterans who had been forced to view their sexuality as political by their discharge from the military. By 1960 San Francisco was one of three major nodes of gay and lesbian organizing, along with New York and Los Angeles.

In the 1960s San Francisco saw events that were unthinkable elsewhere, from a drag queen running for city supervisor in 1961 to a gay dance sponsored by heterosexual ministers in 1964. By the end of the decade, San Francisco's Haight-Ashbury had become the center of the hippie movement, and homosexuality was but one of many deviations in an atmosphere of free love.

Gay and lesbian immigration to San Francisco heavily accelerated in the 1970s, providing neighborhoods such as the Castro and Noe Valley with heavy concentrations of gay men and lesbians. The gay community's political strength could be seen in the election of Harvey Milk as a city supervisor in 1977 and a widely praised coordinated public response to the AIDS crisis beginning in the early 1980s. Today San Francisco continues to be a pioneer: Three of the city supervisors are openly gay or lesbian, and San Francisco City College is the only place in the country where a college student can major in gay and lesbian studies.

9. Was Susan B. Anthony a lesbian?

Susan B. Anthony, the most famous American feminist, never married, dedicated her life to women's causes, surrounded herself with female friends, and had an intense romantic friendship with Anna Dickinson, one of her colleagues. In the first decade of the 20th century, Anthony died holding the hand of Anna Howard Shaw, another unmarried feminist, who lived for many years with Anthony's niece. Whether Anthony was a sexless career woman or as queer as a $1 coin is a question that has confounded lesbian and gay historians.

Mainstream historians have amply chronicled the facts of Anthony's life. She was born in western Massachusetts in 1820 and moved as a young child with her family to upstate New York. Her Quaker parents instilled in her their beliefs in peace, social justice, and equality for all. Like many Quakers, Anthony's father and brothers were active in the antislavery movement. Her father owned a series of cotton mills and always refused to purchase cotton from slave plantations.

Anthony's parents also believed in education for their daughters at a time when few girls learned to read or write. Anthony attended a Quaker academy in Philadelphia but had to leave when the Panic of 1837 bankrupted her father. She returned home and at age 17 became a teacher to help support the family.

She began her activist career in the 1840s, when she started volunteering her time for the Daughters of Temperance, trying to bring public attention to the effects of male drunkenness on women and children. Though she was interested in feminism, Anthony did not attend the famous women's rights convention in Seneca Falls, N.Y., in 1848. It wasn't until a few years later, when she read a newspaper account of a fiery speech by suffragist Lucy Stone, that Anthony began to make the transition from temperance work to women's rights. Without the vote, she realized, women would never be able to influence public policy on other important issues, such as temperance and abolition.

For the next 50 years, Anthony worked tirelessly for the women's rights movement, crisscrossing the country on speaking engagements and appearing before Congress every year from 1869 to 1906 to lobby for a woman suffrage amendment. In addition to public speaking, she wrote extensively on women's rights and published a feminist newspaper called *The Revolution* with Elizabeth Cady Stanton. She and Stanton also coauthored a multivolume work, *History of Woman Suffrage*, which they self-published in installments from 1881 to 1902.

Perhaps Anthony's finest hour came in 1872 in a protest that queer activists a century later might call a "zap." Attempting to test the Fourteenth Amendment, which gave suffrage to black men but not to women, Anthony, three of her sisters, and several supporters marched to the polls in Rochester, N.Y., and demanded ballots. They were successful (Anthony cast her vote for a straight Republican ticket), but two weeks later Anthony was arrested and forced to stand trial. The court found her guilty and imposed a $100 fine—a huge sum in those days, not much less than a woman's annual teaching salary.

Anthony died 14 years before women achieved the vote. Ridiculed in her own time, she is today recognized as an important historical figure. A statue of her and other feminist pioneers was recently moved from the basement of the U.S. Capitol to the rotunda, and she is the only woman to have her image on a U.S. coin (despite its unpopularity and eventual replacement with the Sacajawea dollar). But while mainstream historians have extolled her political contributions, they have generally ignored her personal life, assuming that she had none because she never married. Queer historians, however, have uncovered the romantic friendships of Anthony and other feminists and speculated on these women as protolesbians.

Gay historian Jonathan Ned Katz studied Anthony's unpublished letters to Anna Dickinson, a feminist orator. "My dear Chicky Dicky Darling," Anthony wrote to Dickinson in 1868. "Now when are you coming to New York.... I have plain quarters—at 44 Bond Street—double bed—and big enough to take you in...." In another letter Anthony encouraged Dickinson "not to marry a man" and spoke of wanting to hold her in her arms again. Were Anthony's intimate words merely the way women addressed each other at the time, or are they clues to her sexuality? Some queer historians warn against reading letters like these with 20th-century eyes, while others maintain that any woman who makes a life with other women was a lesbian. There are lively arguments on both sides.

We'll never know what Susan and "Dicky" did in their big double bed. What is clear is that Anthony's ties with her many female friends and companions were central to her emotional life—much as they would be for a lesbian today. She was an independent woman who eschewed marriage and children, sought out and treasured the company of women, and devoted herself to pursuing a feminist social revolution. And that's about as "queer" as a 19th-century woman could get.

10. Who were the "berdaches"?

Beginning in the early 16th century, the Spanish and French explorers who arrived in North America in search of land and wealth came into contact with many Native American societies that had existed for thousands of years. Among those whom the explorers encountered were transgendered "men-women" they called "berdaches," a French term meaning "kept boys" or male prostitutes.

Approximately 130 Native American tribes included some form of berdache, and each tribal language had a specific word for biological men who cross-dressed, lived as women, and often partnered with men. The Sioux, for example, called such individuals *wintkes*, while the Chippewa knew them as *agokwas*. Among the Zunis, the term used was *lhamanas*. Most berdaches were found among tribes living west of the Mississippi River, though they were also present among Northeastern and Southern tribes.

Epitomizing the European view of berdaches, one Spanish explorer described them as "impotent, effeminate men...[who] go about dressed as women, and do women's tasks." But within Native cultures, berdaches played a much more important role, often performing sacred, shamanic functions and occupying places of honor within the various tribes. Among the Navaho, for example, berdaches had special ceremonial duties, such as preparing the food for sacred gatherings. The Sioux *wintkes* chose sacred names for the tribe's male children. "If a *wintke* [was] in a family," one Sioux told ethnographer Walter

Williams, "that family would feel fortunate." Some tribes revered the berdaches as healers, while others sought their advice as matchmakers. Berdaches might also be storytellers, the keepers of tribal lore.

Individuals tended to become berdaches instead of being born into the role. They were not necessarily slight or "feminine" in appearance but were often strong and powerfully built, capable of assuming the most rigorous of women's chores. Usually, boys of about 10 were allowed to choose berdache status if they found themselves inclined toward women's tasks, like weaving and cooking. Their childhood choice, it seems, was made for life. "On reaching puberty, their decision is final," wrote anthropologist Mathilda Coxe Stevenson in her 1896 study of the Zunis.

Tribal members referred to berdaches as "she," which led many of the white Americans who met them to believe they were either biological women or hermaphrodites. Stevenson hosted the visit of We'wha, a Zuni *lhamana*, to Washington, D.C., during a six-month period in 1886, and We'wha was universally treated as a woman. One reporter, however, cast some doubt on the Zuni's gender. We'wha, the *Evening Star* said, was no Pocahontas or Minnehaha, but an individual whose "features...especially her mouth, are rather large; her figure and carriage rather masculine." Despite the disappointment some felt that the *lhamana* wasn't a dainty Indian princess, We'wha was the hit of the capital. The Zuni man-woman gave demonstrations of tribal weaving at the Smithsonian and charmed both President Grover Cleveland and Speaker of the House John G. Carlisle when introduced to them.

But were the berdaches gay? At least in sexual behavior, they seemed to be. Early European explorers wrote with horror of the "lewdness and unnatural acts" of the berdaches. As Mathilda Coxe Stevenson somewhat cryptically wrote, "There is a side to the lives of these men which must remain untold." She further noted that "they never marry women, and it is understood that they seldom have any relations with them." In fact, berdaches were almost always the sexual partners of nonberdache men. In this way they seem like the forerunners of the "fairies" of early 20th-century American cultures, who coupled with traditionally masculine, "nonfairy" men.

In about 30 tribes there were also female berdaches, who dressed as men and acted as hunters and warriors. They too exhibited same-gender sexual behavior and were expected as adults to pair off with other women. The female berdache most often written about was Qanqon, a member of the Kutenai tribe, who lived in the very early 1800s. Accompanied by her wife, Qanqon worked as a guide and interpreter in the Pacific Northwest until falling victim to a Blackfoot attack in 1837. In the mid-19th century, Sahaykwisa, another female berdache (*hwame*) from the Mohave tribe, likewise had several female partners, whom she supported by hunting, farming, and occasionally prostituting herself to white men. Mohave legend has it that after being brutally raped by one woman's jealous husband, Sahaykwisa stopped courting women.

Just as Europeans brought disease and alcoholism to Native American tribes, they also disseminated their negative ideas about the berdaches. In the late 1800s, sequestered on reservations and influenced by Christian missionaries, many Native Americans began to view the berdaches as deviants and no longer as sacred people. By the mid-20th century there were few berdaches left among Native tribes, and homosexuality was considered a white European phenomenon. In the 1970s and 1980s, though, the gay Indian movement sought to restore the berdaches (now commonly called "two-spirits") to their former place of distinction in Native American cultures.

11. Who was Katharine Lee Bates?

For many people in the United States, the song "America the Beautiful" captures the spirit of the country even better than the national anthem. It certainly is a lot easier to sing. On top of that, the lyrics were written by Katharine Lee Bates, a Wellesley College professor who lived for 25 years as "one soul together" with another woman.

Born in Falmouth, Mass., in 1859, Bates was a precocious child who at the age of 9 already had strong likes and dislikes. "I like women better than men," the young girl wrote in her diary. "I like fat women better than lean ones." She also showed her early feminist proclivities: "Sewing is always expected of girls. Why not boys?"

After graduating from Wellesley College in 1885, Bates was invited to stay on and teach English. Pursuing a teaching career was one way that young, middle-class women at that time could become economically independent and remain unmarried if they so chose. In fact, Susan B. Anthony called the last years of the 19th century "the epoch of the single woman" because so many educated women opted not to marry men and instead partnered off with other women in romantic friendships.

In 1887 Bates met another young faculty member, Katharine Coman, who taught history and political economy and later founded the college's economics department. Their friendship grew slowly; it wasn't until 1890 that the two women considered themselves (and were considered by others) to be bound together in an intimate relationship. Their circle of friends included other female academic couples who lived together in "Wellesley marriages."

Because the salary for a female professor was only $400 a year, "with board and washing," Bates and Coman supplemented their incomes by writing books and articles, giving guest lectures, and accepting summer teaching gigs. Throughout their relationship, work often kept the two apart. Bates's travels sometimes took her abroad—once to Spain, where she wrote to Coman, "Such a rainy, sorrowful day. I want you very much." On a research stint at Oxford University, she reminisced about an afternoon they'd shared when "there were two hands in one pocket."

In 1893 Bates took a summer teaching job at Colorado College in Colorado Springs. One day she and some colleagues decided to scale the 14,000 feet of Pike's Peak. "We hired a prairie wagon," Bates recalled later. "Near the top we had to leave the wagon and go the rest of the way on mules. I was very tired. But when I saw the view, I felt great joy. All the wonder of America seemed displayed there, with the sea-like expanse." The opening lines of a poem, celebrating "spacious skies" and "purple mountain majesties," formed in her mind. That evening, Bates completed in one sitting the poem she titled "America the Beautiful."

At first Bates didn't consider the poem good enough for publication, and she waited two years before submitting it to a journal called *The Congregationalist*. When published on July 4, 1895, "America the Beautiful" became instantly popular, and shortly thereafter it was set to a piece of music by composer Samuel Ward. Over the years there were several attempts to adopt the song as the national anthem, but "The Star-Spangled Banner," a much older tune, won out in 1931.

The song lyrics provided Bates with a steady income for the rest of her life. In 1907 she had a house for herself and Coman custom-built near the Wellesley campus. On the third floor was a large, open study in which Coman wrote. Though less well-known than her partner, Coman was a prolific writer who authored six books and numerous articles on American history and economics. Also a social activist, Coman helped to found Denison House, a settlement house in Boston that is still in operation.

In 1912 Coman underwent surgery for a lump in her breast. Another operation soon followed, forcing her to retire from teaching. Bates installed an elevator in their home so her partner could negotiate the house's three floors and continue to live as normally as possible. But in 1915 Coman died at the age of 57.

Overwhelmed with grief, Bates immediately began writing a collection of poems for the woman she had nicknamed "Joy of Life." Published in 1922 in a limited edition of 750 copies, *Yellow Clover: A Book of Remembrance* took its name from the small flowers the two women pressed into the letters they wrote to each other during their travels. The poems were a testament to the deep love Bates felt for Coman:

> My love, my love, if you could come once more
> From your high place,
> I would not question you for heavenly lore,
> But, silent, take the comfort of your face.

Bates authored many other volumes of poetry as well as academic treatises on Shakespearean drama and several children's books, including a popular one about her and Coman's dog. She taught at Wellesley until 1920, when she retired to write poetry full time. Without Coman, though, she told a friend that she was "sometimes not quite sure whether I'm alive or not." She died in 1929 at age 70.

12. What was the Scientific-Humanitarian Committee?

The Scientific-Humanitarian Committee, which pushed for gay and lesbian rights in Germany and around the world during its 35-year existence, was founded in Berlin by the Jewish physician and researcher Magnus Hirschfeld, a leading scholar on sexual matters.

As implied by its name and its motto, "Justice through science," the Scientific-Humanitarian Committee believed that gays could convince the government to end discrimination and harassment by using scientific and medical evidence. The same approach is still being used today, but Hirschfeld's science was somewhat different from that of Alfred Kinsey or Simon LeVay.

Influenced by the writings of Karl Heinrich Ulrichs, Hirschfeld believed that gays and lesbians were neither male nor female but formed an "intermediate sex" that had physical and mental characteristics drawn from the other two sexes. He studied the bodies and minds of people who were attracted to the same sex and concluded that they formed a third sex, perhaps influenced by hormonal imbalances. Since to be an "intermediate type" was neither a matter of choice nor morality—and indeed was an expression of nature—all laws penalizing same-sex relations had to be stricken from the books.

The law Hirschfeld found most noxious was Paragraph 175 of the German penal code, adopted in 1871 when Germany unified. The law promised jail for any male who participates in "criminally indecent activities" with another male. The vast majority of the Scientific-Humanitarian Committee's political work was devoted to repealing Paragraph 175.

Unlike today, the German gay and lesbian pioneers did not hold marches or parades. They lobbied legislators, published journals and magazines, and counseled gays and lesbians dealing with issues of discrimination and coming out. But the focus of their work was on circulating a petition opposing Paragraph 175. The Scientific-Humanitarian Committee solicited the signatures of prominent politicians, artists, writers, scientists, and doctors to be added to a statement that described the offending law as "contrary to progressive scientific knowledge."

The committee enjoyed tremendous success in securing the signatures of Germany's elite for the petition. Albert Einstein, Herman Hesse, Martin Buber, and Käthe Kollwitz all signed. The leader of Germany's prominent Social-Democratic Party spoke in front of the Reichstag in 1898, saying that the presence of gays "is so great and reaches so deeply into all social circles...that if the police did what they were supposed to, the Prussian state would immediately be obliged to build two new penitentiaries just to handle the number of violations against Paragraph 175 committed within the confines of Berlin alone."

The Scientific-Humanitarian Committee, which was male-dominated but did include a number of lesbians, had a tenuous relationship with the German women's movement. Many of the women's groups at the time supported women's rights within traditional families and saw homosexuality as a threat. Other German feminists, however, saw a link between women's rights and repeal of Paragraph 175, especially when in 1910 a government agency proposed extending the law for the first time to apply to sexual acts between women.

After 25 years of circulation, in 1922 the signed petition of nearly 6,000 prominent Germans was presented to the Reichstag. Seven years later a Reichstag committee narrowly approved repeal, and the Reichstag as a whole was expected to follow suit. However, the stock market crash and the Great Depression soon turned Germany's focus to other matters, and the law remained on the books.

But the Scientific-Humanitarian Committee found success in other fields of endeavor. It published dozens of informational pamphlets and articles and arranged for presentations before a variety of organizations, especially trade unions. Also, its members sponsored a film in 1919, *Anders als die Andern* (Different From the Others), that was the first film to address gay subjects. Hirschfeld appeared in the film in a bit part. That same year, the Scientific-Humanitarian Committee moved its offices to the Institute for Sexual Science, housed in a Berlin mansion purchased by Hirschfeld, where the Committee offered legal services to men arrested for violating paragraph 175.

With the rise of Nazism, the Scientific-Humanitarian Committee faced its ultimate challenge. Several meetings were broken up by Nazi thugs in the 1920s, including a meeting in Vienna where a gunman opened fire, wounding several audience members. When the Nazis seized power in 1933, Hirschfeld and his research were one of the new regime's first targets. The Institute for Sexual Science was sacked, and much of the contents of its library publicly burned, along with a bust of Hirschfeld. The Scientific-Humanitarian Committee shut down, as did most non-Nazi organizations in the first year of Adolf Hitler's reign. From exile in France, Hirschfeld watched newsreel footage of the destruction of his life's work and remarked that it was like watching his own funeral. He died two years later.

13. What were Oscar Wilde's trials about?

In the space of a few years in the 1890s, Oscar Wilde went from being Great Britain's most famous playwright to being its most famous convict. With the loss of his family, his money, and his freedom, Wilde's life turned into a drama all its own.

Wilde was born in Dublin in 1854 to an aristocratic family. His mother was a poet whose flamboyant personality and dress greatly influenced her son. Even in adolescence, young Oscar preferred scarlet and lilac shirts. At Oxford his taste and wit stood out as much as his aptitude as a student. "I find it harder and harder every day to live up to my blue china," Wilde observed about the elegant furnishings he chose for his room at Oxford, and the droll comment circulated outside the university and throughout England.

By age 30, Wilde was famous in Europe for the snappy, highly quotable epigrams that filled his published essays and peppered his speech. "I have nothing to declare but my genius," he told a customs officer in New York City, following an 1882 U.S. lecture tour that made him a celebrity on this side of the Atlantic too.

But Wilde was equally well-known for his unorthodox clothing—velvet jackets with a green carnation in the button-hole—and his effeminate mannerisms. The British paper *Punch* pronounced him a "Maryanne," a derogatory word for homosexual, and *The New York Times* labeled him "epicene," another word for unmanly. To silence the gossip Wilde married in 1884 and quickly fathered two children.

Still, he couldn't suppress his sexual impulses. At 32 he began having sex with men and over the next few years became more openly homosexual, a risky business in England at that time. Though sodomy was no longer a capital offense, parliament passed the Labouchère Amendment in 1885, widening the definition of illegal homosexual acts to include "gross indecency"—oral sex—a crime punishable with up to two years in prison.

Wilde at first seemed oblivious to the repressive political climate. His homoerotic novel *The Picture of Dorian Gray* (1891) was attacked in the press for dealing with "matters only fitted for the Criminal Investigation Department." Wilde created an epigram in his own defense: "There is no such thing as a moral or an immoral book. Books are well written or badly written. That is all." Still, he changed gears, writing a number of comedic plays, such as *The Importance of Being Earnest,* for general audiences, which brought him popularity and financial success. His personal style influenced many young men, a number of whom appeared at the opening of *Lady Winder-mere's Fan* in 1892 sporting green carnations.

When Wilde fell for the 21-year-old Lord Alfred Douglas (nicknamed "Bosie") in 1892, their affair proved to be Wilde's undoing. Bosie's father was the powerful Marquess of Queensberry, who decided that Wilde had corrupted his son. When Bosie refused to stop seeing Wilde, Queensberry began harassing the playwright, on one occasion leaving his card at Wilde's club with the message, "To Oscar Wilde posing Somdomite [sic]." Egged on by Bosie, Wilde unwisely sued Queensberry for libel in 1895.

But to win a libel suit, Wilde would have to have proven that Queensberry's innuendoes weren't true. During the trial,

Queensberry's lawyer produced a damning letter from Wilde to Bosie that Bosie had carelessly left in a jacket he gave to a male hustler. In the note Wilde rhapsodized that Bosie's lips were made for "the madness of kisses." The jury decided in Queensberry's favor, and within hours of the judgment, Wilde was arrested for sodomy and gross indecency. Bosie quickly escaped to France. The theaters where Wilde's plays were running immediately deleted his name from their programs.

During Wilde's first criminal trial, ten male prostitutes whom Wilde had solicited for sex testified against him. Wilde's eloquence alone saved him when the prosecutor demanded his definition of a phrase in one of Bosie's poems: the "Love that dare not speak its name." Wilde's powerful speech on the noble, innocent nature of love between men met with applause from the spectators. Because the jury couldn't reach a verdict, another trial was scheduled.

Wilde's friends, including Irish poet William Butler Yeats, hired a yacht to transport him across the English Channel to safety in France, but Wilde stubbornly refused to go. On May 25, 1895, he was found guilty and received the maximum sentence of two years at hard labor. His wife promptly left the country, changing her last name and that of their sons to "Holland." (His grandson announced plans to restore the family name on the centennial of Wilde's death.)

In prison Wilde was at first cruelly denied paper and pen. When he was finally permitted to write, he composed a passionate letter to Bosie, later published as *De Profundis*, in which he blamed himself for what was in fact a social injustice. "Desire, at the end, was a malady, or a madness, or both," he wrote. "I allowed pleasure to dominate me. I ended in horrible disgrace."

After his release in 1897, Wilde went abroad. Drained and bankrupt, he spent three years genteelly begging from friends until his death in Paris in 1900. Wilde's much-publicized ordeal sent many British homosexuals into the closet; even Bosie married. But the injustice Wilde suffered also had some positive consequences for awareness of lesbians and gay men. For the first time, millions of people recognized a famous person as gay, thus fostering the development of a gay consciousness and identity that helped lead to the modern gay movement.

14. What is the history of gay bathhouses?

Bathhouses were in existence as far back as ancient Greece and Rome and even then were sites of sexual encounters between men. But bathhouses specifically aimed at providing rendezvous space for gay men first appeared in the early decades of the 20th century.

Cities like New York and San Francisco created municipal bathhouses as a public health measure in the late 19th century because overcrowding and lack of indoor plumbing had aggravated the spread of disease in poor neighborhoods. Though these baths were also meeting places for working-class homosexuals, the watchful eyes of the bathhouse personnel made it difficult for men to have sexual encounters there.

More conducive to sexual activity were private Turkish baths, which provided a higher level of safety and privacy for gay male sex than parks or tearooms. They were also places where men could make friends. Some baths were gay-friendly and welcomed "the patronage of pansies" as long as the police didn't become involved. Gay men might tip the staff to ignore their sexual goings-on. Sometimes gay men would simply meet at a bathhouse and arrange a later assignation. In these establishments there was often a particular time of day, a certain day of the week, or a specific room in the bathhouse that was especially gay. At Coney Island in the 1930s, gay sexual activity occurred mostly in the steam room of one private bathhouse. An eyewitness recalled "an atmosphere murky with steam. If one stumbles over a pair in the act, one mutters a hasty apology and goes on quickly in another direction."

In addition to gay-friendly baths were those that specifically catered to gay men. These businesses protected their gay customers by keeping out heterosexuals who might make a scene if propositioned. One such establishment was the Ariston, a bathhouse on West 55th Street in New York City that as early as 1902 had an almost exclusively gay clientele. For a dollar, a man was given a sheet, a dressing room, and a smorgasbord of services and activities. Despite the fact that there were private rooms with cots, the dark public "cooling room" was in fact a hotbed of gay sexual encounters.

The police soon discovered that the Ariston was "the resort for persons for the purpose of sodomy." On February 21, 1903, after several hours of undercover work to gather evidence, police officers conducted a raid, arresting 26 men on charges of "degenerate disorderly conduct." One man who had been observed with nine sexual partners received a prison sentence of 20 years.

Other popular gay baths in early 20th-century New York included the Everard (nicknamed the "Ever Hard" and later a favorite of Rock Hudson), which survived until a 1977 fire that killed nine, and the Lafayette Baths, which gay artist Charles Demuth captured in a series of paintings made before 1920. The Lafayette was raided twice, once in 1916 and again in 1929, resulting in the arrest of several dozen patrons. One of those arrested recalled how brutally the police treated the patrons during the 1929 raid, kicking and striking them and pushing them into paddy wagons.

During World War II in San Francisco, Turkish baths provided an important way for servicemen on leave in the city to meet and have sex, since bars were off-limits to soldiers and sailors and hotel rooms were hard to come by. One ex-serviceman recalled that Jack's Baths was "very, very busy. It was all gay. There was never any question about being careful making passes."

By 1950 almost all the bathhouses in New York and San Francisco were gay. But the increase in the number and visibility of these gay bathhouses also led to a McCarthy-era crackdown. The baths, along with other gay establishments like bars, became targets of police harassment. One San Francisco newspaper called the harassment a virtual "war on homosexuals." Because raids were so common, bathhouse patrons often refrained from signing in with their real names for fear that police might turn the names over to the newspaper.

Throughout the next two decades, gay bathhouses flourished. The Club Baths was a chain with a reputation for cleanliness and safety. Started in Cleveland in 1965, it quickly became a national network of 42 bathhouses with 500,000 card-carrying members (one of the largest gay organizations in history). The Club Baths was known for its relaxing atmosphere, complete with fountains and palm trees. "I wanted more than rooms where men could fuck," the owner said of his efforts to create a place where gay men could be themselves.

With the onset of the AIDS epidemic, gay bathhouses were once again the focus of a crackdown. The baths were cited as public health hazards despite the fact that many provided condoms and safer sex information to their patrons. The debate split the gay community, with some activists defending the bathhouses and others demanding they be closed. In 1985, New York City mayor Ed Koch, long considered a friend to the gay community, ordered the closing of the city's bathhouses. Similar closings took place in other cities despite vigorous lobbying by many gay activists for their continued existence.

15. When did American gays, lesbians, and others first start calling themselves "queer"?

The term *queer* has been used by at least one segment of the gay and lesbian community for more than 80 years. The word's exact origin is unclear, although it may have developed from the Old English *cwer,* meaning crooked, not straight or the British slang *quare,* meaning unusual. Some say the word originally referred to 18th-century counterfeit money, which explains the phrase "queer as a $3 bill."

There is plenty of historical evidence that as early as the 1910s, a subset of American men who we might call gay preferred to call themselves queer. Historian George Chauncey, in his book *Gay New York,* explains the overlapping and ever-shifting lexicology of men who had sex with other men in the early 20th century in the nation's largest city. Men who adopted a feminine style in mannerisms and sexual behavior called themselves "fairies." "Trade" were conventionally masculine men who pursued effeminate men for sexual encounters. And *queer* was used by men of both the middle and working classes who categorized themselves as different because of their affection for members of the same sex, regardless of their masculinity or effeminacy.

By the 1930s and 1940s, though, all these terms began to be eclipsed by *gay,* which was particularly preferred by younger and middle-class men. As *gay* became more popular, many men began to reject *queer* as a term that highlights difference and strangeness. By the 1950s the term was heard much more often by belligerent or condescending heterosexuals than self-referentially by gays—although some prominent figures such as Christopher Isherwood and Gore Vidal continued to prefer the term *queer* as opposed to *gay*.

By the late 1980s, though, *queer* was making a comeback, particularly among younger activists. And in 1990 the group most responsible for cementing it as a primary term used by a subset of the gay and lesbian movement appeared: Queer Nation.

Queer Nation was founded in New York City in the spring of 1990 by activists who wanted to use ACT UP–style tactics on issues other than AIDS. Their first major public splash came in June 1990, when they distributed an incendiary pamphlet entitled "Queers Read This," which was best known for its mantra, "I hate straights." The pamphlet, soon faxed and Xeroxed across the country, struck a chord with many—especially young gays, lesbians, and bisexuals—who didn't feel the traditional gay rights movement spoke for them.

Queer Nation soon became known for its irreverent strategies, from pasting QUEERS BASH BACK stickers in public places to "invading" nightclubs and shopping malls not identified as gay or lesbian for "Queer Nights Out."

Central to Queer Nation's public persona was its members' determined advocacy of the word *queer* as opposed to *gay* and *lesbian* or *homosexual*. *Queer*, they said, was inclusive of gays, lesbians, bisexuals, transgendered people, and (sometimes) supportive heterosexuals. Unlike *gay*, they argued, *queer* recognized that their difference didn't always make them happy. Many were unaware of the word's history and felt they were reclaiming a pejorative term and using it in a positive sense for the first time.

This "new" use of the word *queer* brought sharp criticism from other segments of the gay and lesbian community. Some worried that the word would only play into the hands of the gay and lesbian movement's enemies. Others felt the term simply evoked too many painful memories to be used to name something they wanted to feel proud of.

Mostly because of internal divisions and organizational exhaustion, Queer Nation largely ran out of steam by 1992. While the group is no longer the visible force it once was, the term *queer* (and the less blatant letter *Q*) appears to be here to stay. Students and professors debate queer theory in the universities; computer users discuss topics of the day on America Online's onQ area; and thousands of Americans use the term to refer to themselves, either interchangeably with *gay*, *lesbian*, or *bisexual* or as a primary identity.

16. Who was E.M. Forster?

Many of the elegant Edwardian novels of British writer E.M. Forster (1879–1970)—*A Room With a View, Howard's End,* and *A Passage to India*—later became opulent, acclaimed period movies. But his one novel of specific interest to gay readers remained unpublished in his lifetime. Fearing prosecution for obscenity, Forster decided against releasing *Maurice,* saying that the novel could not be made public "until my death or England's." The year after Forster's death, *Maurice* was finally published and is now a classic of gay literature.

To make sense of why Forster opted not to publish *Maurice,* it's necessary to understand the time in which he lived. Forster was an impressionable teenager when playwright Oscar Wilde was tried for "acts of gross indecency" in 1895. The ordeal of Wilde, who was left sick and impoverished, had a lasting impact on young gay men of that age. His name was virtually synonymous with homosexuality for many years after his death. In *Maurice* the protagonist sees a doctor for his "condition" and confesses, "I am an unspeakable of the Oscar Wilde sort." Gay sexual relations remained outlawed in England until 1967. As Forster wrote bitterly in his diary late in life, "Society...wast[ed] my time by making homosexuality criminal."

Forster realized he was gay as a student at Cambridge, where he enjoyed physical closeness—but not sex—with a fellow undergraduate. The object of his affection was known by his initials, H.O.M. (Hugh O. Meredith), who went on to become a well-known economic historian. H.O.M. suggested that he and Forster share rooms, but Forster's mother, who was the overriding influence on him during most of his life, vetoed it. "[H.O.M.] has always been considered a one man friend," she wrote, hinting at what she was afraid to admit openly. Forster declined H.O.M.'s invitation, but the two remained friends. In 1908, Forster dedicated his third novel, *A Room With a View,* to H.O.M.

Forster's passionate friendship with H.O.M. probably provided inspiration for *Maurice,* but it was a visit to the home of gay writer Edward Carpenter and his working-class lover, George Merrill, that actually spurred the writing of the novel. On that visit in 1913, Merrill lightly touched Forster's bottom. "I believe he touched most people's," Forster noted 50 years later. "It was as much psychological as physical...I still remember it." Forster was over 30 and had not yet had sex, so Merrill's affectionate tap on the behind made a lasting impression.

Inspired by Carpenter and Merrill's relationship—and probably envious of it too—Forster began writing *Maurice* that same year. The novel is the story of Maurice Hall, a middle-class youth who attends Cambridge and there has a passionate friendship with Clive Durham. Clive knows he is gay but struggles to be "normal." When Clive marries, Maurice at first contemplates suicide, then tries to follow in his friend's footsteps by finding "a woman...to diminish his lust." But on a visit to Clive's country estate, he meets and begins a sexual relationship with Alec, a gamekeeper. When Alec climbs into Maurice's bed, Maurice "cut[s] himself off from the congregation of normal men." Like Carpenter and Merrill, Maurice and Alec bridge the gap of class difference. Maurice leaves behind family and friends and goes off into the woods to live with Alec. Though the threat of being betrayed to the police always looms over them, Forster did allow his lovers a happy ending.

Forster revised *Maurice* three times, with an eye to posthumous publication, and asked other writers to read and comment on the manuscript. Some gay critics now believe that D.H. Lawrence patterned the lusty *Lady Chatterley's Lover* (1928) after Forster's book. When *Maurice* was published in 1971, reviewers dismissed it as derivative of Lawrence, when in fact *Lady Chatterley's Lover* may have been a heterosexualized *Maurice.*

It wasn't until 1917, several years after the completion of *Maurice,* that Forster's gay identity, writing, and behavior finally came together. While traveling in Egypt he fell in love with a young tram conductor named Mohammed el Adl, and the two enjoyed a passionate affair. "I am so happy," Forster wrote in his diary. "I wish I were writing the latter half of *Maurice* now. I now know so much more." The affair was brief, with Forster worrying constantly that his mother would find out.

The most enduring gay relationship of Forster's life began in the early 1930s, with a young police officer named Bob Buckingham. Though Buckingham eventually married, the marriage did not hamper his relationship with Forster. In fact, the constable's wife, May, seemed to accept the relationship, and Forster was a frequent visitor to their home in Coventry.

Forster and Buckingham were together almost 40 years, until Forster died of a stroke in 1970 at the Buckinghams' home. In an endnote to *Maurice* that Forster wrote in 1960, he said, "I was determined that in fiction anyway two men should fall in love and remain in it for the ever and ever that fiction allows." With Buckingham, Forster had finally found the love that he only imagined when he wrote *Maurice.*

17. Who were Havelock Ellis and Edith Lees Ellis?

British researcher Havelock Ellis is remembered in gay history as the man who made "sexual inversion" a household term. What is less well-known is that Ellis, who was heterosexual, became intrigued with the topic because his wife, Edith Lees Ellis, was a lesbian.

Though Havelock Ellis (1859–1939) was trained as a doctor, he never practiced medicine. Instead, he made his living writing treatises on topics that complemented his socialist politics. In his first book, *The New Spirit* (1890), for example, Ellis spelled out his thoughts about the relationship between men and women. While he abhorred the militancy of the suffrage movement, Ellis's belief that "the average level of women's intelligence is fully equal to that of men's" was unusual for his day.

The book caught the attention of Edith Lees (1861–1916), who traveled in the same socialist circles as Ellis. Friends introduced them in 1890, and Lees and Ellis quickly became close friends. No physical attraction, however, seemed to develop between them. In fact, their sexual passions were for other people. A short time before he met Lees, Ellis had been involved with novelist Olive Schreiner, who left him for another man. Lees's intimate attachments had primarily been with women. What prompted Ellis and Lees to marry in 1891, despite their lack of sexual attraction, seems to have been a common interest in creating an ideal socialist marriage. As Ellis later put it, their union was an "affectionate comradeship, in which the specific emotions of sex had the smallest part, yet a union...able to attain...a passionate intensity of love."

The Ellises had separate incomes and separate residences, though they spent part of each year together. Lees Ellis had a small inheritance, but she also supported herself by giving lectures on feminist topics, which were subsequently printed and sold as pamphlets. In the mid 1890s she began writing fiction and plays, while Ellis started work on his seven-volume opus, *Studies in the Psychology of Sex.*

During the months when she lived away from her husband, Lees Ellis had a succession of "good friends," women whom Ellis soon realized were her lovers. Within a few years of their marriage, Ellis too began having extramarital affairs. Despite the fact that the Ellises chose an open marriage, their correspondence reveals a fair amount of jealousy on both of their parts.

In his autobiography Ellis acknowledged the impetus for his most famous research, which he began in 1892. "I had found," he wrote, "that some of my most highly esteemed friends were more or less homosexual (like Edward Carpenter, not to mention Edith)." Ellis's desire to understand his wife's behavior and to "obtain sympathetic recognition for sexual inversion" compelled him to collaborate with John Addington Symonds on a massive study of homosexuality in men and women. Symonds, a gay man, had written a historical treatise on same-sex love in ancient Greece and amassed a large number of case studies on homosexuality. He had not, however, done any research on lesbians. In order to include women in the study, Ellis interviewed his wife (who appeared in the book as "Miss X," speaking frankly about her lesbian likes and dislikes) and her circle of lesbian friends.

Symonds died in 1893, before the work was completed, and his family fought to have his name and the historical essays he contributed removed from the book before publication. As a result, *Sexual Inversion* (1897), with its 27 case studies of men and six of women, was published under Ellis's name alone. Written primarily for doctors and lawyers, it was the first book in English to treat homosexuality as neither a disease nor a crime but as a naturally occurring phenomenon. Ellis was also the first researcher to consider lesbians worthy of scientific study.

Like her husband, Lees Ellis became a defender of homosexuality. On a lecture tour of the United States, she delivered a much-publicized lecture on sex at Chicago's Orchestra Hall on February 4, 1915. "It is our duty," she maintained, "to see to it that equality of opportunity...is given alike to the normal and the abnormal men and women in our midst." Ever since she was 18, Lees Ellis boldly admitted, "I have studied woman and I have loved her." She ended her oration with a passionate call for "a new love world."

Though it was a historic moment, Lees Ellis's lecture drew harsh criticism from Margaret Anderson, a lesbian who edited the Chicago-based journal *The Little Review*. Anderson was angry that Lees Ellis had been so vague and cautious in her remarks, and she took the initiative to write the first militant defense of lesbianism ever published in this country, an editorial titled "Mrs. Ellis' Failure."

For Lees Ellis, who had been in shaky health for several years, the physical and emotional strain of the lecture tour was too much. She was also bothered by gossip about her husband's affair with birth-control activist Margaret Sanger. Lees Ellis suffered a nervous breakdown that spring, and after a suicide attempt and hospitalization, she died in 1916. Ellis spent the year following his wife's death faithfully chronicling their unusual marriage, a frank account that he only allowed to be published after his death.

18. How gay was the Harlem Renaissance?

The decade of the 1920s witnessed a cultural explosion in the upper Manhattan neighborhood known as Harlem, with African-American literature, art, and music flourishing there like never before or since. Though straight historians rarely acknowledge it, the roll call of artists who created the Harlem Renaissance reads like a who's who of queers from that era.

Previously a Jewish neighborhood, Harlem became predominantly black in the early 20th century, when African-Americans from the South began migrating to northern cities in large numbers. Some of the most acclaimed poets and writers of that age lived in Harlem and formed a queer literary community.

Alain Locke, a professor at Howard University and part-time Harlem resident, was one of the fathers of the new movement. A gay man, Locke fostered the careers of many younger gay poets, including Langston Hughes, Countee Cullen, Richard Bruce Nugent, and Wallace Thurman. Though none of Locke's protégés except Nugent wrote openly about their sexuality, gay critics have begun to read Cullen's poems, especially "Young Sailor" and "Waterfront Streets," for their gay codes. In the 1930s, Cullen taught high school English to another budding gay writer, James Baldwin.

In 1926 several of the young men in Locke's circle lived together in a boarding house that Zora Neale Hurston dubbed "Niggerati Manor" (a playful twist on the term *literati*). There, in the summer of that year, Thurman, Nugent, Hughes, and several others started an experimental journal called *Fire!* Each of them pledged $50 to finance the project. But because most of them lived off small stipends from generous patrons, they couldn't afford to pay up. Thurman, the only one with a day job, thus assumed financial responsibility for the endeavor.

Fire! debuted in November 1926 and was immediately controversial. In addition to gritty poems and stories on jazz and the blues, Nugent's "Smoke, Lilies, and Jade" appeared, the first gay-themed essay by an African-American published in the United States. The autobiographical piece, which he published under his first and middle names only, included veiled but vivid descriptions of a night of passion between two men. Nugent's assertion that "one can love two [sexes] at the same time" shocked Harlem.

The first issue of *Fire!* was the only one ever published. Ironically, a fire in the basement where the printed journal was stored destroyed most of the copies. It took Thurman years to pay off the printing bill, and the group was unable to finance another issue.

Lesbian writers were active in Harlem too. Nella Larsen's novel *Passing* was about a black woman passing for white, but contemporary lesbian critics have also read its main character as a lesbian passing for straight. Angelina Weld-Grimké published plays and poems about race, but she also left behind many unpublished lesbian love poems with suggestive titles such as "To Her of the Cruel Lips."

Like the literary scene, Harlem's nightlife was overwhelmingly queer. Many whites came north for (in their words) "slumming," attending drag balls at Hamilton Lodge or catching shows at the clubs along "Jungle Alley" (133rd Street). Among the slummers was Carl Van Vechten, a wealthy gay writer who became a patron of Hughes and Cullen. Gay celebrities such as Noël Coward and Cole Porter frequented Harlem's "buffet flats," private parties that offered a smorgasbord of sexual possibilities.

Many lesbian entertainers found work in Harlem during this time. One of the most popular was Gladys Bentley, a 200-pound "bulldagger" who got her start playing piano at "rent parties" (private affairs held in apartments to raise rent money for the hosts). Bentley later sang in Harlem clubs in top hat and tails, becoming famous for altering the words of popular songs to create raunchy lyrics about straight sex.

Blues singer Gertrude "Ma" Rainey was even more daring in her choice of material. Rainey wrote and performed "Prove It on Me Blues," a challenge to listeners to "prove" her lesbianism:

> Went out last night with a group of my friends.
> They must've been women 'cause I don't like no men....
> They say I do it, ain't nobody caught me.
> They sure got to prove it on me.

In "Sissy Blues" Rainey sang about a man who "got a sissy, his name is Kate. He shook that thing like jelly on a plate." Other lesbian and bisexual women were regular performers in Harlem and went on to national fame, among them Bessie Smith, Ethel Waters, and Billie Holiday.

In literature and in entertainment, lesbians, gay men, and bisexuals were tolerated in Harlem for their creative accomplishments. They were able to form a thriving subculture that was appreciated and sought out by straight and gay people and that influenced later generations of queer artists.

19. Who were Gertrude Stein and Alice B. Toklas?

On the morning of July 27, 1946, in a Paris hospital, Alice B. Toklas kept vigil at the bedside of her partner of almost 40 years, modernist writer Gertrude Stein. Both women were worried because Stein would soon undergo surgery for cancer. Stein turned to Toklas and asked, "What is the answer?" Toklas was silent. "In that case," Stein continued, "What is the question?" The words have gone into history as Stein's last utterance.

Although each spent her youth in the San Francisco Bay area, Stein and Toklas met and fell in love in Paris. Both had had prior romances with women. Stein met her first lover, May Bookstaver, while studying psychology at Johns Hopkins Medical School in the early 1890s. Bookstaver was simultaneously involved with Stein and a mutual female friend. The romantic triangle caused Stein great pain, which she exorcised by writing a novel about the experience. Because of its lesbian content, Stein put *Q.E.D.* away in a closet, and the novel was not published until four years after her death. Disillusioned by medical school and eager to forget Bookstaver, Stein went to Paris in 1903 to become a writer.

In the 1890s, Toklas was studying piano at the University of Washington and enjoying romantic friendships there with other young women. But both her musical career and the budding of her lesbian sexuality were cut short when her mother became ill and died. Toklas returned to San Francisco to take charge of the household. After ten years of caring for her father and brother, she became fed up and used an inheritance from her grandfather to sail to Paris in 1907. On one of her first days there, she received an invitation to dinner from fellow San Franciscans Sarah and Michael Stein, Gertrude's sister-in-law and oldest brother. Toklas recalled that when she met Gertrude Stein that evening, she heard bells ringing, which she took as a sign that she was in the presence of genius.

Stein and Toklas discovered that they had many mutual interests, like modern art and literature. But their biggest common interest was Gertrude Stein. The two began meeting every day at Stein's apartment, where they discussed her work-in-progress, *The Making of Americans,* and Toklas taught herself to type so she could transcribe the handwritten manuscript.

Toklas soon moved in with Stein, and they settled into married life. Stein's pet names for her lover included "wifie" and "pussy"; in turn, Toklas called Stein "hubbie," "lovey," and "Mount Fatty." Toklas managed all the domestic chores so that Stein was free to write. In addition, she typed Stein's work and scrupulously checked the galley proofs of her books. Since Stein got to fulfill herself and Toklas simply took care of her, some lesbian scholars have criticized their relationship as mimicking the worst heterosexual marriage.

However, both women expressed contentment in their relationship and devotion to each other. Toklas was, Stein said, "all to me." They left daily love notes to each other signed "DD" and "YD" ("Darling Darling" and "Your Darling"). Stein wrote about their seemingly robust sex life, using code words like "cow" for orgasm. "I am fondest of all of lifting belly," reads Stein's *Lifting Belly,* a 50-page tribute to lesbian sex:

> Lifting belly
> So high

And aiming.
Exactly
And making
A cow
Come out...
That is what I adore always more and more.

Though Stein was a prolific writer, most of her work was considered too experimental by large publishers. Her prose, like her poetry, contained many repetitive phrases and not much punctuation. As a result, Stein's early books were either self-published or published by small presses, receiving little public attention or money. Stein and Toklas lived almost solely off their modest inheritances. It wasn't until the publication of Stein's whimsical *Autobiography of Alice B. Toklas* (which was more about Stein's genius than Toklas) and a lecture tour of the United States in 1934 that the author became a celebrity, her writing suddenly in demand and the couple's finances secured.

Over the years, Stein and Toklas were inseparable, dividing their time between Paris and a rented house in the south of France. Together they witnessed two world wars at close range. During World War I, they used their Ford car, "Auntie," as a supply truck and ambulance, hauling equipment, provisions, and wounded French and American soldiers across the country. They received medals from the French government for their war service. In the Second World War, when the Germans occupied Paris, the two, who were both Jewish and by then in their 60s, moved to their country house for safety.

Soon after the end of World War II, Stein was diagnosed with cancer and died during surgery at the age of 72. Toklas lived another 21 years, mostly managing Stein's literary estate. But she also tried her hand at writing, contributing articles on cooking to U.S. magazines and compiling her memoirs of life with Stein, *What Is Remembered*. A reviewer in *Time* magazine called Toklas "a woman who all her life has looked in a mirror and seen someone else." When Toklas died in 1967 at the age of 90, she was buried with Stein in a joint plot in a Paris cemetery.

20. Who was Willa Cather?

Many Americans know her as the author of big, sweeping novels of the Midwestern prairies, a major figure in 20th-century literature, and winner of the Pulitzer Prize. Many have read *My Antonia* or *O Pioneers!* in school. Unfortunately, what most people studying Willa Cather (1873–1947) never learn is that she was a lesbian.

In her groundbreaking biography of Cather, Sharon O'Brien brought to light for the first time the influence that Cather's gender expression and sexuality had on her life and writing. Born in Virginia and raised on the Nebraska plains, Cather early on rejected Victorian femininity and adopted a male persona. As a 14-year-old tomboy, she recreated herself as William Cather Jr., cropping her hair to a crew cut and wearing male clothing. Her unorthodox appearance and low voice made her the talk of Red Cloud, Neb., where years later townspeople incorrectly remembered her as a hermaphrodite. Cather cross-dressed for four years, even entering the University of Nebraska as William. But perhaps because of ostracism from her peers, she soon abandoned male clothing and at the same time began to find her identity as a writer.

Years later, though, William Cather Jr. provided the inspiration for the character Paul in Cather's short story "Paul's Case," written in 1905 while she was living in Pittsburgh and working as the editor of a women's magazine. Like her old William persona, Paul is a sensitive, imaginative boy who doesn't fit into the bourgeois society around him. Cather describes him as

"theatrical" in a way "peculiarly offensive in boys." Paul whistles tunes from operas and dresses like Oscar Wilde, in a jacket with a velvet collar and a red carnation in the lapel. A rebel,
he runs away to New York City, where he spends a day and
night in unnamed activities with "a wild San Francisco boy."
Though it seems obvious to gay audiences, most readers
missed the subtle homosexual subtext of Cather's story.

By the time she wrote "Paul's Case," Cather was very much
in tune with her lesbian desires. Cather had had a crush on a
woman in college, but it was Pittsburgh socialite Isabelle Mc-
Clung who was her first and lifelong love. They met in 1899,
and McClung soon invited Cather to live with her in her family's mansion. The two young women shared a bedroom in a far
corner of the house, where they quickly retreated together
after dinner every evening.

In 1906, Cather made a career move to *McClure's* magazine
in New York City, and within a few years she became managing editor. Though she soon met and began living with Edith
Lewis, the woman with whom she shared the next 40 years of
her life, Cather still returned frequently to Pittsburgh and took
all of her vacations with McClung. On one long trip with Mc-
Clung in 1911, Cather began writing her first novel, *Alexander's Bridge.* She continued to find inspiration with McClung,
writing major portions of *O Pioneers!* (1913) and *The Song of
the Lark* (1915) while staying with McClung in Pittsburgh.
These early works are family dramas set in the Midwest and
filled with strong, independent women characters.

When McClung unexpectedly married in 1916, Cather's
heart was broken, and she described the loss to friends as overwhelming. She even stopped writing fiction for a while, saying
she was indifferent to it. Eventually, Cather returned to writ-

ing full-time, leaving her job at *McClure's* at the urging of her friend and fellow writer Sarah Orne Jewett. She continued to use McClung as the model for her strong female characters. It seems Cather's jealousy of McClung's husband, who was Jewish, made its way into some of Cather's short stories in the form of anti-Semitic portrayals of Jewish men.

And what about Edith Lewis? Lewis was apparently content to play Alice B. Toklas to Cather's Gertrude Stein. She was younger than Cather and in awe of her talent, and Cather seemed to thrive on her devotion. Lewis also worked in publishing, and the couple had very similar tastes and interests. Together they created a warm and nurturing home in New York City's Greenwich Village, where for several years they hosted a literary salon. What Lewis thought of Cather's relationship with McClung is unknown, though after McClung's marriage the bonds between Cather and Lewis grew stronger.

There is no way to know for sure if Cather's intimate relationships with women were sexual. Possibly fearing that exposure as a lesbian would jeopardize her career, Cather fiercely protected her privacy, destroying most of her personal letters and requesting that her friends do the same. She even stipulated in her will that her surviving letters could never be published or quoted from—a tremendous loss to lesbian and gay and literary scholars.

Cather found both critical and financial success with a string of important realist novels set in the Midwest and Southwest: *A Lost Lady*, *The Professor's House*, and *Death Comes for the Archbishop*, to name a few. In 1923 she received the prestigious Pulitzer Prize for her World War I epic, *One of Ours*, beating out Sinclair Lewis's *Babbitt*. After "Paul's Case," though, Cather's fiction never again approached the topic of homosexuality. Still, she couldn't keep a queer sensibility out of her work. The disaffected individuals of her short stories, the independent women of her early novels, and the later male narrators who stand in for her own lesbian desire all suggest connections between Cather's life and her art.

21. What was the Leopold and Loeb case?

Before the O.J. brouhaha, before the Manson killings, even before the Lindbergh baby kidnapping, there was a "crime of the century" involving two amoral male lovers intent on the experience of committing murder. The crime, trial, and punishment of Leopold and Loeb—not to mention numerous literary and cinematic retellings of their deed—have buttressed the link between homosexuality, criminality, and mental illness for generations of Americans. Long before the gay and lesbian community had organized itself in a manner that could respond to negative press, Leopold and Loeb were demonized in newspapers, books, and even by their own attorney as very sick individuals whose homosexuality was directly linked to their criminality.

Nathan F. Leopold and Richard A. Loeb were wealthy Jewish teenagers of exceptional intelligence. Lovers since their early teens, they spent a tremendous amount of time together, often bird-watching or driving around their native Chicago. While Leopold had a very strong sex drive, Loeb was driven by lust of a different sort: He dreamed of committing a "perfect murder"—not out of hatred or revenge or greed but out of sheer curiosity about what it feels like to end another life. Leopold's Eros and Loeb's Thanatos came to a bizarre pact: They would have more sex and commit more crimes.

At first the duo shoplifted, set off false alarms, vandalized property, and torched buildings. But Loeb was not satisfied, and the two decided the time was right to experience homicide. On May 21, 1924, Leopold and Loeb kidnapped 14-year-old Bobby Franks from his schoolyard. Once they had the boy in their rented car, Loeb struck his head four times with a chisel, and Franks bled to death. They drove to a deserted area, stripped the boy naked, poured acid on his face to conceal his identity, and shoved his corpse in a drainpipe.

When they returned home they burned the boy's clothes, cleaned up the car, and called the boy's father to tell him about the kidnapping—and that a ransom note would follow. The note, which arrived the next day, demanded $10,000 in old, unmarked bills. Since the murderers were already millionaires, the ransom was simply for show. But in any event, before the money could be paid, the body was found and identified. The boy's death caused a sensation in Chicago, and a massive investigation began, with both professional and amateur criminologists trying to solve the case. Among them was Loeb, who shared his private theories with the police. He didn't help himself, however, when he told them, "If I were going to pick out a boy to kidnap or murder, that's just the kind of cocky little son of a bitch I would pick."

Soon, a pair of glasses found at the site were traced to Leopold, and the typeface on the ransom letter matched the typeface on other notes Loeb had written. The pair were taken in for questioning. When confronted with the evidence, each confessed but blamed the other. When reports of two wealthy young men who killed for sport hit the newspapers, Chicago residents demanded blood. Fearful that his son would get the death penalty, Leopold's father hired the nation's most prominent and talented defense attorney, Clarence Darrow, to take the case.

Since Leopold and Loeb had already confessed, Darrow had

his clients plead guilty and focused his courtroom work on sparing their lives. His speeches from the Leopold and Loeb trial are still considered a classic argument against the death penalty. He said he could think of something worse than a dead boy in a drain pipe: "I can think of taking two boys...irresponsible, weak, diseased...penning them in a cell, checking off the days, the hours, and the minutes, until they be taken out and hanged."

Darrow did not call his clients insane but insisted that they suffered from a host of mental illnesses that should persuade the court to be lenient. Among those mental illnesses was "sexual perversion." In other words, their homosexuality helped explain and mitigate their crime. Darrow's eloquence triumphed, and Leopold and Loeb were sentenced to life plus 99 years in prison—no death penalty.

Because of their wealth, Leopold and Loeb had special privileges in the Northern Illinois Penitentiary at Statesville—including the right to visit each other often. Leopold became a model prisoner, but Loeb remained predatory, raping several of his fellow inmates. Loeb died at age 28, when a prisoner he attacked fought back and killed him with his own razor blade. Leopold volunteered for an Army malaria experiment, survived, and was paroled in 1958. He moved to Puerto Rico to work in a hospital, wrote a book about his experiences, married a woman in 1961, and died in 1971.

22. Who was Natalie Barney?

Often called "the leading lesbian of her time," Natalie Barney stands out in the history of the early 20th century as an unapologetic, visionary woman-loving woman whose influence extended far beyond the circle of lesbians who surrounded her.

Born into a family of railroad magnates in Ohio, Barney lived a life of luxury as a child and soon found herself studying in Paris, as was the custom among young women of her class. Paris and Barney were a perfect match, and she quickly learned to speak impeccable French and came to love deeply the city where she was to spend the vast majority of her life. Paris was one of the few places in the world where lesbianism was not only legal but looked upon as exotic and fascinating; Natalie Barney fit right in. When her parents died and left her more than $4 million (at turn-of-the-century values), she had the wealth necessary to embark on her unusual career as an openly lesbian intellectual in early 20th-century Europe.

By age 12, Barney had already experienced lesbian sex, and by age 22 she was involved in a passionate affair with the stunning Liane de Pougy, the most prominent courtesan of her time. (A courtesan was a kind of high-class prostitute.) But Barney was never one for monogamy, and while her lover was abroad, she fell in love with another expatriate American in Paris, a poet named Renée Vivien. Barney and Vivien—an alcoholic anorexic who was fascinated with death—developed a certain intellectual symbiosis, and they began to explore in their conversations, letters, essays, and poetry ideas of exactly what lesbianism was or should be.

Much of this exploration centered on Sappho, the Greek lesbian poet who, despite the clear erotic meaning of much of her writing about women, was generally interpreted by male scholars (many of them gay) as a sexual predator or even as a non-lesbian. Determined to reclaim Sappho as a model of unabashed lesbian friendship and love, Barney and Vivien traveled to the isle of Lesbos in 1904 and bought homes, although the relationship soon ended, and Barney retreated to Paris, determined to create a Sapphic society in her adopted hometown.

In the early 20th century, the dominant scientific model of homosexuality either considered lesbians and gays to be sick or classified them as members of a "third sex." Many homosexuals internalized these categories, which were reflected in their dress, mannerisms, and patterns of living. Barney, however, objected to the notion that lesbians should dress or act in any way like men, saying, "Why try to resemble our enemies?"

Indeed, in her sexual appetite she more resembled the stereotype of a gay man than that of a lesbian. She was rarely able to maintain a monogamous relationship with any of her lovers, often living with more than one in her famous home at 20 Rue Jacob. She was known to enjoy sex in all its combinations—outdoors, semipublicly, and on occasion with more than one woman. Her unabashed approach to sexuality combined with her bewitching good looks and her long flowing white gowns earned her the nickname "the Amazon."

Barney completely rejected the notion that as a lesbian she was some kind of sick creature deserving of punishment. She wrote: "Albinos aren't reproached for having pink eyes and whitish hair, why should they hold it against me for being a lesbian? It's a question of nature: my queerness isn't a vice, isn't 'deliberate,' and harms no one. What do I care, after all, if they vilify or judge me according to their prejudices?"

But Barney was perhaps most famous for her salon, held every Friday in her home for more than 60 years. French and American artists, poets, philosophers, and other intellectuals (male and female) gathered to listen to poetry, eat cucumber sandwiches, and discuss the issues of the day. At various times Ezra Pound, Ernest Hemingway, Gertrude Stein, Djuna Barnes, F. Scott Fitzgerald, and James Joyce could be found sipping tea and conversing in Barney's salon.

Barney continued her many affairs—including one with Oscar Wilde's niece Dolly—but entered her most important long-term relationship, with the American painter Romaine Brooks, in 1915. Barney and Brooks remained lovers for more than 55 years, although in 1968 the pair of octogenarians separated because Brooks could no longer tolerate Barney's repeated indiscretions, especially an affair with a younger (69-year-old) woman.

Natalie Barney was not, however, known for her literary ability. Her poetry, both in her day and in ours, was considered mediocre, and much of her writing remains unpublished. But Barney never seemed to care: She once said, quoting Oscar Wilde, "I've put my genius into my life; I've put only my talent into my works."

23. What was the first gay rights organization in America?

Almost 30 years before Harry Hay and his friends founded the Mattachine Society, a nonprofit corporation called the Society for Human Rights paid $10 for a charter from the state of Illinois and took its place as the earliest documented gay rights organization in the United States. The written purpose of the Chicago-based group was so vague that the government clerk who processed the application for a charter undoubtedly had no idea he was helping to make queer history.

The guiding light behind the society was Henry Gerber (1892–1972), whose family had emigrated from Bavaria to Chicago in 1913. Immediately after World War I, Gerber served with the U.S. Army's occupation forces in Germany and there became acquainted with the work of gay rights pioneers, including Magnus Hirschfeld and his Scientific Humanitarian Committee. Gerber was particularly enthusiastic about a group called Bund für Menschenrecht (Society for Human Rights), which advocated for a mass movement of gay people. He began subscribing to German homophile magazines and making frequent trips to Berlin to participate in the city's lively gay culture.

Gerber's experiences in Germany fueled his desire to launch a similar movement in the United States, to strive for what he called "homosexual emancipation." Soon after he returned to Chicago, where a gay subculture was forming, Gerber set out to achieve his goal. Besides wanting to help himself and oth-

ers like him, Gerber also had hopes of fame and glory. "If I succeeded," he wrote later, "I might become known to history as
deliverer of the downtrodden, even as Lincoln."

During breaks from his job with the post office, Gerber
drafted a declaration of purpose for his proposed Society for
Human Rights. The statement's wording was lofty, vague, and
drawn from the idea, prevalent at that time, that homosexuality was an "inversion" of normal sexual behavior. Gerber set
down as the society's main intent "to promote and protect the
interests of people who by reason of mental and physical ab-
normalities are abused and hindered in the legal pursuit of
happiness." Nowhere in the statement could he dare use words
like *homosexual* or *invert*.

Once he'd written the declaration, Gerber had a hard time
finding anyone to sign it, even though it was a nebulous statement about human rights. He finally talked a half dozen of his
friends into working with him, and their seven names appeared
together on the 1924 charter. "The average homosexual," Gerber later complained, "was ignorant concerning himself. Others were fearful. Still others were frantic or depraved. Some
were blasé.... We wondered how we could accomplish anything with such resistance from our own people."

As part of the group's mission, Gerber hoped to institute a
series of educational lectures for gay men on sexual self-con-
trol, "especially urging against the seduction of adolescents,"
he wrote. He also wanted to publish a newsletter called
"Friendship and Freedom" to keep gay people informed about
the group's activities. The publication too would downplay sexuality in order to gain the sympathy of the general public and,
in particular, legal authorities.

Gerber soon found that the gay men who were afraid to

sign the society's declaration of purpose also hesitated to donate money to the group or add their names to its mailing list. He wrote and mimeographed two issues of "Friendship and Freedom" by himself and financed them out of his own pocket. Because of the financial drain on Gerber, only those two issues were published. The newsletters were not widely circulated, and no copies of "Friendship and Freedom" remain.

Gerber's greatest challenge as a gay activist came in the summer of 1925. Although most members of the society were, like Gerber, bachelors, the vice president of the organization, Al Meininger, had a wife and children. When Meininger's wife found out about his double life, she reported him to a social worker, alleging he and his friends performed "strange doings" in front of the children. An article appeared on the front page of the *Chicago Examiner* under the lurid headline STRANGE SEX CULT EXPOSED. The three officers of the society—Gerber, Meininger, and an itinerant preacher named John Graves—were arrested and prosecuted. The policemen who raided Gerber's apartment at 2 A.M. took his typewriter, personal diaries, and all the files of the society. But because the arrests were made without a warrant, a judge eventually dismissed the case, and the three men were released.

Though Gerber got his typewriter and the society's papers back, his diaries were never returned. They were confiscated by postal inspectors who were investigating if "Friendship and Freedom" had violated the Comstock Act, the federal law against sending obscene material through the mail. Gerber subsequently lost his post-office job, and his ordeal marked the end of his fledgling gay rights group. Disheartened, he moved to New York City and reenlisted in the Army, serving for another 17 years.

For the rest of his life, Gerber remained an active gay rights proponent, publishing a number of articles and reviews on gay themes, sometimes under the pseudonym "Parisex" and sometimes under his own name. His account of the founding of the Society for Human Rights in a 1962 issue of *One* magazine is one of the few remaining records of that historic organization. After its demise, more than two decades would pass before American gays and lesbians would once again form political organizations to protect their interests.

24. Who was Janet Flanner?

In the 1920s a thriving lesbian artistic community in Paris allowed women such as Gertrude Stein, Alice B. Toklas, and Natalie Barney to live out their creative and personal lives with unusual freedom. But some of the women who participated in that scene aren't always recognized as lesbians as readily as Stein and Barney are—even though their love lives were just as woman-centered as the more famous expatriates. A good example is Janet Flanner, who was one of the most esteemed journalists of her time and a woman who took what she called a "lesbic approach" to life.

Born in Indianapolis in 1892, Janet Flanner wanted to be a writer from the age of 5. After some setbacks she launched her writing career in 1917, contributing an arts column to the *Indianapolis Star* for $25 a week.

But like many lesbians-in-waiting, she found her hometown stifling, and she took one of the few roads out that were available to women at that time: She got married. In 1918, Flanner tied the knot with a friend from college who had settled in New York City. The marriage didn't last long, but it did change her life. Living in bohemian Greenwich Village with her new husband, Flanner immediately became part of the vibrant feminist community there and found herself attracted to the brilliant "new women" around her. One of these women, a drama critic named Solita Solano, became Flanner's first great love.

Even the big city of New York, though, was not very tolerant of lesbians in the years following World War I. The two women

felt confined by sexual mores and were eager to make a life together in another place. When Solano got an assignment in
Greece in 1921, Flanner jumped at the chance to dump her husband and follow her new love abroad. The couple traveled
around Europe, finally settling in Paris in 1922. Flanner and
Solano became active members of the thriving expatriate lesbian community, frequenting Barney's famous literary salon
and serving as the inspiration for the journalist couple "Nip"
and "Tuck" in Djuna Barnes's 1928 satire *Ladies Almanack*. In a
1973 interview with Mike Wallace on *60 Minutes*, Flanner described Paris in the '20s as "lots of fun," but it was also a place
where women like her could shed sexual and social restrictions
and follow their desires and ambitions more freely.

Flanner lived with Solano for close to 20 years in an open
relationship, which at times seemed to involve some pretty
complicated scheduling. Flanner's biographer quotes a letter
written by one of Flanner's friends in 1932: "Janet is now in
love with Noel Murphy, but she still keeps house with Solita
Solano. Solano has a house in the country where she is in love
with another girl and where Janet visits. Noel has another
friend, some French woman, where she visits until Janet returns from Solita's"—lesbian soap opera, 1930s-style. Although
she and Solano ultimately separated, Flanner retained a lifelong tie to her first love, proving that the tendency for lesbians
to stay in touch with their exes isn't something new. And Flanner had a lot of exes. There was always "some woman who excited and charmed me," she wrote at the end of her life, "and
when her influence waned, another took her place."

It's not just for her lesbian love affairs, though, but for her
remarkable writing career that Flanner deserves attention. At a
time when middle-class women's jobs were confined mostly to

homemaking, nursing, or teaching, Flanner forged a successful and noteworthy career as a foreign correspondent. Her literary connections in Paris got her a number of plum writing assignments, and in 1925 the editor of the newly founded *New Yorker* magazine approached her about doing a biweekly column on French culture and politics. Her "Letter from Paris," written under the androgynous pseudonym "Genet" (a twist on the French pronunciation of "Janet"), ran in the magazine for 50 years and earned Flanner worldwide fame. In the column she tackled everything from tame subjects, like art exhibitions and the theater season, to explosively political ones, like the rise of French fascism.

Her left-of-center work won many prestigious honors, including the Legion d'Honneur and the National Book Award. *Paris Was Yesterday*, a book-length collection of her columns, was an international best-seller. When Flanner died on November 7, 1978, her fans around the world mourned her passing.

Why isn't she better known as one of "our people"? Though open about her lesbianism with friends and colleagues, Flanner didn't discuss—and wasn't asked about—her personal life on the record. Not unlike many of today's semicloseted "dykons," Flanner seemed to think that everyone knew she was a lesbian without her having to announce it. As she wrote in a letter to a 1940s lover of hers, "Darlinghissima, how we burned and so publicly." More publicly than most 1940s lesbians, sure, but hardly "out" by our standards.

25. What was the "Padlock" Bill?

In the 1990s several Broadway plays with gay characters and content, like *Angels in America* and *Rent,* won Pulitzer Prizes and Tony Awards. But seven decades earlier three plays with only subtle queer content caused an uproar that resulted in the passage of the Padlock Bill in the New York State Assembly. This law—passed in the midst of Prohibition—banned the presentation of homosexuality in Broadway productions and remained on the state's books for the next 40 years.

The brouhaha started with the opening of the play *The Captive* at the Empire Theater in New York City in September 1926. Originally written in French by Edouard Bourdet and titled *La Prisonniere, The Captive* concerns the intense relationship between a married woman, Irene, and another female character, Madame d'Aiguines, who never appears onstage but pursues Irene by sending her bunches of violets as signs of her affection. Bourdet wrote the play from the perspective of Irene's husband, Jacques, and saw it as "the story of a man's great sorrow," not as an exploration of lesbian love. Irene finds her own Sapphic infatuation appalling: "It's like a prison to which I must return captive, despite myself," she tells Jacques.

Critics in Paris hailed *La Prisonniere* as a masterpiece when it debuted there in March 1926, and French florists reported a sudden and overwhelming shortage of violets. But when imported to this country, the play's subject matter horrified critics, particularly Brooks Atkinson, the influential *New York Times* drama critic, who labeled the theme "twisted" and "revolting." The "loathsome possibility," Atkinson wrote, of an intimate relationship between two women is "never mentioned, scarcely hinted at, [yet it] hangs over the drama like a black pall." Arthur Hornblow ranted in *Theater Magazine* that *The Captive* was "a sad commentary on the decadent times in which we live."

All the controversy stirred up by the press made audiences swarm to the theater, where many were baffled by the subtle treatment of the play's theme. Still, they gave thunderous ovations to the play's stars, Basil Rathbone, who later achieved movie fame as Sherlock Holmes, and Helen Menken, a respected stage actress married to Humphrey Bogart. *The Captive* was that season's hottest show, carrying a whopping $5 ticket price when most plays cost less than half as much. The *New York Herald Tribune* reported long lines to buy tickets, which scalpers offered for as much as $25 apiece.

The real trouble started when the press learned that two other "immoral" plays were set to open on Broadway in early 1927. *The Drag* and *Sex*, both written and produced by screen siren Mae West, featured gay male characters, who were generally considered even more objectionable than lesbian ones. Interestingly, neither of these plays depicted homosexuality in a positive fashion. In fact, West—whose style would later be copied by many a drag queen—hoped that her plays would "call attention to a tragic waste of life that is spreading into modern society."

Local politicians began discussing the need for censorship of "sex perversion" in Broadway plays. Mayor Jimmy Walker cautioned producers to keep plays "clean." Committees of producers, actors, and playwrights met to discuss ways to "purify" their work to avoid official sanctions. But the New York district attorney felt pressured by conservative religious groups, including the Catholic Church, to take direct action. On the evening of February 9, 1927, police raided *The Captive* and *Sex* (*The Drag* had not yet opened), arresting the producers and casts of both. "Most of the actors became hysterical," Menken later recalled. Because she was a friend of the mayor's, however, he sent his personal limousine to escort her to night court.

West avoided prosecution by agreeing to close *Sex* immediately and to call off production of *The Drag*. But Gilbert Miller, producer of *The Captive,* was determined to keep his show running, and it did in fact play for five more performances after the raid. Miller's bosses finally pressured him to close down, which he did to great financial loss: $80,000 in box-office revenue had to be returned to ticket holders. In the trial that followed, a judge leniently ruled that the treatment of the play's subject matter was delicate and artistic though suitable only for mature audiences.

Plans to revive *The Captive* failed, however, because the state assembly rushed through a bill proposed by the district attorney. The so-called Padlock Bill passed on April 6, 1927, made it a misdemeanor to produce or participate in any play "depicting or dealing with the subject of sexual degeneracy, or sex perversion." In addition, any theater in which such a play appeared risked losing its operating license—hence the nickname "padlock."

Though it was not strictly enforced, the Padlock Bill encouraged a measure of self-censorship in the theater community, resulting in decades of plays with closeted lesbian and gay characters, from *The Children's Hour* to *Tea and Sympathy*. The Padlock Bill remained on New York State's books until a revision of the penal code in 1967.

26. What was The Well of Loneliness?

Radclyffe Hall's novel *The Well of Loneliness* was banned in its time and was at the center of a sensational court trial. Its notoriety made it an international hit, and it was translated into 14 languages, selling at a rate of 100,000 copies a year at the time of Hall's death in 1943. Amazingly, the book has never gone out of print and remains the most famous lesbian novel ever written.

Marguerite Radclyffe Hall (she preferred to be called John) was born into a wealthy British family in 1880. Early on she recognized her attraction to girls and women, which made her social-climbing mother uncomfortable. As soon as Hall came into her sizable inheritance, she headed to mainland Europe to escape her mother's disapproval. There, in 1908, she met her first love, Mabel Veronica Batten ("Ladye"), and the two women lived together until Ladye's death seven years later. Shortly after, Hall became lovers with Ladye's cousin, Lady Una Troubridge, who was still married but soon deserted her husband to set up housekeeping with Hall in Paris.

Over the next few years, Hall developed her own distinctive style, dressing in tailored suits and ties and even smoking a pipe. She frequented Natalie Barney's salon and began to pursue her own writing in earnest, though she had had no formal education. Her first novel, *The Forge* (1924), includes a character based on Romaine Brooks, Barney's lover.

Hall also immersed herself in the work of sexologist Havelock Ellis on the subject of "female inversion," or lesbianism.

Ellis's writings convinced Hall that lesbianism was innate. After the critical success of her second novel ensured her literary reputation, Hall approached Troubridge with an idea for a new novel, one with a political point.

"She had long wanted to write a book on sexual inversion," Troubridge explained in her biography of Hall, "a novel that would be accessible to the general public who did not have access to technical treatises.... It was her absolute conviction that such a book could only be written by a sexual invert." Hall felt she needed her lover's permission to write it because it could mean "the shipwreck of her whole career." Troubridge replied without hesitation that she must write what was in her heart, and *The Well of Loneliness* was born.

Hall patterned her protagonist after the lesbians she had read about in Ellis's case studies. *The Well* is the story of Stephen Gordon, given a man's name at birth because her father wanted a son. A tomboy loathed by her mother, Stephen goes abroad to work as an ambulance driver during World War I. She finds personal fulfillment in her work and meets Mary Llewellyn, the passion of her life. Though the two women spend several happy years together, Mary becomes attracted to a man. In a tearjerker ending, Stephen pretends to have an affair with another woman, thus freeing Mary to marry and lead a "normal" life.

Hall told her publisher that she wrote *The Well* out of duty, "in defence of those who are utterly defenceless, who being from birth set apart...need all the help that society can give them." She did what at that time was unthinkable and unforgivable: She wrote a novel that dared to depict lesbianism as a fact of life, not as a vice. "I am not ashamed of [my love]," Stephen declares proudly. "There's no shame in me."

With a brief introduction by Ellis, the novel was published in England by Jonathan Cape Ltd. on July 27, 1928, and produced an immediate furor. When the British home secretary got a copy of the book, he demanded that Cape withdraw it or be prosecuted under Britain's Obscene Publications Act. Cape discontinued publication but cooked up a plan in which an English-language publisher in Paris would print and sell the novel from there. The plan backfired when British customs seized the first copies of the Paris edition as they were on their way to London.

The book's obscenity trial took place in November, with its 40 defense witnesses representing a virtual who's who of 20th-century British literature, with E.M. Forster, George Bernard Shaw, H.G. Wells, and Virginia Woolf ready to testify to its importance. The judge, however, would not allow their testimony and based his decision on his own reading of the book. To no one's surprise he declared the novel to be propaganda for "the most horrible, unnatural and disgusting obscenity," although it included no graphic sexuality. *The Well* was banned in England, where it remained unavailable until 1949.

The American edition went through its own obscenity hearing in 1929 but emerged victorious on appeal and became a best-seller. Hall later claimed to have received 10,000 fan letters, most from grateful lesbians but many from sympathetic heterosexuals. With its stoic hero and dreary ending, *The Well of Loneliness* set the standard for lesbian fiction for the next 40 years. Ironically, though Hall was branded as a propagandist for lesbianism in 1928, she has been dismissed by many post-Stonewall lesbians as self-hating. Still, *The Well of Loneliness* more than any other work helped at least two generations of lesbians realize that they were not alone.

27. Who was Babe Didrikson Zaharias?

Patty Sheehan and Muffin Spencer-Devlin, golfers on the Ladies Professional Golf Association tour, made headlines in the 1990s by coming out as lesbians. In contrast, in the 1930s Babe Didrikson Zaharias, founder of the LPGA and one of the greatest American athletes ever, purposely created a feminine public image for herself to quash rumors about her lesbianism.

Mildred Didrikson was a Texas tomboy, born in Port Arthur in 1911 and raised in Beaumont. The youngest girl in a poor family, she got the nickname "Baby" at birth, which was shortened to "Babe" as she got older. Didrikson was a natural athlete who excelled at games usually reserved for boys, like basketball, which she played in high school and later as a semipro. When a reporter once ticked off her athletic achievements and asked if there was anything she didn't play, she laughed and replied, "Yeah, dolls." In physical appearance too, Didrikson eschewed traditional femininity until she was well into her 20s, preferring pants and flat shoes and a short, unstyled haircut.

Even as a teenager, Didrikson set for herself the goal "to be the greatest athlete that ever lived," as she recalled in her 1950s autobiography. Her gender and the poverty of her family kept her from getting the quality of training that other athletes received, and she had to improvise. When her father read a newspaper story to her about the 1928 Olympics, Didrikson decided to train for the next Olympiad by hurdling the hedges that lined the yards of her working-class neighborhood.

At the 1932 Olympics in Los Angeles, Didrikson took two

gold medals, in the javelin toss and the 80-meter hurdles, breaking world records in both. She also won the running high jump but in an unconventional way—by diving instead of jumping feet first. The perplexed judges decided to award her a half-gold, half-silver medal, the first and only one ever given in Olympic history.

Didrikson returned home a star, dubbed "the Amazing Amazon" and "the Terrific Tomboy" by the media. After the Olympics she traveled the country taking part in public exhibitions of her prowess in sports like boxing, diving, and tennis. However, she soon focused her energy on golf, which she practiced 12 to 16 hours a day. A 1933 tour with golf legend Gene Sarazen honed her skills and brought her more public notice.

But the press proved fickle. Reporters wrote about her physical appearance instead of her athletic ability. Many of the attacks openly challenged her gender. After losing a round of golf to Didrikson, Paul Gallico wrote snidely in *Esquire* that he wasn't sure "whether to invite the Babe into the men's locker room." The implication of much of the press coverage was that Didrikson was a lesbian.

Stung by these attacks, Didrikson decided she would never make it as an athlete unless she changed her image. In the mid 1930s, Didrikson bought a new, feminine wardrobe, had her hair styled, and began wearing lipstick and rouge. She drew the line at restrictive women's undergarments, though. After playing 18 holes of golf in a girdle, she tore into a friend's house screaming, "Goddamn! I'm choking to death!"

The biggest change that Didrikson made in her image was marrying George Zaharias, a professional wrestler, in 1938. Zaharias retired from wrestling the following year to manage his wife's career full-time. Over the next decade Didrikson Zaharias became one of the most successful and popular figures in women's golf. Always confident, she played to the gallery, often making jokes about her own game. "I hit it straight, but it went crooked," she would quip when one of her powerful drives flew out of bounds. The media once again loved her, and the Associated Press voted her Woman Athlete of the Year six times.

But there were few tournaments for women golfers, and Didrikson Zaharias was frustrated by the lack of competition. In 1950 she and five other women changed that by forming the LPGA. Didrikson Zaharias drew huge crowds, and in the first year she won two thirds of the tournaments on the schedule. That year she also met Betty Dodd, a 19-year-old golfer who quickly became Didrikson Zaharias' friend and protégé.

Though they publicly said they were "buddies," the two women were intimate, inseparable companions. George Zaharias was openly jealous of their relationship, and he and Dodd didn't get along. At one point Didrikson Zaharias asked for a divorce, which Zaharias refused. After that, "he got meaner than a snake," Dodd recalled later. "We always had a lot more fun when he wasn't around."

In 1953 the feud came to an abrupt halt when Didrikson Zaharias was diagnosed with colon cancer. Dodd moved into the Zaharias home in Tampa to care for Didrikson Zaharias after her surgery, and the young woman never left. Though the golf star rallied and made a comeback, winning seven LPGA tournaments in the next two years, she eventually succumbed and died on September 27, 1956, at only 45. Upon her passing, even one of Didrikson Zaharias's early naysayers called her "probably the most talented athlete, male or female, ever developed in our country."

28. Was Eleanor Roosevelt a lesbian?

Eleanor Roosevelt would never have used a word like *lesbian* to refer to herself. Nonetheless, we do have ample historical records to confidently state that Roosevelt had a passionate romantic involvement with at least one woman: Lorena Hickok.

Hickok was a reporter for the Associated Press assigned to cover Roosevelt when her husband was elected president in 1932. The two became close very quickly. While much of the correspondence between them was later burned by Hickok's family, many letters remain, including an oft-cited one in which Hickok writes of how she remembers "the feeling of that soft spot just north-east of the corner of your mouth against my lips."

In addition, many of Roosevelt's friends, particularly in the years following the First World War, were involved in romantic relationships with other women. Many of these women were involved in women's organizations that fought for world peace and social justice.

Do these friendships and her relationship with Hickok qualify Roosevelt as a lesbian? Some historians have angrily said no, insisting on the need for proof of sexual intercourse with another woman. Even without this standard—which is never applied before labeling someone as heterosexual—we should certainly be careful not to casually label as lesbian someone who not only married a man and had children but who also carried on a long-term romantic relationship with a younger man, her bodyguard Earl Miller.

With evidence of her erotic involvement with both men and women, it is tempting to simply categorize Roosevelt as bisexual. But since none of these labels was ever embraced by Roosevelt, it may be safest to avoid labels altogether—and point to Eleanor Roosevelt as a clear example of the fact that many of those whom history has traditionally assumed were straight had enormously complex romantic and sexual lives.

29. What was The Children's Hour?

In 1933 best-selling mystery novelist Dashiell Hammett had just finished writing *The Thin Man* and was looking for his next project. While skimming a collection of British court cases titled *Bad Companions,* he found a subject that he thought would make an excellent play. But instead of writing it himself, he passed the idea to his lover Lillian Hellman, who used it as the basis of her first play, *The Children's Hour.*

The case that Hammett discovered was a Scottish libel trial of 1811. Jane Pirie and Marianne Woods were close friends and former governesses who decided to start a girls' boarding school in Edinburgh in 1809. At first they had trouble attracting students, but the situation changed dramatically with the admission of 14-year-old Jane Cumming. Cumming was the orphaned, illegitimate, half-Indian granddaughter of Dame Cumming Gordon, who, despite her social standing, had been unable to find a school that would accept the young girl of color. When Pirie and Woods admitted the girl, Dame Cumming Gordon was so grateful that she convinced her friends to enroll their daughters too. The future of Pirie and Woods's school seemed secure.

But in November, 1810, young Cumming told her grandmother about "disturbing" events she had witnessed at the school. Outraged, Dame Cumming Gordon immediately withdrew the child and wrote letters to her friends, encouraging them to do the same. The reasons, she wrote, were so shocking that she could only relate them in person. What Cumming had told her grandmother was that Pirie and Woods had been sexually intimate with each other.

It is unknown whether the two women were actually lovers or simply romantic friends who kissed and embraced each other in public, as many women of the day did. But only 18 months after their school opened, Pirie and Woods lost all their students and, with them, their livelihood. They engaged a lawyer and sued Dame Cumming Gordon for libel. At the trial, which began on March 15, 1811, and lasted several months, Cumming's testimony was corroborated by two other witnesses. Cumming provided graphic sexual descriptions of the women's behavior that included making "a wet kind of noise, attended with motions of the body, quick and high breathing, and a shaking of the bed."

Although other witnesses contradicted Cumming's testimony, the jurors were unable to dismiss her vivid story, and they decided for Dame Cumming Gordon. A long, torturous appeal—which wasn't resolved until 1821—turned the tables and found for Pirie and Woods. But after legal fees and court costs, the impoverished schoolmistresses collected only a fraction of the £10,000 Dame Cumming Gordon owed them.

For her play, Lillian Hellman appropriated the storyline of the Pirie and Woods case but moved the drama to 20th-century New England. Her protagonists, Martha and Karen, are college friends who decide to open a girls' boarding school together. When Mary, a malevolent student, sees them hugging innocently, she decides to get revenge on her teachers for a harsh punishment she received. Mary implies to her grandmother, a wealthy and influential woman, that Martha and Karen are lovers, although Karen has a fiancé. The grandmother spreads the rumor; Martha and Karen are ostracized by the community; and they lose all their students. They then sue for libel unsuccessfully. In a twist at the end, Martha realizes that she is indeed a lesbian who has always loved Karen, and she hangs herself in shame.

Although it was illegal to depict lesbianism on the Broadway stage at that time, Hellman saw herself as a risk taker and brought it to the stage anyway. *The Children's Hour* found a producer and opened on November 20, 1934. The manager of New York City's Shubert Theater warned Hellman, "This play could land us all in jail." But audiences loved *The Children's Hour;* the police stayed away; and the show ran for more than 600 performances. Critics applauded the play as "finely and bravely written" and "the season's dramatic high-water mark."

Based on its Broadway success, Samuel Goldwyn paid $50,000 for the movie rights to Hellman's play without any knowledge of its subject matter. When told that it was about lesbians, he supposedly replied, "That's OK, we'll turn them into Americans." Because the strict Hays Production Code policed "morality" on the Hollywood screen, the movie version of the play skirted lesbianism. *These Three* (1936), which William Wyler directed and Hellman herself scripted, heterosexualized Mary's lie: Instead of getting caught hugging Karen (Merle Oberon), Martha (Miriam Hopkins) is accused of "carrying on" with Karen's fiancé (Joel McCrea) in a bedroom near the students' quarters. Unlike in the play, heterosexual Martha doesn't commit suicide, she simply leaves town at the end. Hellman justified the mutilation of her play by claiming *The Children's Hour* had never really been about lesbianism at all but about a lie ruining the lives of innocent people.

Twenty-six years later, when the Hays code loosened, Wyler decided to direct a second film version of Hellman's play, restoring its original title and theme. *The Children's Hour* (1962), starring Shirley MacLaine, Audrey Hepburn, and James Garner, was not the critical or popular success that either Hellman's play or *These Three* had been. The grim ending didn't make sense, complained MacLaine (who played Martha), because Wyler excised important scenes from the script that clearly showed Martha's growing love for Karen.

The Children's Hour is remembered today by lesbian and gay film historians for its early, if negative, depiction of lesbianism. But true to its time and to Hellman's play, the word *lesbian* was never even spoken on screen.

30. What happened to gays and lesbians during the Holocaust?

The experiences of gay men and lesbians in Nazi Germany are only beginning to be fully researched and explained. Much of the literature that exists (particularly in English) is full of exaggerations and unproved assumptions. But the story is an important one, for during Hitler's reign, the most open and politically active gay and lesbian community in the world was utterly demolished.

Under Paragraph 175 of the Reich Criminal Code, sex between men had been illegal in Germany since 1871. Nonetheless, by the 1920s a remarkably diverse gay and lesbian subculture had developed in Germany, centered around Berlin. That city's Institute for Sexual Science provided a museum, library, and counseling center for gays and lesbians. The Scientific-Humanitarian Committee, which began in 1897, educated the public and lobbied the legislature about gay and lesbian concerns. During the 1920s, Germany had six journals for lesbians and 15 for gay men. And Berlin and other cities had dozens of gay bars and nightclubs, as well as lesbian costume balls, gay-themed movies and plays, and other cultural activities.

But homosexuality was considered dangerous by the rapidly growing Nazi party. The Nazis considered healthy but non-reproductive Aryans a detriment to their ongoing world struggle with "lesser" races. Also, any relatively secretive clique within German society was seen as a political threat that had to be stopped. Germany's gay and lesbian subculture was quickly suppressed when the Nazis came to power in 1933. The Scientific-Humanitarian Committee was outlawed; the Institute for Sexual Science was trashed; and gay and lesbian meeting places were raided and closed. Gays within the Nazi party—most notably Brownshirt leader Ernst Röhm—were murdered and denounced in the press.

SS Leader Heinrich Himmler led a campaign against homosexuality, strengthening and vigorously enforcing Paragraph 175. During the 1930s, thousands of gay men were arrested and convicted of Paragraph 175 violations, and many were faced with a cruel choice: castration or imprisonment in concentration camps.

Gay men who were sent to the camps were forced to wear pink triangles to signify the reason for their punishment. Like the other prisoners, they were used as slave labor for the Nazi state and, later, the war effort. They were poorly fed and housed and faced beatings and shootings on a regular basis. Some anecdotal evidence and statistical studies suggest that gay men in the camps were likely to die sooner than other prisoners. The greater mortality rates can be explained by a number of factors, including lack of support from their families and from other prisoners, homophobic and sadistic guards, and fear that helping one another might invite accusations of conducting a same-sex relationship within the camp. Even so, the gay prisoners who died were the victims of overwork, disease, starvation, and shootings—and not the gas chambers and crematoriums of the death camps in Poland.

Sometimes gay men in the camps would be subject to medical experiments, often attempts to "cure" their homosexuality. In a handful of camps, gay prisoners who "proved" that they were no longer gay by performing sexually with prostitutes (often prisoners themselves) could be released. While the persecution of gays continued after the start of World War II, the Nazis seem to have slowed their campaign once German men were desperately needed for the war effort. Nonetheless, at least 5,000 gay men—possibly twice that number—died in the Nazi concentration-camp system.

Less is known about the specific experiences of lesbians in Nazi Germany, but unlike the men, they were not subject to arrest and imprisonment for their lesbianism. Of course, some lesbians were imprisoned in the Nazi concentration-camp system for their political or religious beliefs. But more significant was the fact that lesbian public life and culture—just like that of gay men—was annihilated in Germany and did not really recover until the 1970s.

31. Who were some of the lesbians in Hollywood's golden age?

While it is easy to think of lesbian actresses as a phenomenon of the late 20th century, lesbians actually have a long history in Tinseltown. Some of the most glamorous stars of Hollywood's golden age (from the advent of talking pictures through the 1940s) were part of an underground network of lesbians and bisexual women in the movie industry.

Greta Garbo was one of the most famous movie stars of her time, attracting both male and female audiences with her seductive beauty and enigmatic charm. Starting out in silent films, Garbo's first talkie was *Anna Christie* (1930). Her deep, sexy voice and tough demeanor made her very first lines of dialogue legendary: "Gimme a whisky, ginger ale on the side. And don't be stingy, baby." Garbo's gender-bending role in *Queen Christina* (1933), in which she cross-dressed and kissed her female costar on the lips, has become a cult favorite among lesbians.

"I shall die a bachelor," Garbo as Christina vowed. Like the Swedish queen she played, Garbo never married, and although she had affairs with men, it was commonly believed among Hollywood insiders that she preferred women. After a much-publicized romance with leading man John Gilbert, Garbo fell for screenwriter Mercedes de Acosta in 1931. Garbo later credited De Acosta with inspiring her portrayal of Queen Christina. The suave De Acosta had been in and out of the beds of the most respected stage actresses of the time, including Eva La Gallienne and Katharine Cornell. When Garbo dumped her she quickly took up with Hollywood's other husky-voiced sensation, Marlene Dietrich.

Like Garbo, Dietrich was famous for her androgynous sex appeal and a screen persona that defied strict gender classification. Her characters were always incredibly butch women, though they fell in love with men. Studio publicists promoted Dietrich as "the woman even women can adore." Such Dietrich classics as *Morocco* (1930), in which she donned a top hat and tux and sang in her throaty contralto, and *Blonde Venus* (1932) are particularly memorable to lesbian and gay viewers.

Though she was married, Dietrich's relationship with her husband was long-distance and nonexclusive. He had a long-term mistress, and she had just about everyone else, including Maurice Chevalier, Yul Brynner, and journalist Edward R. Murrow. But she also enjoyed a host of female lovers, like De Acosta and French novelist Colette. Rumors of Dietrich's lesbian relationships had little effect on her popularity or her career, which continued unabated into the 1960s.

Dietrich didn't seem to care what anyone thought about her love life, and Tallulah Bankhead was equally unconcerned about gossip. Bankhead's one-liners about her own bisexuality have become famous in lesbian and gay culture. "Daddy always warned me about men and alcohol," she reportedly quipped, "but he never said a thing about women and cocaine."

Garbo, however, was uncomfortable with public scrutiny. Edmund Goulding, the gay filmmaker who directed Garbo in the classic *Grand Hotel* (1932), once implied that the star retired from movies in 1941 at the age of 36 because the pressure of hiding her lesbianism became too great. Whatever her reasons, Garbo fiercely protected her privacy until her death in 1990, making her classic line from *Grand Hotel*, "I want to be alone," a reality.

Other lesbian actresses were so guarded that they entered "lavender marriages." Barbara Stanwyck, who achieved stardom as the take-charge "dame" of movies like *Stella Dallas* (1937) and *Double Indemnity* (1944), married twice, the first time to gay vaudevillian Frank Fay, whose career collapsed just as hers took off. Their stormy relationship inspired the plot of *A Star Is Born.* Stanwyck's second marriage, to bisexual actor Robert Taylor, was glorified by the studio's well-oiled publicity machine and provided her with a cover long after the two divorced. For many years Hollywood's official line on Stanwyck was that she never remarried because she still pined for Taylor.

Janet Gaynor, the tomboyish lead of the original *A Star Is Born* (1937), was another star who married a gay man, costume designer Adrian. Gaynor's "best friend," Mary Martin, remembered for her role as Peter Pan, in turn married Richard Halliday, who styled his wife's hair and decorated all their homes. Lavender marriages provided a guise of respectable heterosexuality that gossip columnists and biographers honored, and that satisfied the stars' straight fans and nervous studios.

Because so many Hollywood lesbians needed to safeguard their secret lives, they tended to socialize at parties rather than in public spaces like bars. Salka Viertel, a lesbian screenwriter with an absentee husband, hosted tea parties at her Santa Monica beach house, where Garbo first met De Acosta. Stage and film actress Alla Nazimova—whose lovers included Dolly Wilde, Oscar Wilde's niece—opened her Sunset Boulevard mansion, "The Garden of Allah," to private queer get-togethers.

Fifty years later, not much has changed in Hollywood, where actresses still play butch roles but keep mum about their personal lives (Jodie Foster) or make the cachet of lesbianism part of their shtick (Madonna).

32. What is the origin of the phrase "a friend of Dorothy's"?

During the middle part of this century, many gay men and lesbians in the United States used the term "a friend of Dorothy's" as a code word for a gay man. Closeted gays in mixed company could ask each other, "Are you a friend of Dorothy's?" without fear of revelation and awkwardness if the answer was no.

Two possible origins for this phrase have been suggested. The most obvious one suggests that the expression refers to Judy Garland's role in the 1939 film *The Wizard of Oz*. The film has always resonated with gay camp sensibility, and Garland has been a gay icon ever since. Particularly after her well-publicized suicide attempt in 1950, Garland was seen as a beloved and tragic figure by gay men, who flocked to her concerts. Upon her death in 1969, many gay bars were draped in black in memorial. The Stonewall riots, which marked the start of the gay liberation movement, started the night of Garland's funeral.

Perhaps the more interesting explanation points to Dorothy Parker, the American writer whose short stories and one-liners have been popular with gay men in particular. Parker was married to a gay man, writer Alan Campbell, and some have suggested she was bisexual. In any event, she is widely recognized as a master of the one-liner; when asked to use the word *horticulture* in a sentence, she replied, "You can lead a horticulture, but you can't make her think."

As recounted in the recent documentary *Coming Out Under*

Fire, Parker's books were on the list of approved literature for soldiers serving overseas. The language in them is exaggerated and campy, and some GIs used Parker's diction and syntax as a secret gay language in their speech and letters.

33. Who were Ruth Benedict and Margaret Mead?

Margaret Mead is a name most students learn in school, and her most famous book, *Coming of Age in Samoa*, is a classic anthropology text. Her mentor and lover, Ruth Benedict, is less well-known outside of anthropology circles, though she was as famous as Mead in her day.

Born in 1887 and educated at Vassar, Benedict (born Ruth Fulton) started out as an English major and continued to write poetry throughout her life. After an early career as a teacher in private girls' schools, she married and honored her husband's wish that she give up working outside the home. Feeling bored and unfulfilled, however, Benedict decided in 1918 to take graduate courses at the New School for Social Research in New York City. At first she studied education with John Dewey but switched to anthropology after an inspiring course with feminist Elsie Clews Parsons. Several of Benedict's professors recognized her potential and encouraged her to study at Columbia University with Franz Boas, regarded as the father of American anthropology.

In 1922, Benedict became Boas's teaching assistant for a class he taught at Barnard, the women's college at Columbia. In that class was a bright 21-year-old named Margaret Mead, a star undergraduate who was editor of the Barnard newspaper. Mead was well-known on campus for her leftist politics and advocacy of free love.

Fourteen years apart in age, Benedict and Mead were opposites in personality. Benedict, who was shy and easily depressed, was drawn to Mead's exuberance and optimism; Mead, on the other hand, liked Benedict's calm, quiet wit. The two women shared a radical world view, a love of poetry, a commitment to their careers, and a deep, mutual respect.

At first their relationship was strictly one of mentor and student, with Benedict viewing Mead as a daughter figure and counseling her on her career. Mead later remembered, "I continued to call her 'Mrs. Benedict' until I got my degree, and then, almost imperceptibly, our relationship became one of colleagues and close friends." While she was working on her doctorate, Mead spent long hours alone with Benedict, discussing ideas that excited them or sharing favorite poems.

Within a few years their passionate friendship, common among academic women at that time, blossomed into a lesbian love affair. During a trip to the Grand Canyon in the summer of 1925, Benedict and Mead discovered they preferred each other to the men in their lives. (They were both married, and each was having an affair with the same man, linguist Edward Sapir.) Benedict's poems suddenly reflected a concern about age differences between lovers, a preoccupation with the permanency of love, and an implied lesbianism. What could compete, one of her poems asked, "with sleep begotten of a woman's kiss?"

But Mead never believed in the permanence of sexual love in the way Benedict did. Mead tended to fall in love with more than one person at a time, disregarding the gender of her lovers. She reflected later in life, "I've never known the kind of union that made me want to exclude other people.... I've never wanted to belong to another person, nor would I ever want anyone to belong to me."

Mead's dislike of sexual exclusivity was one reason she never lived with Benedict. But her own homophobia also got in the way. Mead worried about an openly lesbian relationship damaging her career. Many years later Mead chastised her daughter, Mary Catherine Bateson, for a romance Bateson had with another woman. "She disconcerted me," Bateson wrote in the 1980s, "by turning...to a discussion of what it would have meant to her professional life if I had been involved in a scandal."

Benedict, on the other hand, began a new life after her affair with Mead. She separated from her husband and found the permanence Mead couldn't give her in two subsequent lesbian relationships. The first, begun in the early 1930s, was with research chemist Natalie Raymond. After they separated in 1939, Benedict became involved with clinical psychologist Ruth Valentine, with whom she lived until her death.

Having found her identity, Benedict spent the rest of her professional life trying to justify homosexuality, hypothesizing in her work that society, not nature, created the categories of "normal" and "abnormal." The overarching theme of her masterpiece, *Patterns of Culture* (1934), was the struggle of the misfit individual against a repressive culture. Mead later wrote that her own exploration of "normality" in *Coming of Age in Samoa* (1926) was "a question Ruth Benedict had taught me to ask."

Until her death in 1948, Benedict remained good friends and close colleagues with Mead. Soon after Benedict died, Mead began writing her mentor's biography, *An Anthropologist at Work,* which took ten years to complete and was published in 1959. Though Mead never acknowledged her relationships with women, in 1974 she wrote a positive article in *Redbook* magazine arguing for bisexuality as "creative." The affair between Mead and Benedict became public knowledge when Mary Catherine Bateson disclosed it in her memoirs, published six years after her mother's death.

34. What were the army drag shows during World War II?

Entertainment for the armed forces during World War II was much more than Bob Hope and the Andrews Sisters touring with the United Services Organization. In 1942, to complement the USO, the Army Special Services Branch set up an all-soldier theatrical program to help boost troop morale. These shows almost invariably included drag numbers and female impersonators, which helped to foster an underground gay soldier community during the war years.

The Special Services Branch took the production of soldier shows very seriously, turning its personnel into "talent scouts" who searched army bases for likely performers among the enlisted men—the barracks' cut-ups or clowns—and also those who might be able to write and direct the productions. Special Services also published handbooks, nicknamed "Blueprint Specials," that offered scripts, music and lyrics, and costume design instructions (including dress and evening-gown patterns) to the soldiers.

But one early soldier revue provided the clearest template for many subsequent army shows. Irving Berlin, who had served in World War I, wrote an all-soldier musical, *This Is the Army*, which debuted on July 4, 1942, at the Broadway Theater in New York City to raise money for the production of other shows. *TITA*, as it was known, later toured other cities and was so successful that it was expanded into a Hollywood musical in 1943, starring Lieutenant Ronald Reagan. The revue featured all the basic elements that would become popular in GI shows, including plenty of men in drag.

At first, drag was incorporated because there were no women in the armed forces, but it remained popular even after the founding of the Women's Auxiliary Army Corps. Many drag routines had few queer undertones and featured bumbling chorus lines of hairy-chested soldiers dressed in tutus or frills. In *TITA*, for example, the spoof "Ladies of the Chorus" involved deep-voiced soldiers in dainty dresses, golden curls, and army boots singing and dancing with men in suits and straw boaters. In a ballet sequence the men proved unable to lift some of the burly "ladies." These burlesque-style skits carefully distanced the performers from any suggestion of homosexuality. In the movie version of *TITA*, one soldier forced to play a chorus girl whines, "Grown-up guys in dames' clothes! What a sad sack of bananas!"

Other musical numbers in *TITA*, however, involved comedy drawn more directly from gay male culture. In "Stage Door Canteen," a chorus of "hostesses," again in dresses and army boots, sang lyrics with what sounds today—and must have sounded to gay soldiers then—like obvious gay subtext, alluding to the rules against homosexuality in the military:

> We could do more for the boys
> And greatly add to their joys.
> But we don't get very far.
> The rules and regulations are
> We mustn't be seen
> Outside the canteen
> With a soldier.

In the final verse the hostesses swore "to never be found / Canoodling around / With a soldier."

The canteen segment also incorporated what had for years been a feature of gay male culture: female impersonation. More so than the broad comedy of chorus-line drag, female impersonation was and is a highly refined art, projecting the illusion of becoming the other gender. The mistress of ceremonies of the canteen was "Jane Cowl," a disciplinarian who warned her hostesses that their guests should have fun, "but don't be fools. / It must be done according to the rules." Miss Cowl introduced to the audience various "celebrities" who were in fact soldiers impersonating some of the stars of the day. One private appeared as stripper Gypsy Rose Lee, and as one reviewer noted, he "studied [her] striptease technique carefully. He is charmingly literary about it...." Another private impersonated stage actress Lynn Fontanne, who issued orders to her stereotypically Milquetoast husband, actor Alfred Lunt. Many gay soldiers had undoubtedly heard the rumors about Lunt and Fontanne's lavender marriage, so the skit provided them with a private joke that straight soldiers missed.

The *TITA* canteen segment "I Left My Heart at the Stage Door Canteen" must have been poignant for many gay soldiers. In this sequence a uniformed soldier sang a love song to his "girl," another soldier in drag. Unlike other drag numbers, the song was unabashedly romantic and not for comic relief. Gay audience members could fantasize about same-sex romance and a day when one man could openly sing love lyrics to another man.

The gay men in the audience weren't the only ones who benefited from these drag numbers. A number of gay soldiers had been involved in the theater in their civilian days and were re-

cruited to perform in the army shows. Often, being thrown together in these revues instilled a sense of camaraderie among
gay enlisted men by affording them an underground social network and a public way to camp it up. On the other hand, fear
of exposure as gay and of dishonorable discharge were sometimes so great that many gay soldiers in these shows were too
scared to "let their hair down," even with each other.

Ironically, while the U.S. military was for the first time discharging large numbers of gay soldiers, their own theatrical
program inadvertently gave many gay soldiers—whether they
were audience members or participants—a way to connect
with each other.

35. What were "blue discharges"?

During the Second World War, military personnel who were removed from service because of suspected or confirmed homosexuality were often given Section 8 discharges on blue paper, which became known as "blue discharges." The struggles of lesbian and gay veterans to overcome the discrimination and prejudice related to their blue discharges were among the first organized political struggles by gays and lesbians in the United States.

Army psychologist William C. Menninger described the typical situation as follows: "A man, on his own initiative or because of noticeable difficulty in adjusting himself, might visit or be sent to a psychiatrist for consultation. When it was found that the basis of the difficulty was homosexuality, if this was reported to his commanding officer, the man probably received a blue discharge, or perhaps would be tried. Objections to this were raised by many homosexual individuals, whose request for help from a medical officer ended up in a discharge 'without honor.' This action undermined confidence in medical officers. Furthermore, the Army required that doctors report even those statements given in confidence in a consultation room."

Blue discharges—which were also given for non–gay-related reasons—fell in a category between dishonorable discharges (which were usually given to military personnel convicted of homosexual acts) and honorable discharges (which were sometimes available to gay and lesbian soldiers with otherwise impeccable records). Still, they carried with them the stigma of

less-than-honorable service, and they presented practical ob-
stacles for the gay and straight soldiers and sailors who received them. Blue dischargees (whose stories are told in detail
in Allan Bérubé's *Coming Out Under Fire*) would be stripped of
their uniforms and medals and forced to return in shame to the
draft boards of their home communities to present their discharge papers. The military justified these procedures, in part,
as a way of discouraging straight soldiers from feigning homosexuality to evade service.

But the worst indignity of the blue discharges was the resulting denial of benefits under the GI Bill. Veterans with honorable discharges received thousands of dollars in monetary
benefits in the areas of education, housing, and credit—no
such Veteran's Administration benefits were available to those
with blue discharges.

Approximately one fifth of the blue-discharge veterans
were African-American, in part because racist commanders
used the blue discharge as a way to punish black soldiers and
sailors in their command. In response to this inequity, black
leaders—led by the black newspaper *The Pittsburgh Courier*—
urged Americans to pressure the government to bring relief to
those denied benefits because of their blue discharges.

Many did, including gay and lesbian veterans who resented
their blue discharges. One lesbian former officer wrote an
anonymous letter to the Army publication *Yank* in which she
complained of having received a blue discharge when a lesbian
affair was discovered. She wrote, "The public in general is un-
educated in the psychology of handling my type of discharge,
hence I find it embarrassing and impossible to elucidate upon
just why I left the [Women's Army Corps]."

A congressional subcommittee chaired by congressman Carl

T. Durham of North Carolina investigated the situation, and its report, released on January 30, 1946, found fault with the system that punished the blue dischargees without due process. It even singled out gay dischargees as victims of unfair treatment, stating that the Veterans Administration should be stopped "from passing moral verdicts on the history of any soldier." Blue discharges should be abolished, the report concluded.

The combination of public pressure and the Durham committee's report led to a temporary reprieve for holders of blue discharges, many of whom found success by appealing their individual cases. In May 1947 the Army abolished the blue discharges altogether, replacing them in most cases with a general discharge for unsuitability. But the good news was not shared by gays and lesbians, who were specifically excluded from receiving general discharges. More than one observer has linked this exclusion with the growing concern about rivalry with the Soviet Union, in which gays were seen as potential security risks.

Without such public "scarlet letters," many gay and lesbian veterans would otherwise have returned to the closet or perhaps opposite-sex marriages and conventional lives. But the very public discriminatory treatment led to group consciousness as experience of the blue discharges led to a growing sense among American gays and lesbians that they were a minority group that suffered official prejudice, and they began to band together to discuss and address their challenges in society.

36. When did the American gay and lesbian press begin?

In the summer of 1947, the hand-typed copies of the first lesbian publication in America began circulating among lesbians in Los Angeles. *Vice Versa* was a far cry from today's professional gay and lesbian publications, but it served much the same purpose—albeit on a smaller scale.

Vice Versa was created by Edyth Eyde, a 26-year-old California woman who had only been part of the lesbian "scene" for about a year. (Eyde never used a byline in her publication but later went under the pseudonym Lisa Ben, an anagram for *lesbian*). Somewhat lonely and eager to expand her circle of friends beyond the "gay gals" who hung out at Los Angeles's If Club, Eyde decided to start a magazine for lesbians. She called it *Vice Versa*, because its readers had been accused of "vice," but she felt their lives were really just "versa" (different) than the rest of the population.

As an underworked secretary for an executive at RKO Studios, Eyde was given explicit instructions to "look busy" at all times, even when there was no work to be done. She therefore had both the time and the equipment to type issues of her new magazine. Eyde used RKO's heavy-duty typewriter to type an original copy of *Vice Versa* plus five carbons, and then she would repeat the process—meaning each issue had a circulation of 12. She would then distribute those copies through friends and at lesbian bars (she stopped mailing copies when a friend warned her she was risking jail time) and urged the women who read it to pass the copy along to other women. Many did, and Eyde once estimated that each copy was read by several dozen women.

A typical issue of the free publication—which at its thickest contained 20 pages—consisted of fiction, poetry, essays, book and film reviews, and letters to the editor. Most of the content was written by Eyde, but after the first few issues, she had several other contributors, though none was ever given a byline.

Many of the issues addressed in *Vice Versa* (subtitled *America's Gayest Magazine*) are still commonly discussed in the lesbian and gay press a half century later. The magazine published a short story about a lesbian wedding, a poem by Eyde which frowned upon butch hair and clothing styles among her fellow lesbians, and a movie review objecting to the movie version of the classic lesbian novel *The Well of Loneliness,* calling it insulting to lesbians.

Vice Versa was unwaveringly upbeat and cheery—a conscious strategy on Eyde's part to combat negative mainstream press accounts of gay and lesbian life. More than 20 years before the first gay pride parade, *Vice Versa* was unabashed in its enthusiasm for homosexuality. One essay stated: "How much more beautiful, in every way, are women than men! I am glad that I was not predestined to be oblivious to and unattracted by feminine charm. How thankful I am to have been born in womanly form and yet to possess the capacity of appreciating to the fullest extent feminine beauty!"

But *Vice Versa* contained no news, no political columns, and not a single advertisement. Eyde was afraid to publicize the locations of lesbian bars, for example, for fear that they would be raided or shut down. Several years would pass before American gays and lesbians explicitly portrayed themselves as a social group with a political agenda.

Although *Vice Versa* was not expressly political, the very act of representing women-loving women's lives in the late 1940s was bold and risky. By creating a conduit by which lesbians could communicate with one another—and perhaps more importantly by helping lesbians think about themselves as part of a community—*Vice Versa* nurtured the seed which would grow in the next decade into America's first lesbian social and political organizations.

The reader response was overwhelming. Without access to a printer, Eyde was forced to deny repeated requests from lesbians for more copies of the publication. The letters to the editor expressed a sense that *Vice Versa* served as an oasis in a desert of misinformation and silence about lesbian life. One woman wrote: "May your jaunt into journalesbianism prove to have the angels' support."

Eyde produced a total of nine issues of *Vice Versa* over nine months, until her job assignment was changed in early 1948. She no longer had access to a typewriter or the time to devote to the magazine. Nonetheless, her personal life had been enriched by the women she met while producing *Vice Versa,* and she predicted that the gay and lesbian press had a bright future, even without her. In an editorial she wrote: "Perhaps even *Vice Versa* might be the forerunner of better magazines dedicated to the third sex, which in some future time might take their rightful place on the newsstands beside other publications, to be available openly and without restriction to those who wish to read them."

37. How gay were Tennessee Williams's plays?

Tennessee Williams created some of the most memorable characters in the history of modern theater. He won two Pulitzer Prizes, and many of his plays also became classic movies. His 25 full-length plays have been translated into dozens of languages and continue to be produced around the world. In addition, Williams dealt with the subject of homosexuality in a relatively direct way at a time when few writers dared to do so. All of these facts should make him one of our prominent gay forefathers. But Williams's place in the gay pantheon is complicated by his years in the closet, his tormented gay characters, and his tragic demise.

As an aspiring young writer, Tom Williams took the name Tennessee to honor the home state of his father's family. He was actually born Thomas Lanier Williams in 1911 in Mississippi and grew up in St. Louis. Williams's life always provided material for his writing. In *The Glass Menagerie* (1945), for example, Williams immortalized his dysfunctional family: absentee father, faded Southern-belle mother obsessed with the past, and mentally unstable sister. Like Williams, the beleaguered son-brother of the play, Tom Wingfield, struggles to write but is overwhelmed by the burden of having to support his family by working in a shoe factory. The pressure finally drives Tom—as it did Tennessee—to leave St. Louis to pursue his writing career.

"Everything a writer produces is his inner history, transposed into another time," Williams said late in life. It wasn't just his tortured family that Williams mined for his work. He knew in college that he was gay when he fell in love with his roommate. But he also understood that being gay was not "normal." His conflicted, often negative feelings about his own homosexuality eventually seeped into his best-known plays.

Homosexuality is the deep, shameful secret at the heart of *A Streetcar Named Desire* (1948), which won Williams his first Pulitzer. Blanche DuBois, one of the great tragic characters of the American stage, is plagued by the fact that her young husband killed himself after she confronted him in public about being homosexual. Her guilt drives her to despair, alcoholism, and eventually a mental breakdown. Blanche has a definite campy side, though, with lines like, "I have always relied on the kindness of strangers," that has led many readers and playgoers to view her as a gay man in drag.

Williams's second Pulitzer Prize winner, *Cat on a Hot Tin Roof* (1955), again has homosexuality and suicide at its core. Though he never appears on stage, the character Skipper—who committed suicide over his sexual attraction to his friend Brick—haunts the play. Brick is unable to reconcile his love for Skipper with his negative ideas about homosexuality, and he sinks into alcoholism, frustrating his sensual and ambitious wife Maggie, "the cat," both emotionally and sexually. Maggie is determined to produce an heir to the fortune of Brick's father, Big Daddy, and by the end of the play takes control by locking up Brick's liquor supply and attempting to seduce him.

Cat became a movie in 1958, but because of the strict film production code, Skipper's suicide and Brick's coldness toward Maggie went unexplained. At the end of the movie, Brick (played by Paul Newman) magically overcomes his sexual ambivalence and eagerly beds Maggie (Elizabeth Taylor). What on stage had been a sad and poignant exploration of the forbidden nature of love between men became, in Hollywood's hands, the triumph of heterosexuality.

Williams's 1958 play *Suddenly Last Summer* presents a much darker picture of a gay man. Like both Blanche's husband and Skipper, Sebastian Venable is dead before the play begins, and his shadowy demise remains at the center of the play. Only his cousin Catherine knows the truth, and she is threatened with a lobotomy by Sebastian's mother if she tells Sebastian's secret—that he used first his mother and then his cousin to procure male sex partners for himself. In the end Sebastian's gruesome death is revealed: He was murdered by a gang of Mexican boys he was attempting to lure.

Given the time in which he was writing and his equation of homosexuality with death and ruin, it isn't surprising that Williams was not publicly out during most of his career. He did, however, have several serious relationships, including a long-term one with Frank Merlo, a former sailor he met while vacationing in Provincetown, Mass. It wasn't until openly gay critics prodded Williams to come out that he finally did so—in his *Memoirs* (1975).

Over the course of his life, Williams became increasingly alcohol- and drug-dependent, and his writing suffered. On February 25, 1983, he was found dead in his New York City hotel room. He had tried to pry off the child-proof cap of a Seconal container with his teeth, and the plastic accidentally lodged in his throat and choked him. It was an ending fit for a Williams play.

38. What was the Kinsey Report?

The Kinsey Report stands as the most famous study of American sexuality ever published, and the name Kinsey has become synonymous with sex. Gay activists have used the report to place the number of homosexuals in the population at 10%, and the phrase "one in ten" is now part of gay culture. But what Kinsey—who himself had a complex sexual life—actually found was different from what passed into gay lore and popular belief.

The world would never have had a Kinsey Report if Alfred Kinsey (1894–1956) had followed his first career goal: to be a pianist. Fortunately, Kinsey liked nature as much as he did music, and in college he turned toward the field of biology. He specialized in taxonomy, the classification of organisms by category; his doctoral dissertation examined thousands of gall wasps. After being hired as a professor of zoology at Indiana University, Kinsey continued his cataloguing of wasps for two decades—a painstaking process that prepared him for his next and more famous research interest: human sexuality.

It was in the late 1930s that Kinsey's interests turned toward the study of sex, a taboo topic in his Victorian-era youth. Although he was aware of his same-sex desires as a boy, Kinsey married Clara McMillen, with whom he had four children. Rebelling against the sexual silences with which they'd been raised, Kinsey and his wife were straightforward with both their children and neighborhood kids about sexuality. In addition, Kinsey advised his students to come to him with questions, since so many of them—even the married ones—had only a rudimentary understanding of sex. He began studying scientific literature on sexuality in order to help his students and to liberate himself from the guilt he felt about his own sexuality (which included, one biographer has suggested, a preference for S/M).

When Kinsey first offered a "Marriage and the Family" class in 1938, most of the 100 students enrolled were women looking for information that had never been available to them. Only in 1937, for example, did the American Medical Association sanction the supplying of advice on and means of birth control to patients. Students soon flocked to Kinsey's office with questions and concerns and, in turn, voluntarily answered his questions about their sex lives, becoming his first case studies. Kinsey broadened his sample by interviewing friends, former students, and his own wife about their sexual experiences. Then, after developing a system that would insure his participants' anonymity, Kinsey ventured out into the field.

In the summer of 1939, he made forays into Chicago's gay subculture. Through personal contacts he initially interviewed 60 gay men about their sexual behavior. Kinsey also collected materials he hoped would shed light on homosexuality, like diaries, love letters, photo albums, and collections of erotic artwork. His experiences in Chicago helped him reconcile his own sexuality, and over the next few years, he continued to interview many more men in gay gathering places like bars and bathhouses.

Until 1941, Kinsey's sexual research was self-financed. By securing support from the Rockefeller Foundation, Kinsey was able to expand his efforts and create the Institute for Sex Research at Indiana University. Crisscrossing the country, Kinsey and three other researchers (one of whom, Clyde Martin, was briefly the lover of both Kinsey and his wife, Clara) collected case histories of 5,300 white men. The data were subsequently analyzed in an 804-page tome, *Sexual Behavior in the Human Male*, published by W.B. Saunders, a medical press, on January 3, 1948.

The entire study was unparalleled in its frank discussion of topics such as masturbation and extramarital sex, with an entire section devoted to Kinsey's findings on homosexual behavior. Thirty-seven percent of the men interviewed had had an adult homosexual experience ending in orgasm; 4% considered themselves exclusively homosexual; and one in eight men (roughly the 10% figure) had been predominantly homosexual over a three-year period.

The Kinsey Report's graphic language made the book a one-handed read and an instant best-seller. The publisher originally printed a modest 5,000 copies, but demand for the book forced Saunders to go back for a second printing of 180,000 copies within two weeks. The "Kinsey scale" (zero to six, with zero being exclusively heterosexual and six exclusively homosexual) became a household phrase.

Five years later Kinsey published the second volume of his research, *Sexual Behavior in the Human Female*, another popular hit. In a sample of 5,900 women, the figures on same-sex activity were lower than for men but still astonishing. Thirteen percent had had a same-sex experience to orgasm; 2% were exclusively lesbian; and 6% had been predominantly lesbian over a three-year period.

Kinsey's two reports ushered in modern ideas about sexuality. In addition, his studies were noteworthy because they called for acceptance of different forms of sexual behavior, even those considered "fringe." Though his statistics on homosexuality were misquoted as the famous "one in ten" figure, his research suggested that lesbian and gay sexual activity was fairly widespread. In this way Kinsey had a profound impact on the birth of the gay rights movement. In the early 1950s, on the heels of Kinsey's reports, activists founded the first lesbian and gay rights organizations, and Donald Webster Cory's book *The Homosexual in America* used Kinsey's findings to argue that homosexuals constituted an oppressed minority.

39. What were the lesbian pulp novels of the 1950s?

Though a time of great repression for lesbians and gay men, the 1950s and early 1960s were actually a heyday for lesbian novels in the United States. Pulp fiction—cheap paperbacks printed on coarse paper—proved to be what one historian has called the "survival literature" of lesbians during that era.

After World War II the rapid development of the technology for producing mass-market paperbacks led to a blossoming of lesbian-themed fiction. It started in 1950, when Fawcett Books made the move to paperback publishing with its imprint Gold Medal Books. The imprint included many genres of fiction, including mysteries and westerns, which were sold in bus stations, drugstores, and even supermarkets for a quarter or slightly more. The common denominator of all the Gold Medal titles was sex, sex, and more sex—including lesbian sex.

The decision to produce lesbian pulps was fueled first and foremost by marketing concerns, not a desire to provide a service to lesbians. In fact, many publishers didn't think of lesbians as the market for these books. Instead, they assumed that straight men would buy them for titillation. Consequently, many of the lesbian pulps published during that era were soft-core porn written by men for men (sometimes pseudonymously), though lesbians avidly read them too. However, the pulp novels that lesbians cherished most tended to be those actually written by lesbians.

In 1950, Gold Medal's first lesbian title, *Women's Barracks,* appeared, written by a lesbian using the name Tereska Torres. A front cover blurb pronounced it "the frank autobiography of a French soldier girl." The cover art was a lurid tease, with three young servicewomen lounging on their bunks in various states of undress. *Women's Barracks* was specifically condemned by the House Un-American Activities Committee in 1952. Though congressmen had read it privately, none of them would quote from it publicly because it was too "pornographic." Of course, the sexual content of most of these novels was quite muted.

Sexy covers and suggestive tag lines like those on Torres's novel quickly became the trademark of lesbian pulp fiction. "A story once told in whispers now frankly, honestly written" read the teaser of *Spring Fire* (1952), a pulp novel written by lesbian Vin Packer. The covers may have been designed to lure male readers, but they also signaled "lesbian" to many young women who felt isolated and alone, unable to claim their lesbianism openly for fear of reprisal.

Though the cover art of pulp novels always depicted ultra-feminine women, the "real" lesbians in the stories were often tomboys or "bad girls" who seduced innocent straight women. Reflecting psychological theories of the time, lesbian pulp writers often presented lesbianism as the result of trauma such as rape or incest. At the end the innocent straight woman almost always returned to a "normal" life with a man. If the lesbian protagonist wasn't also converted to heterosexuality, she usually became an alcoholic, lost her job, or committed suicide. Publishers insisted on these "moral" endings, condemning lesbian sexuality even while exploiting it. In this regard, lesbian pulps followed the formula of torment and sacrifice that Radclyffe Hall established in *The Well of Loneliness* in 1928.

In contrast, *The Price of Salt* was unusual among lesbian pulps. Authored by acclaimed suspense writer Patricia High-smith (*Strangers on a Train*) under the pseudonym Claire Morgan, it is commonly believed to be the first lesbian novel with a happy ending. As Highsmith put it 30 years later, the lovers "came out alive at the end and with a fair amount of hope for a happy future." Highsmith's novel sold an incredible one million copies in the United States during the single year of 1953, the same year the Kinsey report on women's sexuality appeared. "Claire Morgan" was inundated with fan letters from lesbians and gay men, thanking her for the book's positive ending.

Like Highsmith, other lesbian pulp-fiction writers used pseudonyms to protect their identities. Ann Bannon, creator of the Beebo Brinker series, was really Ann Weldy, a married woman and college professor. Weldy, like many of her characters, led a double life, leaving her husband and children on the weekend to frequent lesbian bars in New York City's Greenwich Village. In the early 1980s, when Naiad Press republished the entire Beebo series, its creator finally came out as the author of the novels.

For millions of lesbians in the 1950s, buying a pulp novel could be a courageous public act, one that expressed a desire to explore or claim a lesbian identity in a time of repression. Lesbians hid the books under their mattresses or stashed them in closets, but they also circulated them and discussed them, creating an underground community of lesbian readers. Though the themes were dark and the outlook bleak, lesbian pulp novels played a vital role in the development of lesbian identity before Stonewall.

40. What were physique magazines?

At the turn of the 20th century, Bernarr Macfadden—a publisher, health enthusiast, and presumed heterosexual—began putting out the first male bodybuilding magazine in the United States: *Physical Culture*. The magazine was filled with almost-nude photographs of sculpted, athletic male bodies, which made it understandably popular among gay men. Macfadden, however, didn't intend his magazine for sexual titillation. When he became aware of its homosexual following, he publicly denounced his gay readers as "painted, perfumed, kohl-eyed, lisping, mincing youths" whom he encouraged other men to beat up.

Macfadden's success with the magazine sparked the founding of many copycats, none of which were intended for a gay gaze. Just after World War II, however, gay photographers began to publish their own work celebrating the male body beautiful. Two gay-run photo studios—Bruce of Los Angeles and the Athletic Model Guild—led what became known in gay culture as the "physique movement."

Initially, these photographers peddled their work through their own mail-order pinup businesses; 15 cents bought a full catalog of available photos. Bob Mizer was only 23 when he started AMG and its catalog in 1945. He originally operated out of a spare room in his mother's house. She wasn't particularly happy that he was gay, but she cooperated because she liked the extra income he shared with her. When Mizer's business boomed, he built a separate studio next door to Mom. He recruited models at gyms and along Venice Beach, searching for a particular type: chiseled, muscular, white. Many of the models he hired were heterosexual.

Demand for these homoerotic images grew, and Mizer looked for another way to distribute them. In 1951 he began publishing *Physique Pictorial*, a pocket-size magazine created for a gay audience. By 1958 there were several dozen physique magazines serving as many as 70,000 readers. Illustrations included in these magazines launched the careers of several erotic artists, including Tom of Finland. Gay men signed up for subscriptions or bought the magazines at newsstands, though doing either was considered extremely risky.

Because of the oppressive atmosphere of the 1950s, physique magazines were careful to disguise their homoerotic intent. Postal inspectors and FBI agents were on the lookout for pornographic content such as "excessive genital delineation." They particularly targeted gay publications, trying to indict them for violation of the 1873 Comstock Act, which prohibited the sending of obscene material through the mail. To avoid harassment, *Physique Pictorial* adopted a lofty mission statement: "A fine healthy physique," it claimed, was "a great compliment to our creator who planned for the utmost perfection in all of his universe." A beautiful body, according to Mizer's publication, "makes the soul sing."

A number of early physique magazines—with names like *Grecian Guild Pictorial, Adonis,* and *American Apollo*—tried to cover their tracks by purporting to foster the Grecian ideals of morality, honesty, and physical beauty. Photos of men in G-strings or with carefully placed fig leaves ran next to articles on the development of the mind and spirit, often written by clergy members. "I seek a sound mind in a sound body" was the *Grecian*

Guild Pictorial's credo, "I am a Grecian." The word *Grecian,* however, could easily be read by those in the know as an underground code for *gay.* Over time, *Grecian Guild Pictorial* became increasingly campy and tongue-in-cheek, comparing its images to "the magnificent art treasures handed down from antiquity."

Also popular in the 1950s were "all-American" physique magazines with names like *Vim* and *Trim.* Unlike other physique magazines, all-American ones regularly included images of African-American men. They typically featured photographs of muscle men engaged in weight-lifting contests and carried articles about the benefits of exercise. Though *Vim* and others were geared toward gay men, they camouflaged their purpose by promoting the traditionally masculine, he-man interests of sports and competition.

Despite all these efforts at concealment, physique magazines came under repeated attack from the post office and law enforcement officers and were often required to defend their right to exist in court. In 1965 one case, *Manual Enterprises* v. *Day,* went all the way to the Supreme Court and won a significant victory. The high court ruled against the obscenity charge, stating that the publication lacked "patent offensiveness," even though it was "unpleasant, uncouth, and tawdry."

The court decision in *Manual Enterprises* v. *Day* made way for a flourishing of gay pornography, complete with full frontal nudity. Physique magazines were too tame by comparison and either fizzled out or completely revamped to keep current with the new trend. Mizer began producing low-budget movies with, as *The Advocate* magazine reported in 1970, "hunky actors" and "slapped-together settings" like Marine barracks and locker rooms. These movies were the direct descendants of the first modern gay erotica: physique magazines.

41. Who was Christine Jorgensen?

Today, with the growth of the transgender movement, sex-reassignment surgery is becoming more and more familiar. But in 1952, when George Jorgensen Jr. underwent surgery and emerged as Christine, the story made headlines—especially in tabloids around the world.

Jorgensen was not the first person to have a sex change operation. Experiments in sex-reassignment surgery had taken place sporadically in Europe since the early 1930s. The word *transsexual*, however, was not used to describe those who underwent the surgery until 1949, when D.O. Cauldwell wrote about "psychopathic transsexuality" in the popular journal *Sexology*.

But it took the story of an ex-GI from the Bronx to place transsexuality in the public eye. Born in 1926, George Jorgensen was a slender blond boy who grew up enjoying needlepoint. In school, children laughed at his "sissified" ways. At 19, when he was inducted into the army, he weighed only 98 pounds, with almost no body hair and underdeveloped genitals. Jorgensen worried that he was a homosexual, but as he got older he began to believe that he might be a woman in a man's body—"a sexual mix-up," he told the psychiatrist he consulted after his release from the army in 1946.

Jorgensen studied photography under the GI Bill but spent most of his free time searching for information about his "condition." After reading a book called *The Male Hormone*, he became obsessed with chemical theories about gender and with "conversion" surgery; he even enrolled in medical technician classes to learn as much as he could about his body. While in school, Jorgensen was able to obtain female hormone pills and began experimenting on himself.

Jorgensen slowly saved his money and by April 1950 had enough for a one-way passage to Copenhagen, where hormone treatment and conversion were being done by Dr. Christian Hamburger and his associates. Jorgensen offered himself as a guinea pig to Hamburger, who had a theory that a person could be outwardly a man while his body chemistry and brain remained female. Because the work was still highly experimental, Jorgensen was charged nothing for his treatment, which began in August of that year.

After a year of hormone treatment, during which Jorgensen's physical appearance changed drastically, his doctors recommended surgery. Because Jorgensen was an American, the surgery had to be approved by the Danish Ministry of Justice. In September 1951, Jorgensen underwent his first surgery, which removed his testicles. He then applied for and was granted a new passport under the name Christine—a feminine version of Dr. Hamburger's first name.

Jorgensen had not told his family why he was in Denmark. Ostensibly, he had been studying photography and beginning to earn a living at it. In June 1952, Christine Jorgensen wrote a long letter to her parents, in which she revealed that "nature had made a mistake, which I corrected, and I am now your daughter." She enclosed photos of herself taken after the surgery. Amazingly, her parents were open-minded and accepting, cabling her back immediately: "Letter and pictures received. We love you more than ever. Mom and Dad."

Late that fall Jorgensen had a second surgical procedure.

While still recuperating in the hospital, she found out that a front-page story would be breaking in New York's *Daily News* on December 1, under the headline EX-GI BECOMES BLONDE BEAUTY. A technician at the hospital had tipped off a reporter, who then approached Jorgensen's parents for an interview. In the interest of getting the correct story into print, her parents co-operated with the newspaper, even lending the "after" photos their daughter had sent them and her letter detailing the reasons for her surgery.

When the story broke, Dr. Hamburger received hundreds of letters from individuals seeking treatment. Jorgensen too was bombarded with mail, but many of those who wrote simply wanted to capitalize on her overnight celebrity. Warner Brothers Studios asked her to contact them if she was interested in a movie career. Clubs and theaters from New York to Las Vegas offered her as much as $1,000 a week for an appearance.

Jorgensen had no real talent for performing, but she quickly decided that "if [the public] wanted to see me, they would have to pay for it." She hired an agent who booked her into nightclubs across the country. Introduced by the song "I Enjoy Being a Girl," her act consisted mostly of witty repartee with a comedian named Myles Bell. Reviewers noted that while she couldn't really sing or dance, Jorgensen had fabulous costumes and a flair for "showmanship." She continued on the nightclub circuit well into the 1960s and also did stints in summer stock.

In 1959, Jorgensen made headlines again when her application for a license to marry John Traub was denied—because she had never had her birth certificate changed to read "female." Though the tabloids reported that Traub "dumped" her, she wrote in her autobiography that the two mutually agreed to drop their marriage plans and parted as friends.

Jorgensen died in 1989 after a long bout with liver and bladder cancer. One of her many obituaries was titled "A Girl at Heart." Though trivialized and sensationalized by the media, Jorgensen's story brought transsexuality out of the closet and offered hope to individuals who felt similarly trapped in their bodies.

42. What was the Mattachine Society?

In 1950 a handful of gay men with Communist Party ties began meeting at the home of music teacher and union organizer Harry Hay in the Silver Lake neighborhood of Los Angeles. They created what is now recognized as the first long-standing U.S. organization devoted to advancing gay rights: the Mattachine Society. At its first convention three years later, however, the original leaders stepped down, and the group shifted away from its leftist beginnings toward a more conservative outlook.

The idea for the Mattachine Society occurred in 1948, when Hay, an active member of the Communist Party, attended a gathering for supporters of presidential candidate Henry Wallace. During the party, it became clear that all of the men there were gay. Hay and others facetiously talked about forming a group called "Bachelors for Wallace," which would support Wallace if he added a plank about sexual privacy to his platform. Though Bachelors for Wallace never got off the ground, Hay was intrigued by the idea of a homosexual rights organization and began looking for others to help him make it a reality.

Two years later Hay finally found men who shared his vision. One was his lover Rudi Gernreich, an Austrian-Jewish costume designer who achieved fame in the 1960s as the creator of the topless swimsuit. The others were fellow Communist Party members Bob Hull and Chuck Rowland and writer Dale Jennings. These core members began meeting in secret at each other's homes, calling themselves the Mattachine Society, after an all-male performance troupe in medieval Europe.

Early meetings hammered out the philosophy of the group, one that had never been articulated before: that gay people were an oppressed minority with their own distinct culture, of which they should be proud. In April 1951 the Mattachine founders formalized the group's mission statement, listing as its main purpose the unification of homosexuals in a fight for their own emancipation.

Through word of mouth and by distributing flyers about the organization at gay bars and hangouts, the Mattachine Society grew exponentially during the first few years. Members met in small "guilds" or discussion groups to propose actions that would improve the lot of gay people. The organization quickly expanded to other cities along the California coast. While most members were men, lesbians also became involved, though mostly in the northern guilds. Some guild meetings attracted as many as 200 people. For most newcomers it was the first time they had not felt alone or isolated in their sexual desires.

Several factors brought about important changes in the organization. As the Mattachine Society grew, its membership became more diverse, and some new members didn't share the political vision of the organization's leftist founders. Many were more interested in fitting into society than changing it. Also, in early 1953 the House Un-American Activities Committee held hearings in Los Angeles to investigate alleged Hollywood Communists. Though Hay, Rowland, and Hull had all resigned from the Communist Party, conservative members of the Mattachine Society viewed the leaders' former political ties as a liability to the organization. To make matters worse, an article about the group in the *Los Angeles Times* revealed the Communist background of Mattachine lawyer Fred Snider and raised fears about the secret nature of the society, whose membership the article estimated at 200,000. (It was actually about 2,000.)

The Mattachine leadership called a national convention to restructure the organization as an above-ground one, with a constitution, bylaws, and elected officers. On April 11 and 12, 1953 (and at a follow-up session in May), several hundred gay men and lesbians met at a Universalist church in Los Angeles to discuss the future direction of the Mattachine Society. It was the first large public gathering of homosexuals in U.S. history. The leftist founders decided to step down for the good of the whole, and the organization passed to the more conservative leadership of men like Hal Call and Kenneth Burns. Burns urged the Mattachine membership to follow "a pattern of behavior that is acceptable to society in general and compatible with [the] recognized institutions...of home, church, and state."

Within the next two years, membership dropped off sharply. By 1955 most of the group's efforts went into publishing a magazine called *The Mattachine Review.* New members did not learn about the radical origins of the organization, and throughout the 1950s the Mattachine Society advocated for the assimilation of homosexuals into mainstream America. The national organization finally disbanded in 1961, but several local groups continued to use the name Mattachine well into the 1960s. Several of these, like the Washington, D.C., chapter headed by Frank Kameny, were militant in the style of the original founders, and their activism helped shape the gay liberation movement of the 1970s.

43. How did McCarthyism affect gays and lesbians?

Between 1950 and 1954, U.S. senator Joseph McCarthy (R-Wis.) made headlines with his attacks on communists and other "subversives" he claimed had infiltrated the entire federal government. Although McCarthy was only one of many public figures who crusaded against "anti-American" employees of the federal government, his attention-grabbing stunts and blowhard persona helped lend his name to the phenomenon now known as McCarthyism.

Although the campaign against communists is better known, the McCarthy era also saw a widespread push to root out "perverts" from government service—and the overwhelming majority of those "perverts" were lesbians and gay men. About two weeks after McCarthy's first media splash in which he alleged that hundreds of communists were working in the State Department, a top State Department official indicated that nearly a hundred of his agency's employees had resigned amid concern that they were security risks, adding, "Most of these were homosexuals."

This revelation caused a media stir, appearing on the front page of the next day's *New York Times* and causing many—both inside and outside the government—to ask how widespread was the infiltration of sex perverts within the ranks of government. Few questioned the assumption that homosexuals serving in government positions posed a threat to national security, whether through the risk of blackmail or through the presumed weakness and incompetence of "moral degenerates."

Although other legislators—particularly the prominent Sen. Kenneth Wherry (R-Neb.)—took the lead in investigating the presence of homosexuals in government, McCarthy also pointed fingers. For example, he complained to a Senate subcommittee that one gay man had been protected from losing his State Department job because of political pressure from the Democrats.

Throughout 1950 the investigations continued, and dozens of lesbians and gay men lost their jobs each month. In December of that year, the Senate Subcommittee on Investigations released its report on the "Employment of Homosexuals and Other Sex Perverts in Government," which charged that gays were generally unsuitable for government jobs—in part because they enjoy each other's company and thus "it is almost inevitable that [they] will attempt to place other homosexuals in government jobs." Worse, the report continued, homosexuals' emotional instability "makes them susceptible to the blandishments of the foreign espionage agent."

This report and the other accusations of the McCarthy era were turned into concrete homophobic policies as the 1950s wore on. The FBI began surveillance of gay bars and social networks, and the post office began tracking homosexuals by noting the subscribers to physique magazines and gay pen-pal clubs. Soon after Eisenhower took office in 1953, he issued Executive Order 10450, which made "sexual perversion" acceptable grounds for firing any government employee, from the military to the Library of Congress. According to one estimate, as much as 20% of the American governmental workforce was subject to McCarthy-era rules allowing summary dismissal because of homosexuality.

McCarthy's public humiliation and censure in 1954 (which involved his closeted gay aide Roy Cohn's mendacity and audacity in spending public funds) ended his role as the demagogue of the decade. But the antigay policies of the McCarthy era—along with their inevitable psychological effects on the fragile gay and lesbian community—long outlived the public career of their founder.

It is not a coincidence that those who were most feared in the McCarthy era were communists, homosexuals, and Jews. The three groups share key characteristics that posed a threat to an insecure nation at the outset of the Cold War. Communists, homosexuals, and Jews are not always easy to spot. They may conceal their political opinions, masquerade as straight, or change their last names, but heterodox they remain, often discreetly meeting with fellow travelers. Less than two decades after members of these groups were sent to concentration camps on the other side of the Atlantic, they again found themselves thrown together, this time in a vicious campaign of innuendo, slander, and attack on their livelihoods.

The greatest irony of this historical episode is the fact that McCarthy was often accused, McCarthy-style, of having been gay himself. A bachelor for 45 years until he married a member of his staff in 1953, McCarthy's sexuality was the subject of innuendo both during his life and since. At the height of McCarthy's power, a newspaper publisher who had previously tangled with the senator wrote, "It is common talk among homosexuals in Milwaukee who rendezvous at the White Horse Inn that Senator Joe McCarthy often engaged in homosexual activities. The persons in Nevada who listened to McCarthy's radio talk thought he had the queerest laugh. He has. He is."

44. Who were the Daughters of Bilitis?

The first lesbian organization in the United States was the Daughters of Bilitis, which started as a social group of fewer than a dozen women meeting in members' homes in San Francisco. The group was founded by lovers Phyllis Lyon and Del Martin, who chose the name "Daughters of Bilitis" in reference to a French poem set on the isle of Lesbos entitled *Song of Bilitis.* Lyon and Martin felt the name sounded "like any other women's lodge," such as the Daughters of the American Revolution.

From its founding in September 1955, DOB cast itself as an alternative to the lesbian bar scene, which its leaders saw as destructive to the well-being of women who participated in it. One DOB president wrote, "The defiance, disillusionment, and despair, we all know, lie there under the mask of 'gaiety' which [bar patrons] put on!"

Instead, DOB offered mixers and discussion groups they termed "Gab 'n Javas," in which members would discuss issues such as mental health and, "Should lesbians wear skirts?"

But DOB's mission soon widened into outreach and politics. The main mechanism for outreach was a newsletter "The Ladder," launched in 1956. Initially distributed to all members plus any lesbians the organizers could think of—not to mention lawyers and psychologists listed in the telephone book—"The Ladder" later gained nationwide circulation through subscriptions and newsstands. As such, it provided a key lifeline to other lesbians for women living in isolated areas. "The Ladder"

contained news articles, poetry, fiction, and biographies of famous lesbians from the past.

In 1958, DOB chapters were founded in New York City and
Los Angeles, followed the next year by a chapter in Chicago
and briefly Rhode Island. Most of the groups had a strained but
cooperative relationship with the male-dominated homophile
organizations of the time—the Mattachine Society and One.
The women of DOB felt the male groups tended to treat them
like a "ladies' auxiliary," and some of the men resented the fact
that while their own groups were open to all, DOB was open
only to women. DOB leaders reacted to this situation with a
sense of humor, creating a "men's auxiliary" called the Sons of
Bilitis—and handing out membership cards bearing the initials
SOB to gay and straight male allies.

The first of DOB's five biennial conventions was held in San
Francisco in 1960. The conference was interrupted by local law
enforcement who demanded to know whether the attendees
advocated wearing men's clothing, which was illegal at that
time. The irony was that in 1960, Daughters of Bilitis required
its members to wear "appropriate" clothing to activities and
saw part of its mission as "advocating a mode of behavior and
dress acceptable to society." As Barbara Gittings, who later re-
belled against the conformist DOB style, described it, DOB
members at one national convention persuaded a woman who
had worn masculine attire all her life to "deck herself out in as
'feminine' a manner as she could, given that female clothes
were totally alien to her. Everybody rejoiced over this as
though some great victory had been accomplished—the 'femi-
nizing' of this woman."

This incident illustrates the attitude held by Daughters of
Bilitis until well into the mid '60s. Its four-part statement of

purpose identified, along with education of the public, participation in research projects, and promotion of legal changes, the "education of the varian...to enable her to understand herself and make her adjustment to society." On several occasions psychiatrists and other "experts" who had contempt for homosexuality were invited to speak at DOB events. Even the name of the newsletter implied that DOB existed to bring lesbians out of a debased state and up "the ladder" of acceptance.

In the mid 1960s, Gittings began to use her position as editor of "The Ladder" to encourage a change in DOB's stance. She began to use the word *lesbian* on the cover and wrote columns urging women to come out and criticizing the dependence on medical "experts." Then in May 1965 she printed a long article by Franklin Kameny, the leader of the most aggressive, outspoken wing of the homophile movement. In his piece Kameny debunked the "gay is sick" point of view and urged readers to go beyond supporting research into homosexuality's causes and cures and instead focus on "the often less pleasant rough-and-tumble of political and social activism."

By the late 1960s many members of Daughters of Bilitis had embraced the feminist critique of American society, and much of the energy of American lesbians was dedicated to the feminist and gay liberation movements. DOB was so divided between the old guard and the new style that at the 1970 convention the national structure was dissolved. Within a few years "The Ladder" ceased publication, and the local chapters went their own ways, mostly dissolving. Daughters of Bilitis played a crucial role in breaking the ice for lesbian organizing, but its long-standing insistence on conformity and acceptance by mainstream society made it ill-suited for the feminist 1970s.

45. Who was Rudi Gernreich?

Rudi Gernreich secured a place for himself in fashion history as the designer of one of the most controversial pieces of women's wear: the topless bathing suit. But in gay history books he'll also be remembered as a cofounder of the Mattachine Society.

Born in Vienna in 1922, Gernreich showed early artistic talent. He was introduced to fashion design by his aunt, who owned a dress shop where Gernreich spent many hours after school sketching clothes and learning about fabric. When he was 12 a designer saw his sketches and offered him an apprenticeship in London, but his mother vetoed the move.

In 1938, Gernreich and his mother left Austria, along with thousands of other Jews fleeing Hitler. The Gernreichs had friends in Los Angeles and decided to settle there. Living near Hollywood was a dream come true for the teenage boy. "I'd seen movies and read American magazines, and suddenly I was there!" Gernreich later said. Gernreich quickly became fluent in English and eventually spoke it with no accent. In 1943 he obtained American citizenship.

Gernreich put himself through art school by running errands for various advertising agencies. After graduation his first job was as a costume sketch artist for designer Edith Head (a closeted lesbian) at RKO Studios, but he "hated every minute." Attending a dance performance by Martha Graham led him to make a career shift and join the Lester Horton Dance Troupe. Dance, he later observed, influenced his fashion designs: "[It] made me aware of what clothes do to the rest of the body—to the hands and feet and head."

By the late 1940s, Gernreich recognized his limited dancing talent and returned to designing. Some of his first designs were costumes for his former dance troupe. At the Horton Studio in 1950, he met Harry Hay, whose young daughter took dance classes there. Hay later recalled that Gernreich stared at him from across the studio. They made a date for dinner, and "we fell madly in love, of course," Hay said. Gernreich had only had short flings with men before Hay. Because the designer still lived with his mother and Hay was married, they carried on their romance at hotels and in friends' apartments.

Hay was a Communist organizer who had written a prospectus for a homosexual rights group and was looking for people to help him start it. Hay showed the plan to Gernreich and later remembered his lover's first thoughts about it: "This is the most dangerous thing I have ever read," Gernreich told Hay. "And I'm with you 100%."

Together with several other men, Hay and Gernreich started the Mattachine Society, the first long-standing gay rights organization. They distributed flyers at gay bars and in the gay areas of beaches, trying to recruit members. Meetings were held in secret at members' homes. "The whole group was fearful," Martin Block, an early member, said, "although I think Rudi was more so...because he was an immigrant."

Gernreich and Hay had been lovers for a year when Gernreich temporarily moved to New York City for a design opportunity. The distance hurt their relationship, and when Gernreich returned to California, the pair broke up. Hay speculated that Gernreich's career ambitions clashed too much with Hay's consuming gay political work. Gernreich left Mattachine, and Hay honored the group's secrecy pledge by keeping mum about Gernreich's involvement until after the designer's death.

Gernreich's career soon soared with a line of simple, comfortable women's clothing. In 1952 his "nothing-inside-but-you" bathing suit (without a molded, built-in bra) was both controversial and sought after. It was only a short step to the fashion item that made him famous. In an interview in 1962 in *Women's Wear Daily*, Gernreich stated that many women on the Riviera wore only bikini bottoms, and soon topless bathing suits would be the rage. *WWD* printed his prediction, and concerned that another designer would scoop him, Gernreich produced the topless suit himself. Photographs of the first topless bathing suit, modeled from behind, appeared in *Look* magazine in June 1964 and launched Gernreich into overnight celebrity.

Gernreich's design was denounced by everyone from the Vatican to the Kremlin. In St. Tropez, officials warned that wearing the suit would bring "legal repercussions," and helicopters patrolled the beaches for offenders. Many stores refused to carry the suit, but 3,000 topless suits still were sold by reputable establishments like B. Altman and Lord & Taylor.

The uproar over the topless bathing suit overshadowed Gernreich's other designs, which included the first miniskirts. In 1967 he was inducted into the Fashion Hall of Fame. Throughout his career Gernreich continued to shock the fashion world (he was the first to use models with shaved heads, for example) and to advocate for freedom in clothing.

Gernreich's gay identity was not publicly revealed until his death from lung cancer in 1985. At that time the American Civil Liberties Union announced that Gernreich and his lover Dr. Oreste Pucciani had endowed a trust for litigation and education on lesbian and gay rights.

46. Who was James Baldwin?

"I've loved a few men, and I've loved a few women." That's how noted African-American writer James Baldwin once characterized his sexuality. Baldwin never embraced the word *gay*, though he wrote four novels that stand at the forefront of gay literature.

Baldwin was born in Harlem in 1924 to a single mother. When he was 3 she married a Pentecostal preacher. Religion was an early and powerful influence on Baldwin, who used it as an escape from his abusive stepfather. Baldwin became a preacher at the age of 14, and his first novel, *Go Tell It on the Mountain* (1953), fictionalized his youthful career as a popular and talented orator in a Harlem congregation.

The other strong influence on Baldwin's life and writing was his sexual orientation, about which he expressed confusion at an early age. Friends and family members guessed his sexuality before he did. His younger brother told an interviewer after Baldwin became famous, "Honey, I knew when Jimmy was a little boy. Of course we just knew."

Two of Baldwin's early mentors were black gay men: poet Countee Cullen, who taught him in high school, and painter Beauford Delaney, whom Baldwin met in 1940. For many years Delaney was the most important person in Baldwin's life. Delaney introduced him to music, art, and literature as well as to the gay artistic circles of Manhattan. Whether or not he also introduced him to sex, Baldwin never said. After his informal education with Delaney, Baldwin noted, "Then I could really write."

Living in New York City's Greenwich Village in the 1940s and working odd jobs, Baldwin launched his writing career, distinguishing himself as a critic and commentator for such publications as *The Nation, Commentary,* and *The Partisan Review.* To his disappointment Baldwin found that even in the supposedly bohemian and free-thinking Village, the fact that he was both black and queer made him a frequent target of harassment. In 1948, sick of American racism and homophobia and with just $40 to his name, Baldwin moved to Paris to start over. "It wasn't so much a matter of choosing France," he later told an interviewer, "as it was a matter of getting out of America."

In doing so Baldwin joined a long line of expatriate queer American literati—such as Natalie Barney and Gertrude Stein—who found France a more welcome home for their literary and personal pursuits.

In Paris, Baldwin met "all kinds of very different people," including Lucien Happersberger, a young Swiss man who became his great love and lifelong friend. "I starved in Paris for a while," Baldwin wrote in later years, but he learned he could find love—a goal he had found elusive in the United States. Happersberger, however eager to sample the joys of gay sex with his friend, didn't share Baldwin's dream of romantic love between men and eventually married a woman and had a son he ironically named James.

Unrequited love makes good material, and the experience with Happersberger inspired Baldwin creatively. His second novel, *Giovanni's Room* (1956), was a portrait of gay male love and abandonment that repulsed both his editor, who rejected the manuscript, and his agent, who advised him to burn it. It wasn't that the novel was sexually explicit, which it wasn't, but that Baldwin dared to consider a gay relationship an acceptable topic for fiction. The other shocker was that Baldwin's narrator was white at a time when such racial lines were rarely crossed. The novel eventually found a publisher in England and then in the United States. Despite all the barriers, *Giovanni's Room* was hailed by critics in this country as a masterpiece.

Baldwin went on to write three more novels with gay or bisexual main characters. *Another Country* (1961), a best-seller, put forth the credo of Baldwin's life and career: that love can't be restricted by race or gender. *Tell Me How Long the Train's Been Gone* (1968) and *Just Above My Head* (1979) also depicted gay relationships in a complex, sympathetic, and unapologetic way, foreshadowing the work of today's out gay novelists.

After his death from a stroke on December 1, 1987, Baldwin's body was brought back to New York for a star-studded funeral attended by 5,000 people. A tribute from his family, printed in a pamphlet and distributed among the mourners, recalled Baldwin's membership in "the society of the human heart." That euphemism is evocative of some of the other non-labels the writer used for his sexuality during his lifetime. Despite the positive queer content of his novels, Baldwin consistently rejected both the labels "gay" and "bisexual." He and his lovers, he told a reporter in 1984, were simply people who "moved in the world." Though he lived long enough to witness the many gains of the gay liberation movement, he took no part in it and maintained until the end of his life that his sexuality was no one's business but his own and God's.

47. What was the Boise Sex Scandal?

The 50s were generally a harsh time for gays and lesbians in the United States. The decade of conformity, McCarthyism, and atomic hysteria was also a time of rampant persecution of gay men and lesbians, who were subject to firings, arrests, and imprisonment in cities across the country. Perhaps the most famous episode—and certainly one of the best-documented— took place in 1956 and 1957 in Boise, population 35,000, the capital of the state of Idaho.

As in many other places, some of the male students at Boise High School in the mid 1950s engaged in mutual masturbation. Some of these students, often from the "tough" crowd, would also allow older men to perform oral sex on them for a price ranging from a quarter to $10. By targeting men who were rumored to be gay, some of these teenagers were able to collect ever-higher sums of money with threats of exposure.

This situation, not all that different from informal male prostitution in other cities, became a matter of public concern on Halloween 1955, when three adult men were arrested on morals charges. A few days later the *Idaho Daily Statesman* published a highly inflammatory editorial urging immediate public action, warning that the arrests had only "scratched the surface" and that the youth of Boise were in danger.

According to the analysis of former *Time* and *Newsweek* journalist John Gerassi (whose 1966 book *The Boys of Boise* re-mains the most thorough account of the scandal), the Hal-loween arrests and later prosecutions of several more Boise residents, including highly respected citizens, were a part of an ongoing political struggle among the elite citizens of Boise. A group of prominent men, who Gerassi calls the "Boise Gang," used the arrests and publicity to attack their enemies. But the scandal grew out of control and ultimately hurt members of the gang as well as the reputation of the small city. One member of the gang, whom Gerassi calls "the Queen," was an extremely wealthy gay man who was investigated but never arrested or publicly identified.

Another member of the gang was a city councilman who had hoped the arrests would eventually reach the brother of a city official with whom he had clashed. Instead, the councilman's son was implicated, discharged from West Point, and sentenced to three years in a penitentiary for engaging in gay sex.

The effects of the scandal on Boise were widespread. An investigator, fresh from Washington, D.C., where he had worked in the McCarthyist campaign against homosexuals in the State Department, came to Boise and interviewed hundreds of gay and straight men, many of whom were coerced into naming gay friends. The police were deluged with calls, mostly from nervous mothers, accusing specific men of homosexuality. Straight men went out of their way to avoid incriminating appearances, even inviting women to participate in previously all-male poker games.

With coverage in *Time* and other national outlets, Boise quickly gained a reputation as a locus of gay activity, leading both antigay crusaders and men in the Northwest looking for gay sex to label it "Boysy." But as more men were arrested and convicted to sentences as drastic as life in prison, Boise became anathema to gay men, and many left town for friendlier locales. For years thereafter, Boise symbolized oppression in gay circles. The 1972 travel guide *The Gay Insider* included a description of the scandal in its "Idaho" section, along with the warning "Stay out of Idaho." In 1977, when similar accusations threatened Boston's gay community, an organization formed to oppose a government witch-hunt, calling itself the Boston/Boise Committee.

The situation for gays in Boise has improved somewhat. Boise's first pride parade was held in 1990, although one participant marched with a bag over his or her head. In 1994, Idaho voters narrowly defeated a Colorado-style antigay amendment. And according to the editor of Idaho's largest gay publication, *Diversity*, the city now has three or four gay and lesbian bars, depending on how you count.

48. What was Evelyn Hooker's research about?

Dr. Evelyn Hooker was one of the first American psychologists to use the results of psychological research to argue for the decriminalization of homosexuality. Before Hooker began her work, most research on homosexuality relied on case histories of gays and lesbians who were hospitalized, incarcerated, or sought psychological help. Hooker was the first American psychologist to study well-adjusted members of the gay community.

Hooker was originally an animal psychologist, but in the mid 1940s she befriended a gay student in one of her courses at the University of California, Los Angeles. With his prodding she began to explore the nature of homosexuality in her research. She recruited volunteers through homophile organizations and friendship networks for a study on the psychological adjustment of gay men. She subjected 60 men, half of whom were gay, to a series of personality tests, including the Rorschach (inkblot) test. A panel of "experts" was unable to determine who was gay based on the results of the tests. Hooker argued that her results showed homosexuality was not a sickness. Her research did not include lesbians as subjects, however, mostly because she feared being labeled a lesbian herself.

When Hooker presented her work in 1956 and 1957, her findings were attacked by those who were convinced that homosexuality was pathological. But when Hooker allowed her critics to review her data, they too were unable to identify the homosexuals based solely on the results of psychological tests.

In the late 1960s, Hooker took her science a step further when President Lyndon Johnson appointed her to lead a task force on homosexuality for the National Institute of Mental Health. The report her task force issued called for the repeal of sodomy laws and was one of many influences on the 1973 decision by the American Psychiatric Association to remove homosexuality from its list of mental diseases.

49. What was the Wolfenden Report?

Before the modern gay rights movement, the three traditional ways of understanding homosexuality were as sin, sickness, or crime. A key step in undermining the "crime" approach came in 1957 with the release of the Wolfenden Report in Great Britain.

In the early 1950s, British headlines were filled with scandals relating to homosexuality. Several noted public figures—including a prominent politician, a famous actor, and a respected journalist—were arrested and tried for homosexual offenses. These scandals led to increasing public discussion, and for the first time in British history, legal issues relating to homosexuality were openly debated in the House of Lords. The British government decided to appoint a commission to explore legal issues relating to homosexuality and prostitution. To chair the commission the government tapped Sir John Wolfenden, the vice chancellor of Reading University. One of Wolfenden's qualifications was his admission that he knew nothing of the subject at hand—and therefore could be an impartial leader of the inquiry.

Although the Wolfenden Committee also addressed prostitution (and ultimately advocated harsher penalties for street prostitutes), the focus of the Committee and the public debate surrounding its report was male homosexuality. The committee (which included politicians, ministers, aristocrats, and a judge) met more than 60 times, taking testimony from 200 witnesses before issuing its report on September 4, 1957.

The report's conclusions depended on its assumption that the law exists to preserve public order and decency and to protect the weak—especially children—from exploitation. The Wolfenden Committee said it did not feel the law should "concern itself with what a man does in private unless it can be shown to be so contrary to the public good that the law ought to intervene in its function as the guardian of the public good."

The report then examined the three common objections to reforming laws that would criminalize any male-male sexual act: that such an act "menaces the health of society," that "it has damaging effects on family life," and that "a man who indulges in these practices with another man may turn his attention to boys."

One by one the report debunked these objectives. It asserted that there was no evidence to support the view that homosexuality causes the decay of civilizations. It pointed out that "adultery, fornication, and lesbian behavior" were equally threatening to family life but not criminalized. Finally, it suggested that law reform would actually serve to protect minors because some men who would prefer adult partners may instead have been turning to boys because they felt safer from the threat of blackmail or prosecution.

The Wolfenden Report explicitly outlined a program for the reform of laws that criminalized male homosexual acts. It advocated legalizing consensual sex between adult males (defined as those older than 21), loosening penalties for sex with those under 21, and shortening the statute of limitations for homosexual acts between adults and those under 21 to one year.

Many British gays and lesbians were disappointed at the focus on 21 as the legal age, since lesbian and heterosexual acts were legal at age 16. Nonetheless, they welcomed the report and the promise of greater sexual freedom.

Most of Britain's newspapers also treated the release of the Wolfenden Report favorably, but a public opinion poll showed 47% of the public was opposed to the report's conclusions, with only 38% supporting law reform. Nonetheless, the Wolfenden Report sparked a debate within legal circles and wider society about homosexuality and crime in general that ultimately brought about sweeping change.

Some of these changes showed up quite soon after the report's release. For example, in the late 1950s the British government lifted its ban on theatrical and cinematic portrayals of homosexuality. The plays and films that followed furthered the dissemination of liberal ideas about gays and lesbians.

The Wolfenden report had repercussions in North America as well. It was frequently cited by homophile and (later) gay liberation organizations as evidence that a civilized society doesn't criminalize gay sex.

In Britain, though, the Wolfenden Report carried no force of law, and the ultimate reform of the antigay laws it addressed took a full decade. In the ten years between the release of the report and passage of the Sexual Offences Act of 1967, gay and lesbian activists and their heterosexual allies campaigned in all sectors of society for more acceptance of homosexuality. Public opinion had shifted markedly by 1967, when Parliament voted to decriminalize private adult homosexual acts in England and Wales. (Scottish and Northern Irish gay men still faced criminal sanctions into the 1980s.)

50. Who was Lorraine Hansberry?

"I was born black and female," playwright Lorraine Hansberry (1930–1965) wrote, summing up the influences on her life and work. If she had lived longer, she might have added "and lesbian" to her description of herself.

Both of Hansberry's parents were civil rights activists in Chicago. In 1938 the family moved from a black ghetto to a mostly white, middle-class neighborhood in order to challenge the city's Jim Crow housing laws. "Literally, howling mobs surrounded our house," Hansberry recalled of the occasion when angry white neighbors threw bricks through her family's front window. The Hansberrys fought all the way to the Supreme Court for a black family's right to live where it pleased. Hansberry's landmark play *A Raisin in the Sun* (1959) took its inspiration from her family's experiences with racial discrimination in housing.

In her high school yearbook, Hansberry wrote that her ambition was to be a journalist. After a few years of college at the University of Wisconsin, she moved to New York City and joined the editorial staff of Paul Robeson's radical journal *Freedom*. Following in her parents' footsteps, she became an activist for black rights. Hansberry wrote to a friend that she would "attend meetings almost every night...usher at rallies, make street corner speeches in Harlem." At a demonstration against the exclusion of blacks from university sports, she met Robert Nemiroff, a white Jewish intellectual and music producer, and the two married in 1953.

But the marriage lasted only a few years because Hansberry soon began coming to terms with her lesbianism. Around 1957 she and Nemiroff quietly and amicably separated, though they didn't divorce until seven years later. At the same time Hansberry joined Daughters of Bilitis, the early lesbian organization based in San Francisco, and began receiving their journal, "The Ladder." She also subscribed to *One*, the homophile magazine published in Los Angeles.

In May 1957, Hansberry wrote the first of two thoughtful letters to "The Ladder." Since the policy of the magazine was to identify letter writers only with initials, "L.H.N., New York, N.Y." followed Hansberry's letter. Barbara Grier, editor at that time, identified Hansberry as the writer only after her death. In her letter Hansberry expressed relief at having found the magazine: "I'm glad as heck you exist," she wrote. She also mused about everything from butch-femme culture to the gaps between lesbians and gay men, displaying a feminist awareness that would grow stronger over the next few years.

In August of that same year, "L.H.N." once again wrote the "The Ladder" with more feminist commentary. The connections she drew between sexism and homophobia were ahead of her time, and her political insights stood out from the magazine's other, lighter fare. "Homosexual persecution," Hansberry wrote, "has at its roots not only social ignorance, but a philosophically active anti-feminist dogma."

By 1957, Hansberry was already well into writing *A Raisin in the Sun;* 18 months after her second letter to "The Ladder," she became an instant celebrity when the play opened on Broadway. Accompanying Hansberry on opening night was her close friend James Baldwin, with whom she often went to gay bars and artists' hangouts in Greenwich Village. The two met in 1957, during a dramatic production of Baldwin's gay-themed novel *Giovanni's Room.* "She sat way up in the bleachers," Baldwin remembered, "taking on some of the biggest names in the American theater because she had liked the play and they, in the main, hadn't."

A Raisin in the Sun made theater history for African-Americans and for women. Never before had a black woman writer's work appeared on a Broadway stage. "I had never in my life seen so many black people in the theater," Baldwin marveled of the opening night. After the play, in the alley behind the theater, Hansberry and Baldwin were mobbed by fans. "Lorraine handed me her handbag," Baldwin said, "and began signing autographs. 'It only happens once,' she said." Hansberry became the first African-American and the fifth woman to win the New York Drama Critics' Award. Softened of some of its defiance, the play became a hit movie two years later.

Hansberry's second play, *The Sign in Sidney Brustein's Window* (1964), received only lukewarm reviews, however. She was criticized for writing about white people and straying from "black" topics. She also presented radical ideas about gay activism: "If you don't like the sex laws," Sidney, the protagonist, tells David, a gay male character, "attack 'em.... Please get over the notion that your particular 'thing' is something that only the deepest, saddest, and most nobly tortured can know about. It ain't." Hansberry's words foreshadowed the "gay is good" attitude of 1970s gay liberation.

Sadly, Hansberry's contributions to theater, to African-American culture, and to gay liberation were all cut short. After a bout with ulcers, she learned in July 1964 that there were serious problems with her intestinal system. Six months later she died of cancer at the age of 34. Nemiroff, her literary executor, spent the next 25 years keeping her work alive. But Hansberry's sexual identity remained hidden until lesbian scholars brought it to light in the 1980s.

51. What was the Supreme Court's first pro-gay ruling?

Romer v. *Evans,* the 1996 Supreme Court decision that found Colorado's antigay Amendment 2 unconstitutional, was not the first time the high court ruled in favor of gay people. In January, 1958, the court delivered its first pro-gay ruling in *One, Inc.* v. *Oleson,* a landmark decision that allowed lesbian and gay publications to be sent through the mail.

One, Inc., a homophile educational organization, was founded in Los Angeles in 1952 by about a dozen members (mostly men, with one woman) of the Mattachine Society. The group wanted to publish a monthly magazine, also called *One,* instead of just participating in Mattachine discussion groups. The name was chosen from a quote by 19th-century British essayist Thomas Carlyle: "A mystical bond of brotherhood makes all men one."

One of the magazine's early editors, Martin Block, recalled that for the premier issue, "We thought if we had to, we would write articles ourselves. We called our friends and asked them to contribute." The underlying message of the magazine, Block said, was that people could be proud to be gay. "That in itself was radical," Block noted. "At that time, gay...was thought to be a disease."

One appeared in January, 1953, with the Carlyle quote on the first page. It featured articles on the Mattachine Society and several personal essays. The longest essay, "To Be Accused Is to Be Guilty," was by Dale Jennings, one of the magazine's founders. Jennings described his entrapment in a Los Angeles park by a plainclothes policeman in 1952 and his subsequent trial and acquittal. "The only true pervert in the court room," he quipped, "was the arresting officer."

From the beginning the founders insisted on a professional look for the magazine. Even though they were paying the initial publication costs themselves, they opted to typeset and print *One* instead of mimeographing it, which was how many underground organizations reproduced their publications. *One* distinguished itself with bold graphics, eye-catching artwork, and eventually paid advertising (one of the first ads was for men's pajamas).

To distribute the new magazine, the staff visited newsstands that carried physique magazines (which attracted gay buyers) and asked them to also carry *One.* They found a pool of eager subscribers in the membership of the Mattachine Society, and within a few months *One* was selling 2,000 copies a month. Its readership, of course, was much higher because many gays would pass their copies along to friends after reading them.

Besides drawing gay readers, however, *One* also caught the attention of law enforcement officials. At the height of the McCarthy witch-hunts, FBI agents in Los Angeles began collecting copies of the magazine in hopes of finding obscene or communist content. In July 1953 the FBI initiated a full-scale investigation, sending copies of the magazine every month to national headquarters in Washington. FBI agents even wrote letters to the employers of *One*'s editors, advising them that their employees were "deviants" and "security risks." Despite these underhanded tactics, none of the *One* staffers lost their day jobs, and the FBI never succeeded in shutting the magazine down.

Postal authorities, however, were nearly able to close the magazine several times. The first time was in August, 1953, when the L.A. postmaster seized all copies of *One* on the grounds that its content was obscene. But post officials in Washington decided that *One* did not violate federal law. The following year a Republican senator from Wisconsin, Alexander Wiley, renewed the attack on *One,* writing to the Postmaster General protesting "the use of the United States mails to transmit a so-called 'magazine' devoted to the advancement of sexual perversion." Wiley's letter led to a second effort by the post office to keep *One* out of the hands of its subscribers.

In October 1954 postal officials once again seized the magazine and charged the editors with sending obscene material through the mail, a violation of the 1873 Comstock Act. The post office cited a poem, "Lord Samuel and Lord Montague," and a short story, "Sappho Remembered," as "obscene, lewd, lascivious, and filthy"—obviously thinking one adjective wasn't enough. The poem offended, officials claimed, because it suggested that homosexuality was common among British lords. The short story was "lustful" because it depicted a woman who left her fiancé for another woman.

One's editors hired a straight defense attorney, who argued in federal district court that *One* was educational and strove simply "to create understanding of an extremely knotty social problem." But the judge ruled for the post office, contending that the magazine was intended not to educate but to "stimulate the lust of the homosexual reader." On appeal a second judge concurred, dismissing *One* as "cheap pornography."

Determined, *One* took its case all the way to the Supreme Court. On January 13, 1958, the court delivered an astonishing unanimous pro-gay decision, overturning the rulings of the two lower courts and limiting the power of the Comstock Act. As a result, lesbian and gay publications could be mailed without legal repercussions, though many continued to experience harassment from the post office and U.S. Customs.

Over the years One, Inc. expanded its focus beyond the magazine, publishing books and pamphlets and offering classes. Though *One* magazine folded in 1967, One Institute for Homophile Studies continued the educational mission of the group's founders.

52. What have gays and lesbians experienced in revolutionary Cuba?

In the more than 40 years since Fidel Castro's communist revolution in Cuba, gays and lesbians have faced a series of physical and psychological challenges that have largely excluded them from the dramatic advances in gay and lesbian equality in other countries during this period.

Before Fulgencio Batista's government was overthrown on New Year's Day 1959, gays and lesbians were a prominent part of Havana's notorious underworld of gambling, sex, and drugs. But when the revolution aimed to "clean up" the excesses of the old regime, homosexuality was treated as a capitalist vice the new Cuba could do without. Many gay men in particular sought to leave the country, and others, including many lesbians, retreated to the closet.

In 1961, just two years after the revolution, the first massive roundup of homosexuals took place in Havana. Known as Operation Three Ps for its targeting of "pederasts, prostitutes, and pimps," this campaign advanced the communist government's goal of showing its success in ridding Cuba of decadent bourgeois influences. That same year prominent playwright Virgilio Piñera was arrested for being gay. Although he was soon released, his detention added to the climate of fear for Cuba's gays and lesbians. Soon, gays were barred from joining the Cuban Communist Party—which ended any hope for economic advancement—and gay teachers and students were dismissed from the University of Havana.

But the most notorious antigay action of the Cuban government was the *Unidades Militares Para el Aumento del Production,* or Military Units to Aid Production, camps. Between 1965 and 1968 several thousand gay men, those suspected of being gay, and other politically or culturally suspect individuals were imprisoned in forced work camps in eastern Cuba. These men were forced to work in sugarcane fields by day and to listen to Marxist-Leninist lectures at night.

The UMAP camps garnered media attention in the United States, and a small group of homophile activists even picketed the United Nations in 1965 to protest what they saw as the twin homophobic policies of Cuba and the United States. This protest was an unusual moment in the history of the gay movement in the United States, which has rarely paid attention to the plight of gays and lesbians in other countries.

Even after the UMAP camps were closed (in part due to international pressure), gays and lesbians remained subject to official measures regulating their economic and sexual lives. Hundreds of gay artists, teachers, and actors in particular lost their jobs, often in very public purges that left the victims isolated from their families and communities.

Official Cuban homophobia posed a challenge for the early gay liberationists in the United States. In the post-Stonewall era many advocates of gay liberation embraced leftist thought, an ideology that applauded the socialism of Castro's Cuba. In 1970 a number of members of the Gay Liberation Front joined the Venceremos Brigade, a group made up of several hundred young Americans and Canadians who spent the summer in Cuba to work on socialist farms. While many of their straight compatriots returned enamored of Cuban society, the gay Venceremos were not as impressed. A group of them wrote:

The anti-homosexual policy of the Cuban government does not simply fail to include gay people in the revolutionary process—it specifically excludes them from participation.... A policy of ruthless and incessant persecution of gay people is contradictory to the needs of all people, and such a policy is reactionary and fascist.

By most accounts gay men were disproportionately represented among the refugees who fled Cuba for the United States in the Mariel boat lift of 1979. In some cases the Cuban government actually encouraged gay men to join the boat lift, and it financed a film called *Scum* that portrayed the refugees as effeminate gay men. When thousands of gay Cuban refugees reached Southern Florida, a number of American gay organizations worked hard to find them homes and jobs.

In the 1980s, Cuba came under attack by American gays and lesbians for its reactionary policies on the subject of AIDS. Cuba's official approach to combat the disease has been quarantine, which originally meant imprisoning anyone who tested positive for the HIV virus (a policy that has since been relaxed significantly). Cuba's approach of emphasizing its version of "public health" over human rights has met with some success, though; only a few hundred Cuban residents (mostly heterosexual) have died of AIDS-related complications, a rate far lower than in other Caribbean countries.

On July 28, 1994, about 20 young Cuban gays and lesbians met in a Havana park for Cuba's first gay pride celebration. They founded Cuba's first gay rights organization and penned a manifesto that read, in part, "For the first time we have consciously gathered here in unity. Being afraid can only help the ideas of our detractors. Being afraid is absurd if we want to defend our rights. It is necessary to act proudly, to make a daring gesture; it is necessary to act with courage."

53. Who was Bayard Rustin?

Alveda King, niece of Dr. Martin Luther King Jr., has expended a lot of energy publicly condemning gay people and denouncing the gay rights movement. What she seems to have forgotten is that the man who taught her famous uncle about nonviolent protest and who was a major architect of the black civil rights movement of the 1950s and 1960s was an openly gay man named Bayard Rustin.

Rustin was born in 1912 in eastern Pennsylvania and raised by his black Quaker grandparents. Toward the end of his life, he noted that his activism was rooted more in Quaker pacifism than in being black. After attending two colleges and graduating from neither, Rustin moved to New York City in the mid 1930s and enjoyed a brief first career as a singer and actor, playing opposite Paul Robeson in the Broadway musical *John Henry*.

But activism, not acting, was to become Rustin's life work. In 1936 he joined the Young Communist League but became disenchanted with the party when it abandoned its commitment to the desegregation of the armed forces at the start of World War II. Rustin quickly moved on to work with the Fellowship of Reconciliation, an international Christian pacifist organization. During his early years with FOR, Rustin became a disciple of Gandhian nonviolence. In 1944 he put Gandhi's principles into action when he defied his draft summons and had to spend 28 months in a federal prison. After his release Rustin played an important role on the Committee Against Jim

Crow in Military Service and Training, a group instrumental in the desegregation of the armed forces in 1948.

Rustin became one of FOR's top figures and was rumored to be heir apparent to its leader. But his homosexuality and frequent casual sex hurt his career. In 1953, while on an FOR speaking tour, he was arrested in Pasadena, Calif., on a morals charge when he was caught in a parked car having sex with two men. Rustin maintained that the men entrapped him, but he pled guilty anyway and spent 60 days in jail. Though Rustin had never been closeted, being arrested made him a liability to FOR, and he was asked to resign.

Rustin continued to work in the peace movement, taking a staff position with the War Resistors' League. But in 1956, Lillian Smith, a Southern white lesbian and author of the controversial novel about miscegenation *Strange Fruit,* hooked Rustin up with 27-year-old Martin Luther King Jr., who was trying to organize a bus boycott in Montgomery, Ala. King had academic knowledge of Gandhi's philosophy, but Rustin taught him how to actually employ the techniques of nonviolence. As King's adviser, Rustin and several others conceived the Southern Christian Leadership Conference, the grassroots civil rights organization that propelled King into the national spotlight.

To King's credit he hired Rustin knowing about his sexual orientation and criminal record. King himself "was under such extraordinary pressure about his own sex life," Rustin later explained. "J. Edgar Hoover was spreading stories, and there were very real efforts to entrap him" and thereby discredit the civil rights movement.

Some black activists close to King were not comfortable with Rustin, whose promiscuity, they believed, might compromise the entire movement. At one point and for unknown reasons, congressman Adam Clayton Powell Jr. threatened to go public with the false accusation that King and Rustin were lovers. In 1960, in the interest of preserving the movement, Rustin quietly resigned as King's assistant.

In 1962, however, Rustin was back in the thick of things, at the request of veteran black organizer A. Philip Randolph. Randolph's 1941 threat to bring 100,000 black protesters to Washington, D.C., had convinced Roosevelt to block discrimination in defense contracting, and he was once again planning a march to bring about government action. Recognizing Rustin's extraordinary organizing skills, Randolph asked him to draw up the blueprint for a massive civil rights march on Washington, to be held on the 100th anniversary of the Emancipation Proclamation. Though Rustin was the march's architect, black leaders were hesitant to name him as director, since his ties to Communism, his conscientious objection, and his morals-charge arrest made him vulnerable to attack from civil rights opponents. (Congressman Strom Thurmond eventually did attack Rustin on all of these points.) Randolph became the official march director instead, but he named Rustin as his assistant and turned the responsibilities of organizing over to him. The march on Washington, which took place on August 28, 1963, and culminated in King's "I Have a Dream" speech, was a pinnacle of the black civil rights movement.

Though the march was probably Rustin's finest hour, he spent his entire lifetime as an activist and was arrested over 20 times for acts of civil disobedience. In 1964 he organized a public-school boycott in New York City, in which 400,000 students, teachers, and school employees stayed home to protest the slow pace of integration.

Rustin died in 1987 of heart failure. Well into his 70s, he

was still active in various causes, including the fight against AIDS. "He had work to do until the very end," one of his associates said. "His utter devotion to causes was marked by the use of his last ounce of talent, the driving urge to talk, to plan, to organize."

54. What was NACHO?

In the mid 1960s gay and lesbian activists for the first time initiated a broad effort to coordinate and unite the activities of the America's several dozen homophile organizations by creating the North American Conference of Homophile Organizations, or NACHO (rhymes with Waco, not macho).

In 1963 lesbian and gay groups in New York City, Philadelphia, and Washington, D.C., had begun meeting and planning joint activities under the umbrella of East Coast Homophile Organizations. The many protests and public demonstrations led by activists such as Frank Kameny and Craig Rodwell gave ECHO a "militant" reputation that attracted the attention of gays and lesbians across the country, many of whom felt isolated in their organizing. Consequently, ECHO began to be viewed as a model for a national, united organization.

On the weekend of February 18, 1966, 40 delegates met in Kansas City for the first National Planning Conference of Homophile Organizations. Mostly in their 20s and 30s, those in attendance represented 14 lesbian and gay organizations from different parts of the United States. Ironically, none of them were in Kansas City; the site of the conference was chosen for its central location, not to take advantage of the hospitality of any local organization. But the conference's presence in Kansas City inspired local activists, and within a month the Phoenix Society for Individual Freedom was born.

At the Kansas City conference, the decision on whether to form a national organization was postponed until the next meeting, scheduled for San Francisco six months later. But those assembled did establish a national legal defense fund, begin plans for a series of nationwide protests in May 1966 against discrimination in the military, and start a newsletter to keep each group informed of the activities of the others.

At the San Francisco conference—dubbed Ten Days in August—NACHO was formed. During the four years of its existence, it helped start local organizations in dozens of cities, held an annual summer conference, and wrote studies and position papers on issues of concern to gays and lesbians nationwide. The legal defense fund financed court cases to challenge antigay discrimination in immigration, liquor, and military policy. Still, some activists faulted the organization for having no real authority over its member organizations, viewing NACHO as more of a United Nations of gay groups than an actual union of them. Also, many lesbians felt their issues and needs were rarely addressed by NACHO's male-dominated political structure.

At the 1967 NACHO conference in Washington, D.C., the strains of uniting an extremely diverse movement continued to pose problems. Important homophile groups such as New York Mattachine and One in Los Angeles refused to attend for a variety of procedural and substantive reasons. Particularly at issue was the question of "credentials," the right to vote and be considered an official organization at the conference. Some East Coast members wanted to be very strict about letting questionable organizations participate, out of fear of infiltration by extreme left-wing activists. Others, particularly from California, felt that any organization or individual who wished to participate should be welcome.

NACHO's 1968 conference in Chicago was particularly notable, given that it took place just weeks before the stormy protests outside that year's Democratic convention in the same city. Even though Stonewall was more than a year away, the 1968 conference was noticeably militant, adopting as the NACHO slogan "Gay is good" and pronouncing a five-point Homosexual Bill of Rights. The new slogan, which elicited protests from more traditional NACHO affiliates, was consciously patterned after the black nationalist credo "Black is beautiful"—a reflection of the increasing influence of civil rights activism on the homophile movement. Still, the organization was wracked by internal dissent, and many lesbians who had earlier been willing to put up with NACHO's male-oriented structure refused to participate after the 1968 conference.

By its last two conferences in 1969 and 1970, NACHO found itself increasingly overshadowed in a rapidly changing and expanding gay and lesbian movement. The momentum had clearly shifted to newer, more radical organizations such as the Gay Liberation Front and the Gay Activists Alliance. NACHO was never able to overcome its internal divisions and the fear of many of its member organizations that a strong national group would encroach upon their autonomy. Still, the history of NACHO can serve as a necessary corrective to the widespread notion that gay and lesbian groups before Stonewall were timid, desultory, and irrelevant.

55. What is the origin of the annual gay and lesbian pride events?

Many people know that the gay and lesbian marches, parades, and festivals that take place every summer across America and around the world commemorate the Stonewall uprising of June 28, 1969. But the idea of a gay event every summer actually goes back to the mid 1960s, to the "Annual Reminder" held every July 4th from 1965 to 1969.

The Annual Reminder was organized by the East Coast Homophile Organizations, an umbrella organization of gay and lesbian groups in New York, Philadelphia, and Washington, D.C. The first Annual Reminder took place in 1965 at Independence Hall in Philadelphia as one of a series of demonstrations protesting government policies that considered gays and lesbians to be security risks and unfit for both military and civilian employment.

While ECHO also picketed the White House, the Pentagon, and the State Department in 1965, the Philadelphia protest became an annual tradition, with conservatively dressed gays and lesbians marching a stone's throw from the Liberty Bell on Independence Day five years in a row. Organizer Franklin Kameny, a longtime homophile activist and organizer of Mattachine Society in Washington, insisted that the women wear dresses and the men wear suits and ties. Protesters wore EQUALITY FOR HOMOSEXUALS buttons and carried signs with slogans such as, "Sexual preference is irrelevant to federal employment."

The 1969 Annual Reminder came just days after a series of

clashes between police and gays in New York City, sparked by a raid at the Stonewall bar in Greenwich Village. Most of the 40 or so New York gays and lesbians who had chartered a bus to join the Annual Reminder had "liberation" on their minds, not "equality." The activists who wanted to maintain the decorum of previous Annual Reminders objected when a pair of lesbians were seen holding hands. Kameny tried to separate the pair, much to the dismay of the gay liberationists. Craig Rodwell, a New York activist who had proposed the Annual Reminder in the first place, was furious and led the New Yorkers in breaking the "rules" of the Annual Reminder. For the rest of the demonstration, the New York activists paired off and held hands in same-sex couples.

Rodwell engineered a resolution that passed at the November 1969 ECHO conference to replace the Annual Reminder with a new, annual demonstration shifted a week earlier to commemorate "the 1969 spontaneous demonstrations on Christopher Street." The resolution dubbed the New York City protest Christopher Street Liberation Day and urged other cities to form their own, parallel demonstrations the same day. The new protest was inspired by the broader goals and more confrontational tactics of the burgeoning gay liberation movement, in contrast to the public but polite protests of the homophile movement of the previous decade.

New York's first Christopher Street Liberation Day march was a part of a Gay Pride Week of activities, including dances, political meetings, and an erotic art show. The march, held on Sunday, June 28, visibly reflected the liberationist style, including shirtless, long-haired marchers, GAY POWER signs, and open drug use. As with any march, crowd estimates vary widely, but perhaps 5,000–10,000 gays participated in the

New York demonstration, with hundreds more in Los Angeles and Chicago.

The next year the number of participants at the New York, Los Angeles, and Chicago demonstrations grew sharply, and marches were added in Boston, New Orleans, and other cities. Since then, events have been organized in every major city in America—some of which have continued the march-parade tradition and some of which are more of a picnic or festival. The issues most visibly represented in the pride events have varied widely, from opposing Anita Bryant in 1978 to supporting gays in the military in 1993. But contemporary gay pride events still draw on elements of the both the bold but conservative Annual Reminder and the confrontational, celebratory Christopher Street Liberation Day.

56. Was J. Edgar Hoover gay?

For decades Americans have periodically debated the sexuality of longtime FBI director J. Edgar Hoover, the dominant law enforcement official of this century. In his public life Hoover set a new standard in his zealous pursuit and surveillance of those deemed dangerous to national security. His private life, in turn, has become a lightning rod for both his critics and his defenders. Those who see Hoover as a national hero and freedom fighter tend to vigorously defend him against rumors of homosexuality, while his critics—both gay and straight—often describe Hoover's rumored peccadilloes with glee. Both approaches are historically problematic and, more disturbingly, seem to presume that homosexuality is a character flaw.

Any serious inquiry into Hoover's sexuality has to start with the following basic fact: for more than 40 years, the most important person in his life was another man—Clyde Tolson. Tolson, who was five years younger than Hoover, rose quickly through FBI ranks once Hoover became his patron. Within two years Tolson was assistant director of the bureau, and the pair were inseparable. Hoover and Tolson often traveled together and rarely dined apart. Hoover's photo albums consisted almost exclusively of snapshots of Tolson from their many vacations together. Anyone who knew what a gay couple looked like saw something very familiar when they looked at America's top two G-men.

In addition, making the case that Hoover was heterosexual requires tremendous mental strain. Hoover was close friends with Lela Rogers (Ginger's mother), whose far-right philosophy matched his own. Some people suggest the two may have been lovers, although with far less evidence than that which romantically links the director to Tolson. Other purported girlfriends have been put forth, but it is clear that Hoover never seriously dated any woman nor did he ever give any indication that he wished he had a wife. Those who argue that Hoover was straight sometimes depend on amusing contortions—such as when one writer argued that Hoover must have been straight because he kept a portrait of Marilyn Monroe on his wall. One wonders whether the starlet's picture was kept next to a Judy Garland or a Bette Davis.

But whether we classify Hoover as gay, homosexual, asexual, or even "homosocial," the director's obsession with homosexuality cannot be challenged. During the 1950s and 1960s, when the homophile movement was diminutive and quite powerless, Hoover had his agents keep close tabs on gay and lesbian organizing—even keeping the menus from some gay gatherings in his files. He blackmailed several gay government employees and cracked down on individuals or groups who repeated rumors of his own homosexuality. One woman who told her bridge partners she had heard Hoover was gay was visited by FBI agents who demanded she call her friends and retract her accusation. Perhaps with no sense of irony, Hoover was once quoted as saying, "I regret to say that we of the FBI are powerless to act in cases of oral-genital intimacy, unless it has in some way obstructed interstate commerce."

On the other hand, the "proof" that Hoover was gay that has circulated since the 1920s—and especially since the publication of several "tell-all" biographies in the 1990s—is rarely substantiated by more than one source and often seems exaggerated in order to sully Hoover's reputation. For observers who don't share the assumption that homosexuality is a character flaw, these tales can be somewhat disturbing—even when titillating.

One recent book argued that Hoover never executed a full-frontal assault against the Mafia because they had full-frontal shots of him orally servicing his deputy. This book also gained public attention for its weakly documented descriptions of Hoover attending gay sex orgies in a short fluffy black dress, lace stockings, high heels, and a black curly wig. It quotes a woman who claims to have witnessed the director, so attired, being introduced by Roy Cohn as "Mary." It also tells of Hoover lecturing a 15-year-old male prostitute about his long hair before having sex with him.

While it is probable that Hoover had a sexual relationship with Tolson—and quite possible that Hoover did hire underage male prostitutes and attend gay orgies—the way Hoover's homosexuality has been used to reinforce the negative aspects of his life (wiretapping, blackmail, and selective law enforcement, to name a few) should give gays and lesbians pause. During his life, Washington politicians privately referred to the FBI's leaders as "J. Edna" and "Mother Tolson"—and the jokes have not stopped; even President Clinton suggested when selecting a new FBI director that it would be hard to find someone who could fill J. Edgar Hoover's pumps.

Perhaps Hoover's closet makes him a fair target for such jokes. But if he had been openly gay and candid about a love of cross-dressing, that would not have changed his role as the corrupt policeman of American conformity. If the primary reason for Hoover's continued ignominy is his "queerness" and not his politics, we all lose.

57. Who was Andy Warhol?

Pop artist and avant-garde filmmaker Andy Warhol once wrote in the catalogue for a retrospective of his paintings, "In the future, everyone will be famous for 15 minutes." Warhol enjoyed a much longer time in the spotlight. His career spanned three decades and was punctuated by fabulous art openings, celebrity parties, and an assassination attempt by a disgruntled hanger-on. While Warhol's public life regularly made headlines, his private life was much more hidden.

The man who is generally credited with founding pop art was born Andrew Warhola in Pittsburgh in 1928, the son of Czech immigrants. His coal-miner father died when he was young, and his mother helped support the family by selling tin flower arrangements that she crafted out of cans. Andy showed a talent for drawing and painting as a youngster and took free art lessons at Carnegie Institute. With financial support from his brother, a Good Humor ice cream man, Andy attended college at Carnegie Tech.

After graduation the young artist moved to Manhattan, where he supported himself in commercial art. His first assignment was drawing women's shoes for *Glamour* magazine. By the mid 1950s he had shortened his last name and was earning $50,000 a year. Despite his financial success, however, Warhol was envious of his contemporaries Jasper Johns and Robert Rauschenberg, who were younger but getting important gallery shows. When Warhol tried to break into the snobbish New York City art world, he found that his years in advertising art damaged his credibility as a painter.

He had other liabilities too: his exaggerated, effeminate mannerisms (patterned after his idol, Truman Capote) and his open homosexuality. Warhol's first gallery show was decidedly homoerotic, with paintings of beautiful male faces and of penises decorated with bows. At that time Warhol had sexual relationships exclusively with men. Several of his boyfriends later admitted that Warhol was ambivalent about sex, though he always surrounded himself with handsome young men. Self-conscious about his looks (he lost most of his hair in his 20s and wore wigs thereafter), he steered his energy into his work and his public image. "Sex takes up too much time," Warhol told a friend, and he consequently spent long periods of time being celibate, though he enjoyed voyeurism.

In 1962, Warhol made a name for himself in the art world with his silk-screened paintings of folk objects such as Campbell's soup cans and Coca-Cola bottles. Warhol's pop art brought together his training as a painter, his experience as a commercial artist, and his working-class background. (His mother, he told people, always served Campbell's soup.) Most critics at first thought his work was horrible, but collectors and museums snapped it up anyway. Warhol progressed to celebrity portraits, including a series of Marilyn Monroe painted shortly after her suicide. Within a short time he was a celebrity himself, attending glamorous parties with beautiful young women instead of men on his arm. He created his own public persona: a shy, kind of dumb eccentric with no interest in sex.

Warhol the voyeur soon branched out into avant-garde filmmaking. One of his first projects was *Sleep,* a six-hour movie of his then-boyfriend sleeping. Eschewing professional actors, Warhol's casts were an unlikely constellation of friends, transvestites, and street hustlers. He produced a series of films at a rapid pace at his studio in Manhattan, known as the Factory. His best-known film, *Chelsea Girls* (1966), had a host of queer characters and was the first underground film to receive commercial distribution.

The Factory attracted aspiring artists and filmmakers, and Warhol gave many—especially Paul Morrissey—their start. In 1967, Valerie Solanas, a radical lesbian who was the founder and only member of the Society for Cutting Up Men, or SCUM, dropped off a screenplay called *Up Your Ass,* which she hoped Warhol would produce. Warhol misplaced the screenplay and tried to make it up to her by letting her appear in one of his films. The mentally unstable Solanas continued to hang around the Factory on and off for a year, waiting for her script to turn up and be produced.

On the afternoon of June 3, 1968, Solanas met Warhol outside the Factory and entered the building with him. Warhol later remembered that she was nervously fumbling with a paper bag. Inside, Warhol made phone calls and carried on business as usual. Suddenly, Solanas drew a pistol out of the bag and aimed at Warhol. No one paid attention until she shot the artist three times, almost fatally. Warhol was in fact pronounced dead at the hospital, but a doctor massaged his heart back to life. Though Warhol recovered physically and lived another 19 years, the incident scarred him emotionally. He retreated from filmmaking, exploring other creative avenues such as founding *Interview* magazine.

In 1987, Warhol died of a heart attack during routine gall bladder surgery. Six thousand people attended the public auction of his apartment's contents—everything from paintings by rivals Johns and Rauschenberg to a bizarre collection of cookie jars. The auction netted $25 million. Ironically, appraisers found none of Warhol's own work in his apartment. "It's nothing in the end," he once said dismissively of his paintings. "My work won't last.... I was using cheap paint."

58. Who was Ramon Novarro?

One of the most interesting gay Hollywood lives came to an end the night before Halloween in 1968 when Ramon Novarro, screen legend who once rivaled Rudolph Valentino, was murdered in his Los Angeles home.

Born Jose Ramon Samaniegos in Durango, Mexico, in 1899, the future star was descended from Aztec nobility and Spanish conquistadors. He moved to the United States as a 14-year-old boy and worked as a grocery clerk and café singer before breaking into Hollywood in a series of bit parts. The actor, rechristened Ramon Novarro, had his big break in 1922, when gay director Rex Ingram cast him as the villain in *The Prisoner of Zenda*. At the time America was experiencing a "Latin lover" craze because of Valentino, and Novarro was quickly cast in several more films. In 1925, Novarro played a shirtless, muscular galley slave in the silent version of *Ben Hur*.

Publicly, Novarro was seen as a ladies' man, rumored to be linked romantically with Myrna Loy as well as Greta Garbo, with whom he costarred in 1931's *Mata Hari*. (Novarro was the one who uttered the famous line, "What's the matter, Mata?") Newspaper and magazine writers promoted this heterosexual image, although some noticed another side of Novarro. One described him as "dark, stunningly handsome (although his looks are somewhat effeminate) and seductive."

Novarro, however, took few pains to hide his preference for men. One writer described how studio bosses had to "look the other way when Novarro made a beeline for the electrician with the tightest trousers." The star struck up a friendship/romance with Valentino, who, according to legend, presented Novarro with a black lead art-deco dildo in 1923, with a silver inscription of Valentino's signature. Novarro also threw the wildest sex parties in Hollywood, often tied to current movies. For example, guests at Novarro's *Ben Hur* party wore nothing but Roman sandals and leather headbands. At his *Tarzan* party, the guests wore only leopard-skin wristbands, while their host, clad only in a leather thong, swung back and forth on a vine hanging from the ceiling.

But Novarro's stardom was not to last. In the early 1930s, MGM mogul Louis B. Mayer demanded that the gay star marry, and when Novarro refused he found his contract canceled. He played few roles in the 1940s and in 1950 went to Rome, where he was granted an audience with the Pope. He proclaimed his intention to beg forgiveness of his sins and pray at holy shrines throughout Italy. This religious phase was short-lived, and he returned to Hollywood to take bit parts, including his last role as a Mexican bandito on TV in 1968.

By 1968, Novarro was a 69-year-old fat, bald alcoholic living in Los Angeles's Laurel Canyon and spending his money on hustlers he picked up on the Sunset Strip. His wealth was legendary among the rough-trade set, many of whom had no idea Novarro was even an actor.

Two brothers, Paul and Tom Ferguson, who had run away from Chicago, were living on the streets in Los Angeles, turning tricks and stealing. They heard Novarro had $5,000 hidden in his home, and they hoped to steal that cash and use it to return to the Midwest. On October 30, 22-year-old Tom and 17-year-old Paul arrived at Novarro's home and found the actor nude and passed out from drinking.

As the brothers searched the home for valuables—especially among the screen legend's hundreds of souvenirs from his film career—Novarro awoke and shouted for help. The Fergusons then began attacking him, and Paul grabbed an ivory-tipped cane and struck the former star repeatedly with it. According to one account, in an attempt to muffle Novarro's screams, Tom grabbed the Valentino dildo and shoved it down the actor's throat.

Soon Novarro was dead, and the Ferguson brothers realized they had to plant some misleading clues to avoid being caught and tried for murder. They trashed the house, tied Novarro's body up, wrote the name "Larry" in several places in the house, and scrawled the following message on the mirror: "Us girls are better than fagits."

This feint was less than successful, especially since they stole two of Novarro's outfits and left their own blood-soaked clothing in a neighbor's yard. A few days later they were arrested and charged with murder. They were convicted and sentenced to life in prison but freed on parole just seven years into their sentence.

59. How did the Vietnam War affect gay men?

U.S. involvement in Vietnam was one of the most hotly contested issues of the late 1960s and early 1970s, the era that also spawned the gay liberation movement. Gay men found themselves on both sides of the conflict, as service members and as antiwar protesters.

Many gay men, like Leonard Matlovich (who later became a test case as an openly gay soldier), willingly enlisted for tours of duty in Vietnam. At the time Matlovich felt it was his patriotic duty to "kill a Commie for Mommy." But in retrospect he wondered about his real intentions in enlisting. "I was so dissatisfied with being gay," he later recalled, "that in some ways, volunteering for duty in Vietnam was like a death wish or a suicide pact." Matlovich also noted that he signed up looking for male companionship.

"In country," gay soldiers developed an underground network for finding each other, much as gay men had always done back home. Gay GIs had to be particularly careful because they were in jeopardy of courts martial and prison or dishonorable discharge if caught or turned in. That risk lessened somewhat as the war escalated and the armed forces needed more and more fighting power.

During the war, there were at least two gay bars and several other gay-friendly ones in Saigon, though it was risky for servicemen to frequent them. "You...have to be in uniform when out of quarters," one gay sergeant told *The Advocate* magazine in 1971, "and this makes promiscuous bar-hopping dangerous…. Also, there's a 10 P.M. curfew." But gay GIs claimed the best cruising actually occurred right on the bases— at the USO service clubs in Cam Ranh Bay and Danang and at the military swimming pool near the Tan Son Nhut Air Force base. The verandah of the officers' club at China Beach was also a gay hot spot. At the front there was much less opportunity for privacy and intimacy. Many gay soldiers experienced come-ons from straight comrades who were sexually frustrated by being away from women for long stretches.

Stateside, other gay men did everything in their power to avoid military service. Rey Rivera (a.k.a. Sylvia Rivera), one of the transvestites arrested at the Stonewall riots, was drafted in 1967 at age 18 and decided to report to the local draft board in full drag—high heels, miniskirt, and red nails. The sergeants in charge assumed Rivera was a woman. But Rivera corrected them and was promptly sent to a psychiatrist who asked if there was a problem with his sexuality. "I don't know. I know I like men," Rivera replied. "I know I like to wear dresses. But I don't know what any *problem* is." The doctor quickly stamped HOMOSEXUAL in red across Rivera's draft notice.

Claiming to be gay became a popular way for straight men to avoid the draft. One draft-resisters manual from 1968 dispensed stereotypes and epithets along with advice: "Act like a man under tight control. Deny you're a fag, deny it again quickly, then stop, as if buttoning your lip…. And maybe twice, no more than three times over a half-hour interview, just the slightest little flick of the wrist."

The early gay liberation movement was the scene of both draft resistance and antiwar protest. Gay groups and publications encouraged members to resist serving. "Homosexuals will not fight in a war that fucks us over in all its institutions," read an editorial in a San Francisco gay paper late in 1969, summing up the attitude of many gay leftists. "We will not fight in an army that discriminates against us."

Members of the Gay Liberation Front—which took its name from the Marxist National Liberation Front of Vietnam—had been active in antiwar demonstrations before Stonewall, like the first Moratorium on Washington. After gay liberation took off, they continued the campaign. During the December holidays in 1969, GLF handed out flyers in New York City's Greenwich Village, near the site of the Stonewall rebellion, encouraging people to wear black armbands and to send gifts to GIs in Vietnam in the name of peace. The following spring GLF-ers shouting "Suck cock; beat the draft" joined a protest in Washington, D.C., that ended in a "nude-in" in the reflecting pool in front of the Washington Monument.

In April 1971 a second and larger Moratorium Against the War was held in the capital, with an estimated 10,000 gay people taking part. Later that year 15,000 gay protesters swelled the ranks of antiwar demonstrators in a similar march in San Francisco. GLF members carried signs like soldiers: MAKE EACH OTHER, NOT WAR and BRING THE BEAUTIFUL BOYS HOME. The leftist chant "Ho Ho Ho Chi Minh / Dare to struggle, dare to win" was transformed by gay participants into "Ho Ho Homosexual / The status quo is ineffectual."

But GLF self-destructed from a lack of leadership and organization, and many in the gay movement realized that the Left wasn't concerned with gay liberation. Antiwar protest and support for gay soldiers fighting in Vietnam became low priorities for gay groups, since at home gay people were being harassed, arrested, and denied their rights. The Gay Activists Alliance, which dominated the movement after 1970, focused on issues of more immediate concern to gay people in the States, like legal and electoral politics.

60. What was the role of the Stonewall riots in the lesbian and gay liberation movement?

Among gay organizations today there's everything from the Stonewall Democratic Club to the Stonewall Chorale. In the media there's *Stonewall* the book and *Stonewall* the movie. On the business front there's Stonewall Records, a gay dance music label; Stonewall Inn Editions, a gay imprint of St. Martin's Press; and even a bottled water called Stonewall. A word that once brought to mind only a resolute Confederate general has taken on mythic proportions in lesbian and gay culture. But the widespread appropriation of the name Stonewall doesn't dilute the importance of events that happened in the summer of 1969 in New York City.

The event for which so many groups and products have been named is still a hot topic of debate in gay circles, with much disagreement about what actually precipitated the violence and who took part in it. One legend holds that Judy Garland's funeral, held June 27 in Manhattan, fanned the flames of gay rage. Other versions of the story claim that dozens of sequined drag queens and a mysterious, unidentified butch lesbian were at the forefront of the street rebellion. From contemporary eyewitness accounts, however, a few facts have remained constant.

In the early morning hours of June 28, 1969, New York City police raided the Stonewall Inn, a dingy, Mafia-run "private club" on Christopher Street in Greenwich Village, whose clientele was predominantly gay. The charge was illegal sale of alcohol. It was the second time that week the bar had been targeted by the police, and other gay bars had also been raided in prior weeks. Police officers lined up the Stonewall's 200 patrons to check identification. Most were free to leave, but the staff as well as three drag queens and two male-to-female transsexuals were detained. (It was illegal in New York City to wear fewer than three items of "gender-appropriate" clothing.)

Eyewitnesses recalled that the scene outside the bar was at first campy and festive. Patrons were joined by tourists and passersby, and everyone cheered when a gay person emerged from the bar, dismissed by the police. But when a paddy wagon arrived and the police loaded the bar's staff and the three drag queens inside, the crowd on the street grew surly. One person threw a rock through a window, and eventually garbage cans, bottles, and even a parking meter were used to assault the building. Someone set a fire with lighter fluid. By newspaper accounts 13 people were arrested and three police officers sustained minor injuries in the confrontation.

Later that night and into Sunday morning, a crowd again gathered in front of the ravaged bar. Many young gay men showed up to protest the flurry of raids, but they did so by hand holding, kissing, and forming a chorus line. "We are the Stonewall girls," they sang, kicking their legs in front of the police. "We wear our hair in curls / We have no underwear / We show our pubic hair." Police cleared the street without incident, but another street altercation occurred a few days later.

Even more significant, though, was what happened later in the summer. At the end of July, gay activists circulated copies of a flyer calling for a mass "homosexual liberation meeting." The headline of the flyer read, DO YOU THINK HOMOSEXUALS ARE REVOLTING? YOU BET YOUR SWEET ASS WE ARE! The alliance that formed from the meeting held on July 24 adopted the name Gay Liberation Front, and its members viewed themselves as radicals breaking away from the accommodationist thinking of homophile groups like the Mattachine Society. Among GLF's demands were not only an end to police harassment but also a broader vision of gay rights: job protection for gay employees, the repeal of sodomy laws, and local and national antidiscrimination laws.

Soon, numerous other organizations, like the Gay Activists Alliance, and a host of gay liberation publications, like *Gay Power*, emerged, first in New York City and then across the country. Estimates suggest that at the time of the riots, there were a few dozen gay organizations in the United States. Within a few years the number had risen to more than 400. With this surge of gay activism came a new visibility. In the fall of 1969, *Time* magazine profiled "the homosexual in america" for a national cover story on the nascent gay movement.

Today, Stonewall is shorthand for a struggle that has mobilized gay people to action. For example, the protests that followed police raids on gay bathhouses in Toronto in 1981 are often called the Canadian Stonewall. Other cities and countries also point to their own "Stonewall" moments. It almost doesn't matter who threw the first rock on Christopher Street or who was involved in the fight. What matters is that the gay community interpreted events at the Stonewall Inn as revolutionary and used them to create a global gay political movement.

61. What was the Gay Activists Alliance?

In the aftermath of the Stonewall riots of June 1969, a gay liberation movement quickly began to emerge, with organizations sprouting up first in New York City and then in cities around the country. These new groups used the word *gay* proudly in their names instead of the more cautious terms like *homophile* favored by earlier gay rights organizations.

At the front of the pack was the Gay Liberation Front, which got its start a month after Stonewall. GLF's name was meant to echo that of the National Liberation Front of Vietnam, a Marxist group, but also to signify a far-ranging movement instead of one monolithic organization.

GLF staggered early on, suffering from a lack of structure and leadership. Meetings could be freewheeling and fragmented, with lots of in-fighting. Some of those involved became dissatisfied that the founders wanted to extend the group's focus to include issues like peace and ecology. Many women were disgruntled by the sexism they encountered in GLF. Some transgendered individuals also found themselves unwelcome. Before long GLF members began to splinter off and form other groups. In December 1969 approximately ten defectors from GLF worked up a constitution for a new organization they named the Gay Activists Alliance.

Unlike GLF, GAA declined to address nongay issues. It also created a hierarchical structure of officers, committees, and members, with meetings run according to Robert's *Rules of Order*. GAA embodied what one gay journalist called "middle-of-the-road radicalism." The group used radical tactics like sit-ins and heckling and perfected the "zap," a surprise disruption. But GAA was less interested in affecting sweeping social change than in improving the lot of lesbians and gay men through legislative and electoral means.

GAA grew quickly after the group took a leading role in the demonstrations that followed the March 1970 controversy over the impaling of Diego Vinales, which set off a protest on which GLF and GAA cooperated but which GAA largely orches-trated. A major coup for GAA was the enlistment of congress-man Ed Koch in trying to end police harassment of gay bars.

Shortly after the Vinales incident, GAA noisily disrupted sev-eral of New York City mayor John Lindsay's public appearances. In April 1970 they zapped the mayor's speech at the Metropol-itan Museum of Art and also the taping of his weekly TV talk show. One GAA man rushed onto the stage crying, "Homosex-uals want an end to job discrimination!" Other GAA-ers joined in, interrupting the mayor's conversation with guest Arthur Godfrey on pollution. "What good is environmental freedom if we don't have personal freedom?" a lesbian shouted.

Within days of the disturbance, GAA obtained meetings with both the deputy mayor and the chair of the city's Com-mission on Human Rights to discuss antigay discrimination and harassment. GAA initiated demands for a city gay rights ordinance, though it took a full 15 years for such a bill to pass the city council.

In 1971, GAA set up headquarters in downtown Manhattan. The Firehouse, which opened on May 6, was an abandoned, turn-of-the-century fire station in Soho that the group leased and transformed into a gay social and cultural center. On the first floor was a large mural depicting various aspects of the lesbian and gay story—portraits of forefathers and foremothers like Walt Whitman and Gertrude Stein, a gay man behind bars, couples holding hands—interspersed with slogans of the day, like "Gay Power."

In addition to general membership and committee meetings, the Firehouse hosted popular community dances. On Saturday nights the meeting hall was transformed into a dance space that pulsed with disco music and attracted as many as 1,500 dancers, mostly men. Since gay bars in New York were still owned by the Mafia, the Firehouse provided an alternative to the seediness and danger of the bar scene at that time. For $2 admission, gay people could dance all night and drink unlimited beer and soda.

Despite its accomplishments, GAA remained a very white, male organization that fell under heavy criticism for its insularity and lack of attention to racism and sexism. Some women of color referred to the Firehouse as "a white boy's playhouse."

Over the next few years, GAA's focus became increasingly more social than political. In 1974 the Firehouse was burned by arsonists, and GAA never fully recovered from its loss. It finally disbanded in 1981.

The legacy of GAA, however, has lived on in lesbian and gay organizations like the National Gay and Lesbian Task Force and the Human Rights Campaign, in the zaplike tactics of ACT UP and the Lesbian Avengers, and in gay community centers that dot the country. Like its predecessor, the New York Lesbian and Gay Community Services Center continued to charge only $2 a head for social and cultural activities through the 1990s and still serves as the hub of gay activity in the city.

62. Who was Yukio Mishima?

Yukio Mishima was one of Japan's most popular 20th-century novelists, whose writings include some of the first modern Japanese explorations of gay identity and gay subculture. His disturbing suicide in 1970 drew attention to his unusual philosophy, which combined right-wing nationalism with the veneration of the male body and a fascination with violence.

Mishima was intensely proud to have descended from samurai warriors, and he aimed to make his life follow that of the ideal Japanese warrior, with a finely honed sense of both the martial and the fine arts. Although he generally looked down upon anything non-Japanese, even as a student he was a fan of the essays of the previous century's gay literary savant, British writer Oscar Wilde.

Perhaps Mishima's most famous—and certainly his most personal—novel was *Confessions of a Mask.* Published in 1949, it told of a boy's growing awareness of both his homosexuality and his fascination with sadomasochism. The protagonist's inability to make himself aroused by his girlfriend puzzled many postwar Japanese readers, some of whom considered the book to be an attempt at parody. Few recognized (until years later) its autobiographical nature—Japan's first "coming out" novel.

Two years later Mishima published *Forbidden Colors,* a second novel with gay themes. This one, however, had a broader setting, introducing its readers to the diverse gay subculture in 1950s Tokyo, with its bars, cruising spots, and gay parties. One of the main characters is a gay man who uses a younger man to wreak vengeance on women who wronged him in the past.

During the 1960s, Mishima continued to write and to develop the philosophy that ultimately led to his violent death. He believed the emperor was central to Japanese society and that no two people could love each other without first loving the emperor. He also believed that to live with honor meant to be prepared for war, to be unafraid of violence, and to be intensely loyal to one's colleagues.

Sometimes these beliefs had bizarre manifestations. In 1967, Mishima led a ceremony for about a dozen university students in which all of them drew blood from their little fingers and poured it into a cup. They then used the blood as ink to sign their names to a pact. The ceremony finished with Mishima adding salt to the cup and drinking from the blood, after which each of the students followed suit.

In his writing Mishima frequently praised the Japanese samurai who ended their own lives by performing seppuku (also known as hara-kiri), a ritual form of suicide in which the warrior takes a short knife and disembowels himself, after which a fellow warrior cuts off his head. It became clear to many who read his works (which by the late 1960s were among the most celebrated of any Japanese writings) that Mishima hoped to end his own life in such a fashion. Seppuku was clearly erotic for Mishima, who once called it (just months before his death) "the ultimate masturbation."

However, Mishima felt that ritual suicide was not honorable unless one's body was in peak physical condition. Though he was skinny as a young man, he started a strict regimen of bodybuilding at age 30 that he continued through his death at age 45, by which time he was extremely muscled. With such a body Mishima posed for many erotic photographs and even acted in a Japanese gangster film.

But Mishima is probably best remembered for the last day of his life. On November 25, 1970, along with some of his right-wing nationalist followers, he stormed a Japanese military headquarters (the army was then called the Japan Self-Defense Force) and demanded to speak to the troops outside. When they assembled he exhorted them to rise up and overthrow Japan's postwar pacifist regime and replace it with a government that once again emphasized military might. When the troops laughed at and heckled Mishima, he returned to an office inside, where he shouted his undying loyalty to the emperor and proceeded to cut open his abdomen with his sword. His protégé Masakatsu Morita—widely believed to be his lover—then cut off Mishima's head and committed seppuku himself.

63. Who was Diego Vinales?

The riots that took place at the Stonewall Inn in June 1969 have come down in history as the impetus of the lesbian and gay liberation movement. But a gruesome incident several months later also roused the fledgling movement, making the name Diego Vinales a rallying cry to action.

In the early morning hours of March 8, 1970, New York City police raided a bar in Greenwich Village called the Snake Pit. Much like the Stonewall Inn, the Snake Pit was a dark, dingy, overcrowded "private club" operated by the Mafia without a liquor license. The licensing violation was the ostensible reason for the raid, though Sidney Pine, the police inspector in charge, told reporters that people in the neighborhood had also complained about noise.

Pine and his officers had closed two similar bars the night before. Both of those raids had occurred early in the evening, however, before many customers arrived. The police sent the handful of clients home and arrested only the management and employees.

In contrast, the Snake Pit was in full swing when the police arrived. Officers hauled a total of 167 people, staff and customers alike, off to the precinct house. Pine, also responsible for the Stonewall raid eight months earlier, was aware of the danger of "a riotous crowd milling around outside," he told a *Village Voice* reporter. "Our purpose in making the arrests was to get them out of there."

Paddy wagons arrived to transport the men to the police

station. Reports of what actually happened at the precinct house varied wildly. "Things were terribly disorganized," one eyewitness later said. Some men asserted that they were never read their rights or apprised of the charges against them. Others said the police verbally abused them by calling them "faggots." Still others claimed the police were incredibly polite and referred to them as "gentlemen."

In this confusion a 23-year-old Argentinean national named Diego Vinales panicked. Worried about deportation and the fact that his family didn't know he was gay, Vinales raced up the stairs to the second floor of the station and either leaped or fell from a window. An iron fence surrounded the building, and Vinales was impaled on six 14-inch spikes. Inside the precinct house the gay men arrested with Vinales listened with horror to his screams.

Amazingly, Vinales was still alive when the police got to him. Because they couldn't move him off the fence without causing further injury, the fire department's special rescue squad was called in. Using an electric saw, the rescue team cut away the section of the fence on which Vinales was impaled and brought him to the hospital with the fence prongs still imbedded in his thigh and pelvis. During a two-hour surgery, doctors dislodged the spikes from Vinales's flesh.

News of Vinales's grisly ordeal spread quickly. The Gay Liberation Front and the Gay Activists Alliance, two organizations who usually had different priorities, worked together to rally people for a march on the precinct. In addition to holding an all-day phone-athon, activists distributed 3,000 flyers in bars and on the streets. "Any way you look at it," the flyers read, "that boy was pushed! We are all being pushed!" One activist, Allen Warshawsky, recalled how Vinales's fall made him and

others feel: "I [began] to feel an anger welling up inside me....
An anger at the stinking, rotten, corrupt system that defines,
fosters, and promotes my 'criminal' status."

At 9 o'clock that night, 500 gay people marched en masse
to the Sixth Precinct. GLF carried its banner, while other signs
read GAYS ARE GETTING ANGRY. Shouts of "Say it loud: Gay is
proud!" and "Stop the killings!" went out from the crowd, but
the demonstrators were in general orderly and well-behaved.
After a protest at the police station, the crowd continued on to
St. Vincent's Hospital, where they held a "death vigil" for
Vinales.

Miraculously, though, Vinales didn't die, though he underwent surgery several times and spent more than three months
in the hospital. Arthur Bell, a reporter for *Gay Power*, visited
Vinales in the hospital and found the young Argentinean unwilling to talk about the incident in detail, perhaps out of fear.
"His family may now know of the Snake Pit incident," Bell
wrote. "He has not heard from them."

In the aftermath GAA emerged as a leader of the movement. It achieved several major coups, like winning the support
of then-congressman (and later mayor) Ed Koch, who wrote an
impassioned letter to the police commissioner calling for an
end to police harassment of gay people. Vinales's tragic fall
galvanized the lesbian and gay community as nothing since
the Stonewall riots had.

64. What was the Lavender Menace?

In the late 1960s and early 1970s, some straight feminists—most notably National Organization for Women founder Betty Friedan—worried that feminism's public image would be marred by a too-visible lesbian presence. In Friedan's choice phrase, lesbians represented a "lavender menace" to American feminism.

It was a loaded slogan. From the perspective of the mid 1990s, it is easy to forget the mind-set of the Cold War and the hysteria linked to such phrases as "red menace." Although Friedan later backed off and said the lesbian issue was just a "lavender herring" to divert attention from the real issues facing women, lesbians understandably felt stung by both phrases.

Complicating Friedan's statements was evidence of actual discrimination within NOW, where lesbians in positions of leadership were being silenced or forced out of office. A group of women from the Gay Liberation Front felt that the feminist movement needed some consciousness-raising and planned an incident that would mark a turning point in the relationship between lesbians and the women's movement. It would also be one of the most creative direct actions in the early history of the gay liberation movement.

On Friday night, May 1, 1970, the lights went out on the hundreds of women gathered for the second annual Congress to Unite Women. When they came back on, 20 women in purple T-shirts which proclaimed LAVENDER MENACE stood in front of the auditorium, and there were signs along the walls which read TAKE A LESBIAN TO LUNCH and IS THE STATUE OF LIBERTY A LESBIAN? The "menace" demanded the microphone from the stage and accused the women's movement of internalized sexism and of discriminating against lesbians.

The rest of the scheduled speakers were canceled, and the assembled women spent the rest of the evening listening to the concerns of lesbians. Although the event had its angry and emotional moments (such as when some lesbians came out publicly for the first time), for the most part the Lavender Menac kept a sense of humor about what they were doing, which helped relax many women present who had never been exposed to open discussions of lesbianism.

When the lesbians who had prepared remarks finished speaking, an open microphone was declared, and one of the women who chose to come forward and talk about her struggles with her own sexuality had actually been a scheduled speaker (on another topic) for the evening. She was the well-known sculptor and author Kate Millett, who herself would later become a lightning rod for debates over sexuality in the women's movement.

During the rest of the weekend, the Lavender Menace put together well-attended discussions and workshops on issues related to sexual orientation and feminism. On Sunday the congress even passed a tongue-in-cheek "menace" resolution declaring, "Be it resolved that Women's Liberation is a Lesbian plot."

The Lavender Menace action was a landmark in an ongoing struggle within the lesbian movement. Many political lesbians in the early 1970s were feeling increasingly like tokens or showpieces in male-dominated groups like the Gay Activists Alliance and the Gay Liberation Front. Yet at first the National Organization for Women, the Redstockings, and other groups had tried to silence lesbian issues. After the 1970 Congress to Unite Women, the women's movement was more open to lesbian concerns, and just 16 months later NOW passed a resolution declaring "the oppression of lesbians as a legitimate concern of feminism."

It took Friedan many more years to come around to support lesbian rights, and she is said to have told a reporter in 1973 that lesbians in NOW had been sent there by the CIA.

As for the Lavender Menace themselves, they did not disappear after their highly public debut. They marched in that summer's first-ever New York City Christopher Street Liberation Day Parade and under the name Radicalesbians published an influential essay, *The Woman-Identified Woman*.

65. What was the Alpine County Project?

In October 1970 the *Los Angeles Times* ran a story about a plan by the local Gay Liberation Front to establish a gay colony in Alpine County, Calif. The ensuing brouhaha—which spread to the national media and caused an uproar in the tiny, snow-bound county—is a fascinating episode illustrating the utopianism, the folly, and the media savvy of the early gay liberationists.

The plan originated with a speech by underground newspaper reporter Don Jackson at a December 1969 gay liberation conference in Berkeley. Jackson's speech, later reprinted widely in the gay and underground press as "Brother Don Has a Dream," envisioned "a place where gay people can be free...where a gay government can build the base for a flourishing gay counter-culture and city." He urged gays to move en masse to California's least populous county, register to vote, and elect an all-gay government that could then use tax dollars to create a gay civil service, community college, museum, hospital, and other public facilities and services.

Jackson's plan was dismissed by many as a quixotic fantasy. But it was nonetheless exciting to many gays and lesbians precisely because the legal and demographic hurdles to actually setting up a "gay county" seemed relatively small. A recent California supreme court decision had required counties to allow new residents to register to vote after only 90 days. Also, Alpine County, nestled in the Sierra Nevada Mountains ten miles south of Lake Tahoe, had only 367 registered voters in its population of 450. It seemed to Jackson and a small group of supporters that the plan required only a few hundred gays and lesbians willing to make a three-month experiment.

Meanwhile, many members of the Los Angeles GLF were frustrated by the lack of media attention given to their movement. Despite their attempts at public protests and pleas for gay and lesbian equality, the most attention they got from the *Los Angeles Times* was an occasional story written by its medical reporter.

So a group of GLF members decided to use the Alpine County idea as political theater in hopes of gaining the attention of the *Times* and other mainstream news outlets. Unlike Jackson and some of his idea's boosters, the Los Angeles GLF treated the Alpine County project as a publicity stunt, not an actual plan. They called a news conference at the GLF office to announce that hundreds of gays and lesbians were already preparing to move to Alpine County. Only the medical reporter from the *Times* covered the conference, but his article quickly gained national attention, with stories soon appearing in the *Wall Street Journal, Time* magazine, and on every network news broadcast.

The GLF members continued to string out the hoax, announcing new developments in their plan and even sending a scouting party up to Alpine County during Thanksgiving 1970 to make "preparations" for the gay colony. Some GLF supporters—men and women—who read about the plan in the papers or saw it on the news took it seriously and even started planning to move. One lesbian couple from Long Beach told *The Advocate* magazine that they were planning to open a "little country store" in Alpine County.

When the longtime residents of Alpine County heard about

the plan, however, they were not amused. The chairman of the Alpine County board of supervisors noted the cold climate of the region and said that "no fruit is very welcome up in our particular county." The county began to explore the option of merging with the more populous neighboring El Dorado County. The project found enemies nationwide, including a New Jersey fundamentalist preacher who announced plans to counterbalance the Alpine project by flooding the county with missionaries who could out-vote the gays. One GLF member claims that the Alpine County board traveled to Sacramento to ask Gov. Ronald Reagan to stop the gays from moving to Alpine but that Reagan said there was nothing he could do under the Constitution. Another GLF-er remembers differently—that Reagan threatened to call out the state militia to keep the gays out.

In any event, by February 1971 the plan had lost steam. The GLF issued a statement that they were abandoning Alpine County for a "more temperate county" with better soil and rivers. The media attention had died down, although the GLF had achieved its goal of being taken seriously by the press as a political force, not a medical issue. The project was not publicly revealed as basically a hoax until many years later.

66. What was the first gay-themed TV movie?

The first gay-themed TV movie was *That Certain Summer*, which aired November 1, 1972, on ABC. The movie starred Hal Holbrook, playing a character whose 14-year-old son comes to spend the summer with him and discovers that Dad is in love with Martin Sheen. It appeared at a time when television was beginning to explore controversial topics—including, later that month, the decision by the title character on Maude to have an abortion.

But *That Certain Summer* was extremely tame, especially when compared to films that had recently played in cinemas, such as *The Boys in the Band* and *Sunday, Bloody Sunday*. Sheen and Holbrook played the very model of an "acceptable" gay couple: They never touched; they denounced open displays of affection; and they wondered out loud if homosexuality was a sickness. At the end of the film, the son leaves his weeping father and—unlike in the original script—doesn't even show any regrets.

Gay and lesbian reaction to *That Certain Summer* was mixed. Some gays and lesbians were thrilled to see any portrayal of their lives on television and relished the opportunities for conversation with their families that the show—and the surrounding controversy—afforded. Others were offended, such as the man who wrote to *The New York Times* to complain that Holbrook's character's tears at the end of the film were a "repudiation of the life he had chosen for himself."

That Certain Summer also provoked the usual protests from

offended religious conservatives. But it was probably more important for alerting gays and lesbians to the power of television to shape straight perceptions of gays and lesbians. Two
years later the Gay Activists Alliance and the National Gay Task
Force protested a homophobic episode of *Marcus Welby* before
it even aired—and the Gay and Lesbian Alliance Against
Defamation continues such activities today.

67. What are some of the products gays and lesbians have boycotted over the years?

Boycotts have been a useful form of political action for the American gay and lesbian community in the last several decades. While petitions and marches bring some measure of publicity and visibility to participants, boycotts are much quieter. They allow a lesbian in rural America who would be terrified if her neighbors knew she favored gay rights to register her protest by simply ceasing to buy orange juice or visit Colorado.

One of the first nationwide efforts by the gay and lesbian community to boycott a specific product came in 1973, when gays and lesbians around the country began to boycott Coors beer. As with many boycotts, this one spread by word of mouth more than by organized political action. Reasons for the boycott included unfair labor practices at Coors (including asking potential employees if they were gay) and antigay donations by the Coors family. The local Coors boycott in San Francisco was organized by none other than future supervisor Harvey Milk.

In 1977 Coors took out ads in *The Advocate* magazine declaring that the company and the Coors family did not give money to antigay organizations, but the boycott continued. In 1982 the company even filed an unsuccessful lawsuit against Solidarity, a gay organization pushing the boycott. In 1987, when the AFL-CIO settled its labor disputes with Coors, the boycott fizzled, but some gays and lesbians still refuse to drink Coors, and some community bars still don't sell its brand of beer.

Another major beverage boycott by gays and lesbians came

in 1977, when Florida orange juice spokeswoman (and former pop singer and Miss Oklahoma) Anita Bryant began her crusade to repeal nondiscrimination laws in Miami and other parts of the country. To protest the Save Our Children campaign, Bryant opponents stopped purchasing and drinking Florida orange juice. Some gay bars even displayed signs that insisted, "We use California orange juice only." In 1980, Bryant was dropped by the Citrus Commission, and Florida orange juice reappeared on the breakfast tables of same-sex households throughout America—at least until Rush Limbaugh was hired by the Florida Citrus Commission in 1994.

Probably the biggest gay and lesbian boycott in recent years hasn't been of a product but of a state: Colorado. On election day 1992, just as gays and lesbians around the country were celebrating the election of Bill Clinton, Colorado voters approved Amendment 2. This measure, sponsored by the group Colorado for Family Values, sought to forbid any jurisdiction within the state from protecting gays and lesbians from "any claim of discrimination." The very next day activists announced their plan to boycott Colorado's tourism industry, which continued until a court suspended the initiative.

Unlike the Coors and orange-juice boycotts, however, the Colorado boycott generated significant controversy within the gay and lesbian community. Some gays and lesbians have questioned whether by boycotting the state, activists were abandoning Colorado when it needed outside help most. Others questioned the wisdom of boycotting Gay Ski Week in Aspen—a city that had passed a nondiscrimination law that Amendment 2 had voided—and instead vacationing in Park City, Utah, which never protected gays from discrimination in the first place.

On the other hand, the boycott deprived Colorado of millions of dollars in convention and tourism revenue. More than simply punishing the state for its 1992 vote, Colorado's loss of funds has sent a financial warning to other states and cities considering such initiatives.

68. Who was Norma McCorvey?

On January 22, 1973, the U.S. Supreme Court handed down a decision in *Roe* v. *Wade*, establishing a woman's constitutional right to terminate a pregnancy. Only a few people knew the true identity of Jane Roe, the plaintiff in this historic and controversial case. Roe was, in fact, Norma McCorvey, a lesbian from Dallas.

McCorvey was born Norma Leah Nelson in 1947 to a working-class family. Ironically, her mother had wanted to abort her, which was illegal, but consulted the local backroom abortionist too late. Norma's father deserted the family when she was a child, and the girl suffered physical abuse from her mother. Angry and unhappy, Norma ran away with a girlfriend when she was 10 years old, using money she stole from the gas station where she helped pump gas.

At a motel in Oklahoma City, Norma and her friend had their first lesbian sexual experience. When they were picked up by police several days later, Norma's friend said Norma had forcibly sodomized her. Norma was sent to a girls' reform school for that offense and for robbing the gas station. The reform school, McCorvey later wrote in her memoirs, was more of a home than she had had with her own family.

After her release at age 15, Norma began working as a carhop at a drive-in restaurant. There she met Woody McCorvey, a smooth talker whom she married after a brief courtship. Their marriage proved almost as brief. When McCorvey told her husband she was pregnant, he beat her up, and she left him to return home.

Though it may seem like an unlikely time to come out as a lesbian, it was during her pregnancy that the 16-year-old Mc-Corvey discovered a local lesbian bar and began to frequent it. She found a home within the lesbian and gay subculture of Dallas. Though she had several relationships with women, she also continued to have occasional sex with men. After the birth of her first daughter, she came out to her mother and paid a price for her honesty: Her mother was able to take the infant daughter away from her.

When McCorvey became pregnant again after a week-long affair, she carried the baby to term but gave it up for adoption. Norma's third pregnancy, from another casual fling, made history. That time she sought an abortion but was unable to find a doctor to perform one. She tried unsuccessfully to abort with a homemade potion that made her sick. Finally, an attorney she consulted about adoption referred her to two young lawyers who changed her life, Sarah Weddington and Linda Coffee.

Weddington and Coffee were feminists who wanted to build a case challenging Texas's antiabortion laws, with an eye to setting a precedent that might overturn all existing abortion laws. Weddington had a personal stake in such a case: She'd had an unwanted pregnancy in law school and had gone to Mexico for an abortion. In order to make their case, Weddington and Coffee needed a pregnant woman who wanted an abortion. Enter Norma McCorvey.

In February 1970, McCorvey was two-and-a-half–months pregnant and desperate. She saw the two attorneys as her last hope for an abortion. When McCorvey met with them, she was honest about her sexual orientation and saw the confusion on the women's faces. Afraid they might not take on her case,

McCorvey lied and told them she had been raped. Because she was concerned that her lie would be discovered later on, McCorvey opted to use the pseudonym "Jane Roe" for the trial.

McCorvey didn't understand the legal system, and Weddington and Coffee failed to tell their client that the suit would take too long to benefit her. By the time the case was tried and won, McCorvey was six-months pregnant. She put her third and last child up for adoption. After a period of despondency in which she tried to commit suicide, McCorvey met her life partner, Connie Gonzalez, and got a fresh start.

Roe v. *Wade* was appealed by the state of Texas and went all the way to the U.S. Supreme Court. In early 1973, by a vote of 7–2, the justices held that a woman's right to an abortion was part of her constitutional right to privacy. It wasn't until 1987 that McCorvey revealed herself as Jane Roe and admitted her lie about being raped. A television movie starring Holly Hunter was made in 1989—but with McCorvey's lesbian identity left out.

In 1995, after several years in the public eye, speaking out for abortion rights, and writing a pro-choice memoir, McCorvey became a born-again Christian and abruptly recanted her position on abortion. She also became an outspoken advocate for Operation Rescue, the militant antiabortion group.

69. What is the history of Naiad Press?

In January 1973, Barbara Grier and Donna McBride, a young lesbian couple from Kansas City, Mo., had only one manuscript and a $2,000 loan from friends with which to start a publishing company. More than 25 years later that company, Naiad Press, is the country's largest, most successful, and oldest lesbian publisher, with almost 400 books to its credit and annual revenues approaching $2 million. Its name—which means "water nymph"—has become, in Grier's words, "a synonym for *lesbian.*"

Grier and McBride met and fell in love in 1972. McBride was working as a librarian, and Grier was a bill collector by day and editor of the Daughters of Bilitis lesbian journal, "The Ladder," by night. Grier had joined that publication's staff in 1956, after having an epiphany the first time she saw the journal. "I remember thinking," Grier said recently, "*This is what I'm going to do for the rest of my life.*" "The Ladder" folded in 1972, but Grier and McBride were soon approached by friends—one of whom was novelist Sarah Aldridge—with the idea of starting a lesbian publishing company.

With money from Aldridge and her lover and the hard work of Grier and McBride, Naiad Press published its first title in 1973—Aldridge's novel *The Latecomer,* the start of a long line of Naiad romances. At a time when only a handful of women's bookstores existed, Naiad relied heavily on mail orders. Naiad inherited the mailing list of "The Ladder," which had grown from 150 subscribers in 1956 to 3,800 at its demise, and Grier and McBride did four mailings in the first year, marketing their one and only book. The income from the mailings kept the press going. As of 1998 about 500 "Ladder" subscribers were still receiving Naiad's catalog along with more than 25,000 other lesbians. And according to Grier, many of those 500 original subscribers own everything the publishing company has ever published.

From the beginning Naiad had no trouble finding manuscripts to publish. Many lesbian writers approached the company with their novels, and Grier also used her prior experience as a "skip tracer" (a trade term for bill collector) to track down lesbian novelists of the past whose work she admired. That way the novels of Ann Bannon and Gale Wilhelm got second lives as Naiad reprints.

In 1980, Grier and McBride relocated to Florida, where they held full-time jobs while operating Naiad out of their home. "We got up at 5 A.M.," Grier recalled, "and Donna would go out to pack books in an unheated shed while I made breakfast." After work they would do Naiad business until 10:30 at night. It wasn't until 1982 that Grier took a leap of faith and quit her day job. McBride followed suit six months later. There was a recession that year, and Grier and McBride held on through several months with no income. But because the women were able to devote all their time to the press, the company flourished.

A succession of popular titles ensured Naiad's future. Some of the press's early best-sellers are now lesbian classics, like Jane Rule's *Outlander* and Sheila Ortiz Taylor's *Faultline*. In 1982, while on a book tour with one of their authors, Grier met "a shy, tall woman with a white Afro," who came up to her in Los Angeles's Sisterhood Bookstore and said she had a novel to submit. Grier was tired and grouchy and snapped, "Tell me,

Does anything happen in this novel?" The woman turned out to be Katherine V. Forrest, and the book was *Curious Wine*, which sold out its first print run of 8,500 copies in less than a month. Forrest went on to become a Naiad superstar.

But the title that really established Naiad was *Lesbian Nuns* (1985), a nonfiction book about life behind convent walls that made Naiad and authors Rosemary Kurb and Nancy Manahan $500,000, a remarkable sum in small publishing. The book was reviewed in everything from the *Navaho Times* to *The New York Times* and was translated into many languages. Bette Midler held a copy of it on screen in the movie *Down and Out in Beverly Hills*. Naiad was finally able to move its office out of Grier and McBride's house and into a separate building, and the company thrived while many other women's presses failed.

Today, Grier attributes Naiad's long life to other factors too. The press has diversified its list to include videos and books on tape, and Grier, an aggressive marketer, has successfully sold foreign rights for many of its books. Most importantly, she says, "We genuinely like what we're doing. And I have an absolute inability not to win."

70. Did Bette Midler really get her start by singing in a gay bathhouse?

In the early 1970s, Bette Midler was a featured performer at the Continental Baths in New York City, where her popularity reached beyond the men who had sex in the cubicles and playrooms of the upper floors of the bathhouse. Straight and gay audience members in full evening dress would sit in the basement dance floor–theater and watch Midler sing and camp it up, sometimes accompanied by Barry Manilow at the piano. Particularly after the favorable comments of *Rolling Stone* magazine in 1973, watching Midler at the Continental Baths came to epitomize chic decadence, and hundreds of New Yorkers would line up for the chance to watch "the Divine Miss M" perform—and to gawk at handsome young men in towels at the same time.

Her popularity at the Continental helped her land a guest spot on *The Tonight Show,* and Midler was soon starring in feature films, including *The Rose* (1978), in which she did a lesbian scene. Midler also performed at gay and lesbian pride celebrations, most notably at New York City's 1973 pride rally, in which she helped smooth over tensions between two segments of the gay and lesbian community. Some drag queens were furious at lesbian feminist Jean O'Leary's speech attacking transvestites for mocking women, and Midler's performance of "You Got to Have Friends" aimed to appease the ruffled feathers.

But Midler has had a mixed relationship with the gay and lesbian community, particularly given some of her statements reported by the media. In 1976 she denied having gay fans and told the *Chicago Tribune* that she "wouldn't know a homosexual if [she] saw one." She also told *Vanity Fair* in 1987 that she felt sorry for what she considered to be her contribution to the spread of AIDS by performing at a bathhouse: "I was helping to make it seem fun."

Still, Midler has performed at a number of AIDS fund-raising events and is widely considered a gay icon for her campy sensibility. She remains one of the most popular targets for impersonation by drag performers.

71. Who was Dr. Howard Brown?

Nowadays, its seems like every few months a major public figure discloses her or his homosexuality. While the press attention varies depending on the extent of the person's celebrity—from coverage limited to gay publications to Ellen DeGeneres's announcement, "Yep, I'm gay," on the cover of *Time* magazine in 1997—the idea that some famous people are lesbian or gay is unremarkable.

That wasn't true in 1973. When Dr. Howard Brown (at best a minor public figure as the ex-head of New York City's public health department) talked about his homosexuality to a New Jersey symposium on human sexuality in October 1973, the disclosure was front-page news precisely because many people were surprised that a prominent physician could be gay.

When Brown was appointed by Mayor John Lindsay as the chief health officer of New York City in June 1966, the rumors of his homosexuality had already begun. One newspaper described him as "a 42-year-old bachelor who lives in Greenwich Village"—code for "homosexual" to anyone paying attention.

Nonetheless, Brown felt that if he acted carefully, he could keep his private life from threatening his very public professional life as he worked to consolidate the city's disparate health agencies and supervise a budget nearing a billion dollars annually. His lover, also a physician, moved out and set himself up in an apartment around the corner. He had his phones checked and rechecked for bugs, and he avoided being seen socializing with the other closeted gays in Lindsay's administration.

Still, just six months into Brown's tenure, one of the mayor's aides visited him at home and asked about the truth of a rumor that linked him romantically to another man serving in the Lindsay administration. Brown truthfully denied the link, but he was put on notice that he needed to continue being careful.

In 1968, Brown was in the hospital recovering from infectious hepatitis when his brother-in-law, a reporter for *The New York Times*, visited him and let him know that a *Times* investigative reporter was working on a story that would expose homosexuals in the Lindsay administration. Afraid of exposure and exhausted from illness, Brown sent a vague letter of resignation to the mayor the next day.

In the years that followed his resignation, Brown taught medicine at Albert Einstein College and then at New York University beginning in 1970. At the same time gay liberation had arrived, starting with the Stonewall riots and continuing with the protests and parades organized by the Gay Liberation Front and the Gay Activists Alliance. Brown felt alienated from these activities by people he saw as mostly young, mostly poor gay men and lesbians. When a student group at NYU proposed gay dances on campus, he opposed the idea despite overwhelming support from his straight colleagues.

But he soon decided to help the gay activists, particularly in the area of fund-raising. He approached his wealthy gay friends for contributions to the GAA. Most contributed but only by writing checks to Brown, who in turn wrote checks to the Alliance. Brown later attributed his ultimate decision to come out publicly to the "magnificent fighters for human rights" of the GAA. Another factor was a heart attack he suffered in June 1972 that made him reevaluate his fears of public exposure and the legacy he wished to leave.

He agreed to address a symposium on human sexuality in New Jersey in October 1973. Six hundred physicians gathered to hear a series of speeches about sexual behavior. To set a tone of openness, the symposium began with a series of films of explicit sexual acts. Brown later wrote, "As I watched the explicit sex in film after film, I wondered how my speech would be received. A film on female masturbation left me feeling like a middle-aged prude.... We were worried that our earnest speeches might be a letdown after the 'action' of the films."

Nonetheless, Brown's talk garnered tremendous attention. Homosexuals are everywhere, he proclaimed. "I have met far more homosexual physicians than I have homosexual nurses, more homosexual politicians than homosexual hairdressers, more homosexual lawyers than homosexual interior decorators." He went on to criticize the studies that treated homosexuality as a sickness.

The New York Times treated the revelation as front-page news, and Brown was deluged with requests for interviews—as well as thank-you letters from gay men and lesbians around the country who considered him a role model.

In the fall of 1973, Brown was the most prominent American in any field to be openly gay. This prominence led him to be appointed the first-ever chair of the board of a new breakaway group from the GAA that called itself the National Gay Task Force. He headed that organization, which is now the National Gay and Lesbian Task Force, until his death from heart disease in February 1975 at the age of 50.

72. How did homosexuality lose its official status as a mental illness?

In what was indisputably a key turning point in the struggle for gay and lesbian equality, the American Psychiatric Association experienced a tumultuous internal debate in late 1973 and early 1974, ending in the decision to remove homosexuality from the APA's list of mental disorders. The episode, whose lasting impact on public perceptions of gay people has been tremendous, was a political saga and a public spectacle.

For early 1970s gays and lesbians, the "official" status of homosexuality as an illness listed in the APA's "Diagnostic and Statistical Manual of Mental Disorders" was a pressing concern. The adjective *sick* along with *sinful* and *criminal* formed a triumvirate of labels that posed significant barriers to both gay self-esteem and civil equality.

As early as the 1960s, some gay men and lesbians were beginning to publicly reject the sickness label as insulting to a group of people who mostly led happy, healthy lives tainted only by prejudice. In addition, the work of non–gay-identified researchers like Evelyn Hooker, Alfred Kinsey, and Judd Marmor lent credibility to such claims. But starting in 1970, an orchestrated campaign by gay and lesbian liberationists was the spark that convinced many psychiatrists to finally reevaluate homosexuality's official status. One of the first "zaps" against the psychiatric status quo took place at the 1970 APA convention, when a bearded man in a red dress grabbed the microphone from antigay psychiatrist Irving Bieber and shouted,

"We've listened to you long enough; you listen to us. We're fed up with being told we're sick. You're the ones who are sick. We're gay, and we're proud." Other gay liberationists adopted the chant, "Stop it! You're making me sick!"

The next year demonstrations continued, with longtime gay activist Frank Kameny disrupting the event's convocation by shouting "Psychiatry is the enemy incarnate!" into a microphone and lesbian and gay activists protesting the inclusion of an aversion-therapy booth in the convention hall. But in addition the APA, in hopes of preempting pro-gay demonstrations, scheduled a panel at its conference entitled "Lifestyles of Non-Patient Homosexuals," which gay activists soon began to refer to as "Lifestyles of Im-Patient Homosexuals." For the first time, psychiatrists at their annual convention did not just talk about homosexuals; they listened to them as well.

At the 1972 convention another panel was held, but this one included an unusual spectacle: a gay psychiatrist, wearing a wig and rubber mask, with a microphone rigged to disguise his voice. "Dr. Henry Anonymous" spoke to 500 of his colleagues attending the session about his experiences in the closet, and observers were moved by his talk, however farcical the circumstances.

By the 1973 convention in Honolulu, more and more psychiatrists publicly supported deleting homosexuality from the diagnostic manual, but significant opposition remained. The breakthrough came with a compromise proposed by a heterosexual psychiatrist named Robert Spitzer, who proposed that homosexuality per se be deleted but that a category called "Sexual Orientation Disturbance" be retained to cover those lesbians and gays who were unhappy in their orientation and wanted to change. Although many gay activists found the new category insulting, they made a tactical decision to support the compromise, declare victory, and ignore the lingering diagnostic category.

On December 15, 1973, the APA's board of trustees unanimously approved Spitzer's compromise and went a step further by calling for the decriminalization of homosexuality and the passage of civil rights protections for gays and lesbians. It was an unprecedented endorsement of what gays had been asking for by one of the very groups they had seen as their oppressors. Gays and lesbians had just begun to celebrate their victory when a reversal seemed all too possible. Bieber and his fellow antigay colleague Dr. Charles Socarides (whose son Richard later became Bill Clinton's top gay aide) invoked a procedural maneuver that would bring the diagnostic change before a vote of the APA's 20,000 members. Before the mail-in vote, gay activists from the National Gay Task Force orchestrated and paid for a letter (whose gay funding was not noted) from all three candidates for the APA presidency as well as other leading psychiatrists to the entire APA membership urging them to support the board's position in order to avoid embarrassing their profession.

The results were announced on April 8: 58% of those voting supported the board's decision, and 37% opposed it, while the rest abstained. It was a clear vindication of the idea that homosexuality per se is not a mental illness—but at the same time, it meant that thousands of doctors still treated (as many still continue to treat) gays and lesbians as inherently sick individuals.

73. Who was Oliver Sipple?

Oliver Sipple was a disabled ex-Marine who saved the life of the president of the United States. On September 22, 1975, Sipple was standing near the entrance of the St. Francis hotel in downtown San Francisco, hoping to get a glimpse of President Gerald Ford, who had just finished addressing the World Affairs Council inside. When Ford stepped out of the hotel, Sipple noticed a gray-haired woman who aimed a gun toward the president. He wrestled her to the ground, and although the gun went off, no one was injured.

When questioned by the Secret Service, he begged them not to release his name to the press. They did so anyway; the near-assassination of President Ford by Sara Jane Moore was a major national story. Soon, Sipple faced the public revelation of something he hoped to keep out of the newspapers: the fact that he was gay. Harvey Milk—who later became San Francisco's first openly gay elected official—is said to have contacted *San Francisco Chronicle* columnist Herb Caen, who promptly included a brief item about Sipple in his column. Caen wrote of the celebrations of Sipple's heroism in a gay bar the night of the assassination attempt—and listed Sipple as a volunteer in Milk's campaign for office.

Several other newspapers followed with stories about "the gay vet" and the "homosexual hero," and when Sipple's family found out they refused to speak with him. Sipple responded by suing the *Chronicle* and other newspapers for invasion of privacy, but the courts rejected his case, arguing that by choosing to save the president's life, he had become a public figure.

President Ford—embarrassed by the affair—did not invite Sipple to a Rose Garden ceremony or grant him a Presidential Medal of Honor. After weeks of waiting Sipple finally received a brief note of thanks for his heroism.

74. Who was Sgt. Leonard Matlovich?

Long before Keith Meinhold, Tracy Thorne, and Zoe Dunning dominated the gays-in-the-military headlines, Sgt. Leonard Matlovich brought attention to the military's policies of discharging homosexuals, whatever their service record.

The son of a career Air Force serviceman, Matlovich joined his father's branch of the service a year out of high school, in 1963, and immediately volunteered to go to Vietnam. In the year before he was granted his request, he became involved in Republican politics, campaigning for ultraconservative presidential candidate Barry Goldwater. Despite his Catholic faith and conservative politics, Matlovich's private sexual thoughts were exclusively toward other men.

His service in Vietnam was exemplary by all accounts; he won both a Bronze Star and a Purple Heart. But contrary to military expectations, he continued to find himself drawn to his fellow servicemen. These feelings troubled Matlovich because they distracted him from his primary motivation to serve his country with honor. Eager for a way of life that was even more hierarchical and authoritarian than the military, Matlovich was baptized into the Mormon Church in the South China Sea in 1968.

But Matlovich continued to struggle with gay feelings that became politicized after he began teaching racial sensitivity courses to service members as part of the military's efforts to combat racism among the troops. At one point he asked his students who the most discriminated-against group in America was, and when they answered "blacks" or "Jews," he wrote the word *homosexuals*. Soon, Matlovich's class was debating the military's exclusion of gay and lesbian personnel, and one of the students mentioned the name of a local gay bar. Intent on doing "research," Matlovich went to it one evening, met another man, and had his first sexual experience.

Increasingly, Matlovich wanted to integrate his burgeoning homosexuality with his loyalty to the armed services. He also recognized that his medals and his all-American background made him an ideal test case in a court challenge to the ban on openly gay service members. So he contacted Franklin Kameny, a longtime Washington, D.C., gay activist who had successfully challenged the government's discrimination against gay employees. Kameny urged Matlovich to consider the implications of coming out on his career, but once Matlovich indicated he was sure he wanted to mount a challenge, Kameny helped Matlovich find a lawyer.

In March, 1975, Matlovich delivered a letter to his superior officer in which he indicated that "my sexual preferences are homosexual as opposed to heterosexual" and urged a waiver of the military's antigay policies in light of his continuing abilities to perform his duties.

At first the Office of Special Investigations didn't even believe him. Its agents demanded that Matlovich offer proof that he was actually gay and not just trying to make a political point. While the sergeant refused to "out" other gay personnel, he did write a letter in which he indicated he had engaged in specific sexual acts.

While awaiting an administrative hearing on whether Matlovich should be discharged, the sergeant faced decidedly mixed reactions from other military personnel. Several of his nongay coworkers at Langley Air Force Base, particularly those who were African-American, came to his defense, insisting his case was one of civil rights. Others were less supportive, and Matlovich even received threatening phone calls and gunfire aimed at his home. At one point Matlovich was ordered to conduct an after-hours inspection of a barracks of young servicemen, and he was convinced he was being tested to see if he would stare at the half-naked bodies under his command. But the reaction of many service members was disbelief, as expressed by the sergeant who told Matlovich, "You can't have a Purple Heart and a Bronze Star and suck cock."

By this time Matlovich's case had attracted broad media attention, and he became the first openly gay man to be pictured on the cover of *Time* magazine.

At his hearing, testimony on the nature of homosexuality was offered along with the inconsistent fashion in which the Uniform Code of Military Justice was enforced. (Adultery and wife-swapping allegations were never investigated, the defense pointed out, unlike charges of homosexuality.) But the presiding judge made it clear that the board would have to base its decision on whether Matlovich was violating current regulations, not the fairness or constitutionality of those regulations. Matlovich lost and was given a general (less than honorable) discharge.

Matlovich appealed, and in December 1978 the U.S. Court of Appeals ruled that his discharge had been illegal—and that a lower court should determine whether he should be reinstated. Almost two years later a judge ordered the Air Force to reinstate Matlovich, but the Air Force—desperate to keep Matlovich a civilian—offered the former sergeant a tax-free $160,000 settlement. To the surprise of many observers—and the rage of many gay activists—Matlovich took the money, citing his dim prospects of winning a government appeal to an increasingly conservative Supreme Court. He used the money to open a gay bar in the Russian River resort area north of San Francisco.

In 1988, Matlovich died of AIDS-related complications. His gravestone in Washington's Congressional Cemetery reads, "When I was in the military, they gave me a medal for killing two men, and a discharge for loving one."

75. Who were some of the first openly gay elected officials?

In the mid 1970s the gay and lesbian movement reached a new phase when the first openly gay men and lesbian women began to win election as public officials. Gays had campaigned for public positions as early as 1961, when openly gay drag entertainer Jose Sarria received 5,600 votes in his bid for a position on the San Francisco board of supervisors. Other openly gay individuals ran for office in the next 13 years, and at least one of them won: Kathy Kozachenko of the Ann Arbor, Mich., county council.

But in late 1974 one gay man and one lesbian burst onto the political scene as openly gay legislators. In November of that year, Elaine Noble was elected as a state representative in Massachusetts, and one month later Minnesota state senator Allan Spear revealed his homosexuality in a newspaper interview.

The openly lesbian Noble—a former cocktail waitress, educator, and community volunteer—ran as a Democrat for a seat in the Massachusetts house representing Boston's Fenway district. She narrowly won the primary and defeated her Republican opponent in November with nearly 60% of the vote.

In office Noble found herself torn between her goals as a legislator representing a mostly straight, elderly, and poor district and the demands of the gay and lesbian community that she focus on "their" issues. On more than one occasion, she was accused of "selling out" and acting against the best interests of gays and lesbians. For example, when two dozen gay men were accused of pedophilia in Boston, she quickly held a news conference and condemned the accused men, most of whom were never convicted. In 1976 she flew to a fund-raiser in San Francisco to raise money for the straight, pro-gay politician who was running against Harvey Milk for the California assembly.

On the other hand, Noble did try (albeit unsuccessfully) to pass a statewide job-protection bill for gays and lesbians and certainly helped break down barriers and stereotypes among legislators in Massachusetts and nationwide. After she served two terms, the district lines were redrawn and she found herself in the same district as her ally, then-closeted gay legislator Barney Frank. Rather than face off against Frank in a primary, Noble ran for the U.S. Senate in 1978, but she lost the primary to future presidential contender Paul Tsongas.

Noble left elected office with some bitterness toward the community that had both embraced and scorned her. She told *The Advocate* magazine, "I guess more than anything I'm just exhausted and very, very tired and probably disillusioned because I really tried the best I could and it wasn't good enough for the gay community. To be honest, I don't know what 'good enough' is."

In part, inspired by Noble's November 1974 election, Allan Spear granted a front-page interview to the *Minneapolis Star-Tribune* soon after his reelection to a second term as a state senator in which he declared he was gay. This announcement was not met with universal acceptance. One state senator indicated during a committee meeting that he thought the state should appropriate money to help Spear get his homosexuality "cured." Nonetheless, many of Spear's fellow senators were supportive, although most expected him to lose his 1976 bid for reelection. Spear's Republican opponent in that race spent so much time denying homosexuality was an issue in the race that it became clear it was. Spear won with nearly 70% of the vote.

In the years that followed, Spear made a name for himself fighting for strict drunk-driving laws and expanded child care services. He also pushed for a gay rights bill that met strong opposition from religious conservatives but was ultimately passed in 1993. By that time Spear had risen through the ranks of Minnesota's senate to become that body's president.

In the two decades since Noble and Spear became openly gay elected officials, dozens of gay men and lesbians have come out in office or run as openly gay and lesbian candidates. In 1991 the Gay and Lesbian Victory Fund was founded to help raise money to elect openly gay and lesbian candidates—and by the end of that decade, hundreds of gay men and lesbians had been elected to public office.

76. When did American gays and lesbians first wear pink triangles as a political statement?

The pink triangle—originally a cloth patch the Nazis forced homosexual men to wear in German concentration camps—has become the most prominent symbol of the gay and lesbian community in America.

The Holocaust was a repeated metaphor in gay and lesbian rhetoric in the decades following the Second World War, with early gay rights organizations consciously comparing American homophobia to that of Nazi Germany and 1970 gay liberationists screaming "Genocide!" at psychologists who advocated aversion therapy as a treatment for homosexuality.

But the pink triangle was not widely worn as a political statement until 1975, when the emblem was chosen as the symbol of the campaign by gay and straight New Yorkers to pass a citywide ban on antigay discrimination. Ira Glasser—a heterosexual Jew who later became the executive director of the American Civil Liberties Union—led a coalition of groups which lobbied the city council. He wrote an impassioned and frequently reprinted op-ed piece in *The New York Times* that evoked the memory of the Danish king wearing a yellow star in solidarity with the besieged Jewish citizens of his country (this never happened, by the way). Glasser went on to point out that the Nazis killed nearly a quarter million homosexuals (an exaggeration by at least a power of ten) who were forced to wear pink triangles. Glasser then urged that gay and straight New Yorkers wear pink triangles in solidarity with the gay civil rights bill.

The use of the pink triangle spread to other political campaigns, particularly those against Anita Bryant's crusade to "save our children" from gays and lesbians. Most of Bryant's battles were fought in Florida, and activists there made a conscious decision to highlight the pink triangle as their symbol in an attempt to win Florida's large Jewish vote by an appeal to shared persecution in the Nazi era.

In the late 1980s, ACT UP inverted the pink triangle and combined it with the Holocaust-conscious slogan "Silence=Death" to create one of the most powerful visual symbols of the fight against AIDS and the social conditions that allowed it to spread.

Any cursory glance at a gay newspaper or parade reveals the central place of the pink triangle as a community symbol. There is a Triangle Inn catering to gays vacationing in Palm Springs, Calif.; gift shops in gay neighborhoods sell Pinky, a plush pink triangle with arms, legs, and eyes; and Pride Personal Lubricant features a large pink triangle on its label—all of which demonstrate just how far the symbol has come from its original meaning.

77. Who were the first major-league athletes to come out?

The phrase "openly gay athlete" brings to mind Martina Navratilova, Greg Louganis, Patty Sheehan, and other stars of individual sports such as tennis, diving, and golf. But years before any of these sports figures came out, two major-league athletes had already made gay history.

Football is a brutal game that is associated with "traditional" masculinity. But it is also teeming with homoerotic undertones. The players huddle head-to-head, arms wrapped around each other. At the start of a play, the quarterback grabs the ball from between the center's legs. After a touchdown the players hug and pat each other's behinds.

Within this dual male sphere of aggression and bonding, David Kopay, a Catholic young man originally from Chicago, found a niche for himself. He played ball throughout high school and won an athletic scholarship to the University of Washington, where he was a halfback and cocaptain of the Rose Bowl–winning team in 1964. At the end of his college career, Kopay was drafted as a running back by the San Francisco 49ers. Over the next ten years, he played for the Detroit Lions, the Washington Redskins, the New Orleans Saints, and the Green Bay Packers. In his final years in the National Football League, he was both a player and a coach.

At the same time Kopay harbored a secret. "I always knew I was a bit different," he later said, "but I kept it kind of quiet." Kopay had his first gay sexual encounter with a Redskins teammate, tight-end Jerry Smith (who died of AIDS-related complications in 1987). Though they had sex only once, the two remained friends and often roomed together when the team traveled. For a while Kopay tried different ways of "curing" his homosexuality, even marrying briefly, but he eventually realized that he was and had always been gay.

Rumors about Kopay's homosexuality spread in the NFL. As his years on the playing field ended, Kopay found himself without any coaching offers and unable to get a sports-related job. "By the time I spoke out" about being gay, he recalled, "I really had nothing left to lose.... I just had to do it."

One morning Kopay opened up his copy of the *Washington Star* and spotted an intriguing headline: HOMOSEXUALS IN SPORTS. The story was an interview with an anonymous NFL player who talked at length about his double life in sports. Kopay recognized the player as his former roommate and lover Smith and decided to offer the reporter an interview. But unlike Smith, Kopay agreed to let the paper use his name. On December 11, 1975, Kopay's own story as a "queer football player," as he later put it, made headlines. He was the first professional athlete to come out publicly.

Kopay didn't experience any direct backlash from coming out, though he never got the coaching job he wanted and eventually settled for a job as a linoleum salesman. In 1977 he published his autobiography, which became a best-seller. Kopay received positive letters from lesbians, gay men, and gay youth in particular thanking him for his courage. He was also invited to speak at universities across the country. Though the movie rights to the book were sold, no film was ever made. "I think the NFL maybe had something to do with discouraging anyone from doing a film version," Kopay speculated.

Around the same time that Kopay came out, another major-league athlete was making a name for himself in the all-American sport of baseball. Glenn Burke, an African-American from Oakland, Calif., started playing professional ball for an Los Angeles Dodgers farm team in 1972 and became an outfielder for the Dodgers four years later. In 1977 he invented the "high five" during the Dodgers' final game of the season. When the Dodgers made it to the World Series, Burke reached the pinnacle of his career.

The Dodgers had high hopes for Burke. When he signed on, one coach said, "Frankly, we think he's going to be another Willie Mays." But playing for the Dodgers was complicated because Burke felt like an outsider instead of part of the team. He was trying to hide his homosexuality, which he had known about for years.

Burke developed a "too close" friendship with Tommy Lasorda Jr., the openly gay son of the team's manager. In 1978 the Dodgers' vice president pulled Burke aside and suggested he get married like his fellow players. But Burke remained single and soon found himself traded to the Oakland A's.

Halfway through his second season with the A's, Burke was released from his contract for reasons he never understood. He suspected homophobia, but his modest batting average may have also contributed. No other team picked up Burke's contract, and at 26 he found himself without a career and unprepared for a life outside of baseball.

Two years after his release from the A's, Burke confirmed the rumors of his homosexuality in *Inside Sports* magazine, becoming the first baseball player to come out. "It was more important to be myself than a baseball player," he said. Burke became active in San Francisco's gay community, playing on a gay softball team and joining the group Black and White Men Together.

Still, Burke remained bitter about his firing and began taking drugs to cope, eventually becoming addicted. As he later put it, leaving baseball "took a chunk out of my heart." He died of complications from AIDS in 1995 at the age of 43.

78. Who was Sal Mineo?

On the evening of February 12, 1976, a resident of a West Hollywood apartment building heard someone in the street crying out for help. Hurrying downstairs, the man found actor Sal Mineo bleeding to death from stab wounds, the victim of a bungled robbery attempt. In a sad twist of fate, Mineo's life ended just as he was beginning to reconcile his homosexuality with his career.

The child of Sicilian immigrants, Mineo was born in the Bronx in 1939. He was a tough kid growing up, much like the characters he later played on screen. At age 8 he was expelled from parochial school for being a troublemaker. He subsequently joined a street gang and by the age of 10 was taking part in robberies. Trying to keep him off the street, his mother enrolled him in dance and acting classes, where Mineo immediately shined. In acting school an agent spotted the 11-year-old's potential and cast him in the Broadway run of Tennessee Williams's play *The Rose Tattoo.*

Mineo appeared in Williams's play for over a year, then took the role of the young prince in *The King and I,* opposite Yul Brynner and Gertrude Lawrence. In 1965, with those impressive stage credits behind him, Mineo went to Hollywood, where he made his first movie, *Six Bridges to Cross,* launching his career as a celluloid juvenile delinquent. But it was his second film, made that same year, *Rebel Without a Cause,* that made a star of the teenager. For his compelling portrayal of the anguished Plato, Mineo received an Academy Award nomination for Best Supporting Actor.

The character of Plato is significant in gay filmography because he was the first gay teenager in Hollywood history, a sensitive kid with photos of movie star Alan Ladd taped inside his school locker. Plato was also achingly in love with his best friend, Jim, played by James Dean. Like many gay characters in films of that era, Plato died a violent death at the movie's end, while Jim went on to a heterosexual future with Judy, the character played by Natalie Wood.

In subsequent films during the 1950s, like *Crime in the Streets, Dino,* and *The Young Don't Cry,* Mineo continued to be cast as a street punk or disaffected youth. His roles earned him the nickname "the Switchblade Kid," and his rebel persona made him a hero among teenagers. When at 20 he launched a brief career as a rock-and-roll singer, Mineo's first single, "Start Movin'," stayed in the Top 40 for 13 weeks and eventually went gold.

Mineo got a chance at a few meatier film roles as he entered his 20s. In 1959 his performance as jazz drummer Gene Krupa was a critical success. The following year Mineo's portrayal of a young Auschwitz survivor in *Exodus* with Paul Newman and Eva Marie Saint garnered him a second Oscar nomination.

But with his teen years and baby-faced looks behind him, the good roles began to dry up for Mineo. In the mid 1960s, Mineo observed that he was "on the industry's weirdo list," offered roles mostly as psychotics in forgettable films like *Who Killed Teddy Bear?* In 1971 he played his last movie role, in *Escape From the Planet of the Apes*—as an ape.

Several factors worked against Mineo in Hollywood. His dark Italian features immediately set him up for ethnic typecasting. In addition, Mineo talked openly about his sexuality. Commenting on the death of his *Rebel Without a Cause* costar James Dean, Mineo was quoted as saying, "We never became lovers, but we could have—like that." He also admitted, "I like them all—men, I mean," though he added, "and a few chicks now and then."

When his film career waned, Mineo took sporadic television roles but found greater success back on the stage. He directed the Los Angeles and New York productions of *Fortune and Men's Eyes,* the John Hubert play about homosexuality behind prison bars. Mineo also appeared in a San Francisco production of *P.S. Your Cat Is Dead* as a bisexual cat burglar. He was set to reprise that role in Los Angeles, but it was on his way home from rehearsal that he was fatally stabbed.

Rumors flew about Mineo's murder, all of them suggesting that to live as a gay man was to court danger. The most widespread story was that he was killed by a hustler he had brought home for sadomasochistic games, but in fact he was murdered by a stranger who was attempting to rob him. Mineo's assailant was arrested, convicted, and sentenced to life imprisonment in 1979. The teen idol and two-time Oscar nominee left an estate of only $8,500.

79. What is the history of the Michigan Womyn's Music Festival?

The Michigan Womyn's Music Festival is a part of the calendar's rhythm for thousands of lesbians and other women who gather each August at a secluded campsite outside Grand Rapids. The festival has achieved mythic status in lesbian communities both for its empowering and liberating affect on its participants and for the controversies that have arisen year after year over its rules and boundaries.

In recent years "Michigan," the loving shorthand lesbians use for the event, has drawn between 6,000 and 8,000 women to a 650-acre forest campground in which the action on the various sound stages—by many of the biggest names in women's music—is just one of a whirlwind of activities. Dozens of workshops, from drumming to signing to spirituality, coincide with a crafts bazaar and an international film festival. The festival models itself as a prototype of a nurturing community—how the world would be if women got to design it. As such, a complex geography of care has developed. "The Womb" attends to festivalgoers' physical needs (sunburns, especially), while "the Oasis" attends to their emotional needs. There is a camp for girls on-site, and sons of participants who are under 10 can attend Brother Sun Boys' Camp. More than a dozen sign-language interpreters provide a connection to the music and workshops for hearing-impaired women, and three vegetarian meals are provided daily. And even in 1997 no woman paid more than $300 to stay for up to six days.

From its beginnings on a 20-acre site rented for $400 in the summer of 1976, Michigan has been a communitarian venture. All participants sign up for two four-hour work shifts, from helping with childcare to maintenance to cooking.

The mid 70s, when Michigan was founded, was a period of explosive growth in women's music. The women who started the festival had attended similar events in 1975 and wanted to start their own in Michigan. They chose the spelling *womyn*, with a *y*, to make it clear that their venture would rely not at all on men—an approach that has been strictly adhered to for two decades. Even listening to "male music" on radios or tape decks is forbidden on the festival grounds.

In its second year the festival moved to a larger, rented site in Oceana County, Mich., where the women braved a near tornado. In the early years threatened invasions by hostile local men were a recurrent problem, although no actual violence occurred. Several of the organizers felt a permanent, owned site was essential, and in 1982 the current parcel was purchased. Because the current site is surrounded by a quarter million acres of the Manistee National Forest, many festivalgoers attest that they have never felt safer or freer. Indeed, clothing is optional throughout the festival.

The first of the many Michigan controversies centered over whether participants could bring their sons. Despite official rules against it, in the first years some women brought boys as old as 14, some of whom felt so disoriented by the female-privileged society that they picked on some of the younger girls. The current strict policy of no boys over 3 on the main festival grounds and no boys over 10 at the festival at all developed as a compromise, although it left some mothers unhappy.

Another point of controversy has been sadomasochism. In

the late 1970s and early 1980s, a subset of the lesbian community began openly embracing leather-dyke identities, to the horror of women who identified violence with maleness. For the 1980 festival public sex and open displays of sadomasochism were banned, creating a furor among women who felt nobody's sexuality should be restricted. Eventually a compromise was reached where a separate "Twilight Zone" was set up for the leather set.

The most recent—and perhaps the most wrenching—major debate has been over the participation of postoperative male-to-female transsexuals at the event. One such transsexual, Nancy Burkholder, participated clandestinely at the 1990 festival. But the next year, when she began to share her history with other participants, security guards escorted her from the premises—despite her offer to "drop her drawers."

By 1993 the "womyn-born womyn only" policy was a source of significant controversy. Camp Trans was set up outside the gates of the festival to protest the exclusion of "men-born womyn," and several opponents of the policy wore FRIEND OF NANCY buttons. But the festival organizers and many participants insist that by excluding anyone born as a male, they are creating a uniquely safe and affirming space for the thousands of women who participate. Or as one woman put it, "It's the dick in their heads I don't want here."

Although the controversies have provided for hours of debate for women—both during Michigan and the other 51 weeks of the year—many festivalgoers have grown tired of each new issue and simply want to enjoy the festival for its scenery, its sense of community, and of course its music.

80. What were the civil rights setbacks of the late 1970s?

The decade after Stonewall was a heady time for the American gay and lesbian civil rights movement. Gays and lesbians were more visible than at any previous time in American history, and laws that penalized private same-sex behavior were repealed in many jurisdictions. In addition, more than 40 municipalities passed laws protecting citizens from discrimination on the basis of sexual orientation. Although conservative forces opposed these changes from the start, the battle was not truly joined by them until 1977 and 1978, when a series of cities across the country voted on whether to keep such gay rights laws on the books. The strategies used by both sides in these referendum campaigns helped set the boundaries and the tone for hundreds of future skirmishes over laws protecting gays and lesbians from discrimination.

The site of the first such popular vote on gay and lesbian rights was Dade County, Fla., whose nondiscrimination ordinance drew the ire of orange-juice spokesperson and former Miss America runner-up Anita Bryant. In January 1977, Bryant testified before the Dade County commission that a proposed gay rights ordinance threatened "the rights of the overwhelming number of Dade County constituents." When her emotional testimony failed to sway the commission, she formed an organization, Save Our Children, to begin collecting the 10,000 signatures necessary to force a proposition on the June ballot.

At first many gays and lesbians did not take Bryant's cam-

paign seriously. But when the 37-year-old singer's organization collected more than six times the number of signatures
necessary, gays and lesbians in South Florida and around the
nation began organizing for the June election. Led by Jack
Campbell, who owned a nationwide chain of gay bathhouses,
the Miami gay and lesbian community raised $350,000 in con-
tributions from around the country. Hundreds of gay bars
stopped serving orange juice, and dozens of volunteers flew to
Miami to canvass neighborhoods and work the polls. An elaborate media strategy was developed, emphasizing broad
themes of human rights and freedom.

But in the end Bryant's message was more convincing: Gays
and lesbians were a threat to America's children, and any law
that prevented employers from firing homosexuals increased
the opportunities for a new generation of children to be recruited into the gay lifestyle. The expected opposition of traditionally liberal constituencies such as blacks, Jews, and working-class voters did not materialize, and the ordinance was
repealed, 202,319 votes to 83,319. Gays and lesbians in South
Florida were devastated.

But the war had just begun. Bryant, thrust into the limelight
by the Dade County battle, began a nationwide tour of cities
that had passed gay rights legislation. Organizations similar to
Save Our Children formed in many municipalities to fight the
gains of the gay and lesbian movement.

The spring of 1978 was a particularly difficult time for gay
and lesbian rights. In April, St. Paul, Minn., the capital of a
traditionally liberal state, repealed its gay rights law by a
nearly two thirds popular vote. The next month Wichita, Kan.,
repealed its gay rights protections by almost five to one.
Within weeks gay rights were also repealed overwhelmingly

in another liberal haven: Eugene, Ore.

In each city national forces on both sides sent money and personnel, but the defeat of job protections was ultimately based on a simple message to local voters: gay rights are bad for your children. For example, the antigay forces in Eugene included the following line in their literature: "Other areas adopting pro-homosexual legislation have observed an increase in V.D., public indecency, and boy prostitution. Vote YES to protect your family, job, and community."

The momentum against gay rights laws finally hit a fire wall in the fall of 1978, when two antigay measures were defeated on the West Coast: California's Briggs Initiative and Seattle's Initiative 13. The Briggs Initiative sought to prevent gay and even pro-gay teachers from teaching in public schools, and Initiative 13 threatened to repeal Seattle's nondiscrimination law. Each measure lost because of specific, local reasons, but the overall effect was to stall the movement against local gay rights laws. In California, while early polls showed the Briggs Initiative with a comfortable lead, a concerted campaign by gays and straights throughout the state combined with a late endorsement of the "no" position by California's most prominent conservative, Ronald Reagan, led to the initiative's defeat. In Seattle a strong emphasis on the value of the "right to privacy" for gays and straights alike worked in concert with the negative publicity for the initiative's backers when one of the police officers who initiated the measure killed a black youth while on duty.

The widespread publicity over these antigay initiatives caused the issue of nondiscrimination to be the first public battle over homosexuality in the post-Stonewall era—which perhaps explains why "gay rights" and "nondiscrimination laws" have become virtually synonymous in America's lexicon. Even though the two decades since Bryant's first battle have been wrought with controversy over AIDS funding, the military, marriage, and adoption, the assumption that gay equality means simply adding or keeping sexual orientation as a protected category along with race, sex, and religion has been quite resilient.

81. What was the National Women's Conference?

From November 18 to 21, 1977, 20,000 women, men, and children gathered to herald International Women's Year at the National Women's Conference in Houston. The event's keynote speaker, anthropologist Margaret Mead, called it "not only a historic occasion in the women's movement but in the history of the world." The conference also proved to be a significant moment in lesbian-feminist herstory since it marked a 180-degree turn in the way the straight feminist mainstream of the women's movement dealt with the issue of lesbian rights.

The conference was the brainchild of Bella Abzug, intrepid congresswoman from New York City. Abzug engineered a bill setting aside $5 million in federal funds to finance International Women's Year. From 1976 to 1977 individual states held women's conferences to elect delegates for a national conference in Houston. The purpose of the Houston conference was to adopt a set of feminist resolutions and recommendations for President Jimmy Carter, urging him to pay attention to women's issues.

It would have been easy for the straight feminist majority at the conference to skirt lesbian issues altogether; they'd been doing it for almost ten years. In the late 1960s, when groups such as the National Organization for Women were first firing up, a common "charge" leveled against feminists was that they were man-hating lesbians. There were, in fact, many lesbian activists who helped build the second wave of feminism and found groups like NOW. But homophobic straight feminists shuddered at the idea of being called lesbians and were quick to deny the accusation.

Straight feminists—pre-Houston—frequently tried to impose a gag order on the lesbians in their ranks. If lesbians openly discussed the need for lesbian rights, the straight majority reasoned, it might "discredit" the entire women's movement. Better for everyone to concentrate on more universal issues, like the Equal Rights Amendment. In other words, lesbians could dedicate their time to the feminist agenda, but they shouldn't try to set it.

All this in-fighting took its toll on the women's movement, sending many lesbians running in the other direction, often working at first for gay rights groups and later, when faced with sexism from gay men, establishing their own network of lesbian liberation organizations. By 1977 the deadline for states to ratify the ERA was rapidly approaching, and the women's movement desperately needed the boost of a national women's conference to continue the fight.

The Houston conference turned out to be one of the high points of the contemporary women's movement. The official delegation of 1,442 was a model of diversity, with lesbians and straight women, white women and minority women—all represented roughly in proportion to their numbers in the general population. The delegates ranged in age from 16 to 84, with students, homemakers, prostitutes, nurses, politicians, and scientists represented. A quarter were poor women, many on welfare. Many men and children also attended in support of the women in their lives.

In all, the delegates passed 25 resolutions, with a statement on "sexual preference" one of the most hotly debated. To the surprise of many of the lesbians in attendance, Betty Friedan backed off her initial opposition to lesbian rights, warning delegates that "because...there is nothing in the ERA that will give any protection to homosexuals, we must pass this resolution." Though the resolution used the word *preference* instead of *orientation*, its no-nonsense call for full civil rights for lesbians—and by virtue of its gender-free language, gay men too—was way ahead of its time. It outlined for the president a strategic plan of national and local legislation to ban discrimination based on "sexual or affectional preference" in employment, housing, the military, and other areas; the repeal of all sodomy laws; and protections for lesbian mothers in cases of child custody and visitation.

But Carter failed to take the conference or any of its resolutions seriously. The Christian right, however, did take action, holding a "pro-family" rally in Houston on November 19. In a newspaper ad for the rally, an "innocent little girl" asked, "Mommy, when I grow up, can I be a lesbian?"—clearly a shocking idea to the crowd of 15,000 who gathered to protest the conference. Speakers included Phyllis Schlafly, Bob Dornan, and, on film, Anita Bryant. Jesse Helms sent a supportive telegram. A leaflet passed among the rallygoers declared, "The ERA will legalize homosexual 'marriages' and permit such 'couples' to adopt children." Though a few of the players have changed in the last 20 years, the rhetoric of those who oppose the lesbian and gay movement has been quite consistent.

82. What was the Body Politic raid?

On Friday, December 30, 1977, the staff of *The Body Politic*, at that time Canada's largest gay newspaper, got an unwelcome surprise. Waving a search warrant, five police officers arrived at the newspaper's Toronto office to hunt for evidence supporting a charge that *The Body Politic* (which was collectively operated) had violated Section 168 of the Canadian criminal code: "use of the mails for the purpose of transmitting or delivering anything that is obscene, indecent, immoral or scurrilous." The raid and the ensuing brouhaha marked a turning point in the maturation of Canada's lesbian and gay community.

The incident actually started a month earlier, when *The Body Politic* published its December–January issue. In it was an article by collective member Gerald Hannon titled "Men Loving Boys Loving Men" that explored the controversial topic of man-boy love. Hannon argued that men who had sex with boys were not child molesters, as a homophobic society tended to view them, but responsible citizens performing an educational service for gay youth—liberating their sexuality. The real victims of molestation, rather, were all gays and lesbians. "Every homosexual's sexuality has been interfered with," Hannon wrote, "impeded, strangled, diverted, denounced, 'cured,' pitied, punished. That is molestation."

The Body Politic's staff was well aware that Hannon's take on the subject might cause an explosion of public outrage, both from outside and inside the lesbian and gay community. Consequently, the paper opted to run a preamble to the article explaining that Hannon's piece had been typeset and laid out for nearly six months before the staff could agree to publish it. They had finally made the decision to run it because "the 'climate' will never be right...but the discussion must be opened up."

The political climate was in fact extremely volatile. The Ontario legislature was considering passage of a gay rights bill, and the issue was being hotly debated in the mainstream press. Opponents of the bill painted lesbians and gay men as child molesters, much as Anita Bryant and her followers had successfully done in their Save Our Children campaign in Dade County, Fla., earlier that year. In addition, a public furor had followed the August 1977 killing of a 12-year-old Toronto boy by four men, a crime the tabloids sensationalized as a "homosexual orgy slaying." It was in this atmosphere that *The Body Politic* printed Hannon's article—which from their perspective was an attempt to set the record straight on child molestation.

Predictably, the attempt backfired. The mainstream Toronto press had a field day with Hannon's article. In five separate editorials the week before Christmas, one of which was titled "Bawdy Politic," the *Toronto Sun* blasted the gay newspaper. One conservative columnist who had often attacked the lesbian and gay community in print personally lobbied the attorney general to take action against *The Body Politic.* On December 30, the day the *Sun* announced in a headline, CROWN TO STUDY SEX MAG, police officers raided *The Body Politic*'s office. More than three hours later, they carted off 12 boxes of manuscripts, correspondence, financial and advertising records, and subscription lists.

The week after the raid, the Canadian government brought criminal charges against the paper's nonprofit publisher, Pink

Triangle Press, and three of its officers, one of whom was Hannon. Canada's lesbian and gay community was split in opinion about the case. There were those who believed that *The Body Politic* had provoked the raid by publishing the controversial article, while others were alarmed about the dangerous precedent set when police were able to seize a gay publication's records, particularly subscription lists. Many thought the charges had been trumped up in order to damage the chances of the gay rights ordinance.

It took a full year for the case to come to trial. By that time much of the hostility against the paper had died down, largely because Toronto's new mayor, John Sewell, publicly supported *The Body Politic* and denounced all attempts at censorship of the press. In February 1979 the newspaper was acquitted of the charges. The publication promptly reprinted Hannon's article in its next edition, along with analysis by lesbian novelist Jane Rule and an assessment of the controversy by three staff members.

But the case wasn't over. The Canadian government appealed the decision, and the officers of the paper were retried in May 1982. Once again they received an acquittal, and the charges were finally laid to rest. At that time the materials confiscated by the police in the 1977 raid were finally returned to the paper.

The ordeal cost *The Body Politic* 100,000 Canadian dollars in legal fees and six years of aggravation. Though the collective attempted to regroup and start over, the paper never fully recovered from its financial problems. In February 1987, after celebrating its 15th anniversary, *The Body Politic* closed shop. Ironically, just two months earlier, the Ontario legislature finally passed a provincial gay rights ordinance banning discrimination on the basis of sexual orientation.

83. How gay was the disco era?

According to popular myth, the musical genre called disco was imported to the United States from Europe in the 1960s. The word *discothèque* indeed came from France, where it meant any club that played recorded dance music. However, disco music got its start in the black gay dance clubs of New York City in the late 1960s.

To placate their clients, many of whom wanted to dance all night, black gay DJs began experimenting with records by groups like the Temptations and the O'Jays. They phased records in and out, splicing soul with another style called "Philly." The result was disco, which had an insistent, pulsing, 120 beats per minute. Good disco music was nonstop; as one critic put it, the music saturated dancers and the dance floor.

Disco music, however, didn't achieve wide public attention until white gay men adopted it, creating dazzling dance clubs for feverish, continuous dancing. In the summer of 1970, in the early days of the gay liberation movement, the Ice Palace in Cherry Grove on New York's Fire Island was one of the first clubs to set up a DJ booth, gigantic speakers, a mirror ball, and elaborate lighting that pulsed in time with the music. *Disco* became synonymous with the clubs where the music played. Over the next decade in New York City, Los Angeles, and other cities across the country, vast, empty factories and warehouses were transformed into gay male pleasure palaces. Paradise Garage, the Flamingo, and the Saint were some of the glittering favorites of gay New York, while Studio One dominated Hollywood during disco's heyday.

With its open eroticism, disco music was a tangible reflection of gay sexual liberation. Song lyrics often suggested sex, with an emphasis on fleeting romantic encounters. Disco dancing, with its wild bumping and grinding, offered up the possibility of casual sex to gay men whose sexuality had long been controlled by the dominant culture. In disco clubs, *The Advocate* magazine reported in 1975, "Nobody cared who did what to whom, just as long as you didn't stand still." In this sense, disco fostered a sense of gay community centered around the idea of personal sexual freedom. Gay historian Allan Bérubé has recalled having "a spiritual moment or vision" while dancing in a gay club during the 1970s. He thought, *This is what it could be like...if we were totally free.*

As with many pop-culture movements, disco gradually moved beyond its underground community, becoming a profitable enterprise. Clubs turned into expensive, members-only establishments. Record producers discovered the sound and in turn introduced it to straight America. The hits of straight recording artists like Gloria Gaynor ("I Will Survive") and Donna Summer ("Love to Love You") were embraced in the gay disco scene because so many of the lyrics could be imbued with gay meaning. But disco also saw its share of gay performers whose popularity crossed over to straight audiences.

One such performer, Sylvester, began his career in the 1950s as a child gospel singer. In the late 1970s he became an openly gay disco star, performing in evening gowns and boas and recording hits like "Disco Heat," "Fever," and writing the gold record "You Make Me Feel (Mighty Real)," which is still a standard in gay clubs and at gay pride events. Sylvester contributed most of his earnings to AIDS organizations before suc-

cumbing to the disease in 1988 at age 40. His female backup
singers, Two Tons o' Fun, found their own popularity in gay
male clubs with the disco hit "It's Raining Men."

The Village People presented a parody of both traditional
masculinity and urban gay male culture by performing in costumes as macho "types": a construction worker, an Indian, a
cowboy, a cop, a leatherman, and a soldier. To gay listeners the
group's biggest hits, like "Macho Man" and "YMCA," had obvious referents. But straight people who didn't know (or want to
know) that YMCAs had historically been places for gay men to
cruise each other and have sex could miss the double meaning
of lyrics like, "It's fun to stay at the YMCA / They have everything for young men to enjoy / You can hang out with all the
boys." At one point the group's song "In the Navy" was even
used in television commercials for the U.S. military.

Although their manager, Jacques Morali, was an openly
gay man, the Village People weren't sold to the public as gay.
Their 1980 film *Can't Stop the Music,* for example, featured
the "Indian," Felipe Rose, coming on to women. "If you become too political, you become provocative," Morali said, "and
you risk provoking a backlash." The movie's producer, Alan
Carr, was more blunt: "You don't spend $13 million to make a
minority movie."

Hollywood, in fact, significantly watered down and transformed disco for straight consumption. The 1978 hit movie
Saturday Night Fever marketed disco in a neat package and
presented it to middle America as a new heterosexual fad. Like
all fads, disco eventually faded, though it has recently been enjoying a revival in books and movies that tend to ignore the
role of gay culture in creating the genre.

For many gay men disco music was more than a passing fad,

and it still holds a place in gay culture. The coming of the AIDS crisis may have forced many disco clubs from the landscape, but disco music has remained a symbol of gay sexual liberation.

84. What were the White Night Riots?

On the morning of November 27, 1978, Dan White, a member of San Francisco's board of supervisors, came into the office of the city's liberal mayor, George Moscone, through a side door, argued with the mayor, and then shot him two times in the chest. When Moscone fell White shot him twice more in the head. After reloading his .38, White rushed across the hallway to the office of Supervisor Harvey Milk, the city's first openly gay elected official, and shot him a total of five times—like Moscone, first in the chest and then through the head. Both Moscone and Milk died instantly of their executionlike wounds.

Like Milk, White had served only 11 months as supervisor. An Irish Catholic ex-cop who had won election on a "traditional values" platform, he was an ultraconservative supervisor who unsuccessfully tried to stop the city's gay pride celebration. White was also the only supervisor on the 11-member board to vote against San Francisco's landmark gay rights ordinance. Milk told friends he suspected that White's aggressive homophobia stemmed from his being "a closet case."

Politically disillusioned and citing his insufficient salary as supervisor, White resigned his post in early November 1978. But his supporters quickly urged him to stay on. Within a few days of his resignation, White decided he did indeed want his job back. But he found that he simply couldn't rescind his resignation; Moscone had to decide to reappoint him.

At first Moscone leaned toward reinstatement, but Milk

lobbied aggressively against it. Moscone set November 27 as the day on which he would announce his decision publicly, but word leaked out that White would not be reappointed because "an unnamed supervisor" had opposed him.

To most people it looked like White planned the killings in advance as revenge. White evaded City Hall metal detectors on the 27th by climbing through a side window, and he carried several extra rounds of ammunition in his pocket. After shooting Moscone he reloaded and entered Milk's office, casually asking, "Say, Harv, can I see you?" In addition, White shot both his victims in the head at close range to make sure they were dead.

The prosecution in the Moscone-Milk murder case saw White's actions as clear-cut first-degree murder. But White's lawyers drew a completely different picture. According to the defense, White was an exemplary person, a hardworking and wholesome family man who under normal circumstances would never have killed anyone. However, White was extremely depressed because of his finances, and that made him act irrationally. The night before the shootings, one psychiatrist testified, White consumed an enormous amount of junk food—mostly Twinkies and Cokes—and his fluctuating blood-sugar levels had exacerbated his depression. "The pot had boiled over," his defense attorney said.

What probably decided White's case was a tactical error by the prosecution: the playing of White's tape-recorded confession in court. On the tape White broke into sobs as he described how he just "wanted to talk to [Milk]" but that Milk "started kind of smirking 'cause he knew, he knew that I wasn't going to be reappointed."

The prosecution hadn't gauged the homophobia of the jurors, all of whom were white and heterosexual. Gays and peo-

ple of color had been excluded during jury selection as too bi-
ased. When the jury heard White's tear-choked confession—"I
just got all flushed and, and, and hot, and I shot him"—several jurors wept openly in sympathy for the killer. On May 21, 1979,
the jury found White guilty of involuntary manslaughter, for
which he received a sentence of eight years in prison. With
good behavior he would be out in five.

The city exploded in rage. Many people of color who had
supported Moscone and Milk believed that White received le-
niency because he was a white man. The lesbian and gay community—which had initially reacted to the murders with more
pain and sadness than anger—was now furious. The lesbian
and gay community believed that if the heterosexual Moscone
had been the sole victim, White would have been imprisoned
for life. The verdict sent a message that a gay man was ex-
pendable, and the lesbian and gay community responded with
anger and violence.

That night 3,000 demonstrators shouting "We want justice!" and "Avenge Harvey Milk!" marched to City Hall. The
protest quickly escalated into a riot. Protesters smashed store
windows and set police cars on fire. Shortly after, the police re-
taliated by raiding a gay bar in the Castro district. They entered
the Elephant Walk swinging their nightsticks, injuring several
people and destroying property. In total about $1 million in
damages occurred on the night of May 21 in what became
known as the White Night Riots.

Gay rioters stood by their actions. "Until we display our un-
governable rage at injustice," lesbian activist Sally Gearhart
said, "we won't get heard." Harry Britt, the gay man appointed
to Milk's seat on the board, had at first tried to calm the rioters but then admitted he understood their rage. "We're react-

ing with anger because we're angry," he told reporters.

Despite bitter protests, White's sentence held, and he served only five and a half years for the murders. He received no psychiatric treatment in jail. In 1985, the year after his release, White committed suicide by asphyxiating himself in his wife's car.

85. When did the three marches on Washington for lesbian and gay rights take place?

Mass demonstrations on Washington, D.C., reached their heyday during the civil rights and antiwar movements of the 1960s and 1970s. Crowds in the hundreds of thousands regularly gathered in the nation's capital in support of progressive causes. African-Americans rallied in Washington in 1963; protesters against the Vietnam War staged a massive moratorium in 1969; and women and men marched for the Equal Rights Amendment in 1978. That same year lesbian and gay organizers began preliminary plans for a march on Washington to appeal for civil rights legislation for gay people.

Held on October 14, 1979, the first lesbian and gay march on Washington attracted approximately 100,000 participants from around the country. New Yorkers chartered a train they dubbed the "Disco Express," complete with a "back room" for sexual encounters; San Franciscans boarded the "Gay Freedom Train" for a 3,000-mile journey. Lesbians led the procession from the U.S. Capitol to a rally in front of the Washington Monument, belting out, "When the dykes come marching in." At the rally singer Holly Near captured the tone of the day with her lyrics, "We are a gentle, angry people / And we are marching, marching for our lives."

The following day, a contingent of activists presented a list of five demands to Congress: the repeal of antigay laws, passage of H.R. 2074 to extend coverage of the 1964 Civil Rights Act to gay people, the issuing of executive orders banning antigay discrimination in federal employment and in the military, protection from child custody battles for lesbian and gay parents, and protection of lesbian and gay youth from harassment and discrimination.

From first-person accounts the 1979 march was festive and hopeful. But two years later the AIDS crisis struck. Then in 1986 lesbian and gay rights received a crushing blow from the Supreme Court in its antigay decision *Bowers* v. *Hardwick*. When lesbians and gay men gathered for a second march in 1987, their mood had changed to one of gloom and rage.

Under gray skies, lesbians and gay men descended on Washington once again on October 11, 1987. The U.S Park Service estimated attendance at 200,000, but march organizers counted more than three times that number. This time the tone was set by streams of marchers who wagged their fingers at the Reagan White House, chanting "Shame! Shame! Shame!" and by the many participants who pinned photographs of deceased friends and lovers to their jackets.

Lesbians and gay men also invoked the spirit of the 1963 black civil rights march, singing "We Shall Overcome" while marching and listening to Jesse Jackson speak at the rally. A civil disobedience action was staged at the Supreme Court. "We vow to spend our dollars, our votes, and our nights in jail," asserted Virginia Apuzzo, then the executive director of the National Gay and Lesbian Task Force.

First on the list of demands this time around was the legal recognition of gay relationships, and same-sex couples staged a mass wedding in front of the IRS, officiated by the "gay pope," the Rev. Troy Perry of the Universal Fellowship of Metropolitan Community Churches. But the most moving part of the weekend for many people was the unveiling of the Names

Project AIDS Memorial Quilt. The size of two football fields, the quilt filled the mall between the Capitol and the Washington Monument and consisted of almost 2,000 panels, each for someone who had died of AIDS-related complications.

After the 1987 march activists Ron Eichberg and Jean O'Leary got the idea to hold an annual remembrance called National Coming-Out Day. Eichberg had been disheartened to find that many of the march's participants went home and immediately reentered the closet. NCOD was designed as a day when people could help end gay invisibility. Held first on October 11, 1988, the anniversary of the march, the commemoration has continued and grown every year since.

The third march on Washington occurred on April 25, 1993, and was the biggest by far—approximately three quarters of a million people. Unlike the first two, this march received substantial mainstream media coverage. At that time the furor over President Clinton's attempt to end the ban on gays in the military had reached its height. Clinton declined to speak in person at the rally, though he sent a letter that was read aloud and booed by many. Comedian Lea DeLaria set a cynical tone, drawing reproach for her controversial joke (telecast on C-SPAN) that Hillary Clinton was "a First Lady you could fuck" and singing a humorous rendition of "We Are a Gentle, Angry People" from the first march.

At the heart of the event, though, were gay Coloradans, who were waging a fierce battle over the passage of Amendment 2, an antigay referendum eventually overturned by the Supreme Court in 1996. The Colorado delegation marched with stark, black-and-white banners that read UNDER SIEGE and GROUND ZERO.

86. What were the Cruising protests?

One of the most provocative and controversial gay-themed films in history, *Cruising* (1980) starred Al Pacino as a rookie New York City cop who goes undercover to investigate a series of killings in the gay leather underworld. During the summer of 1979, hundreds of gays and lesbians who heard that the script was violently homophobic attempted to disrupt filming.

The film's content was first publicized to gays and lesbians by openly gay *Village Voice* columnist Arthur Bell, who complained that the script he had read showed Pacino increasingly enticed by the sadomasochistic gay life until he becomes both gay and murderous himself. (The final version of the film was ambiguous on this point.) Bell singled out the film's director, William Friedkin, as particularly homophobic (Friedkin had directed *The Boys in the Band* a decade earlier) and urged gays and lesbians to interrupt the on-location filming in New York City's Greenwich Village and protest the film's distributors. Bell later told a reporter that he sparked the protests because "this movie is a message to go out and kill, mutilate, and decapitate gays."

The furious protests against the film—which drew upon members of activist groups like the Gay Activists Alliance as well as the more moderate National Gay Task Force and gays unaffiliated with any group—have to be seen in the context of the time in which they took place. The summer of 1979 was less than two years after Anita Bryant first sparked repeals of gay rights laws across the country and only half a year after Harvey Milk's murder. Gays and lesbians were particularly sensitive to attacks on their rights and their persons—and *Cruising* was seen as kicking them while they were down.

A few days before filming was scheduled to begin, several hundred gays, lesbians, and supporters gathered in a Greenwich Village church to plan the *Cruising* protests. During the last week of July and the first week of August, activists protested filming day and night. Loud whistles were blown at key moments, forcing expensive retakes, and activists handed out flyers calling the film "a genocidal act." One protester charged, "This movie glorifies fag-killing. It's going to encourage violence against gays."

Particularly galling to the protesters were the dozens of gay men who served as extras in the bar scenes of the film, receiving $60 a day (more if they were willing to simulate sex acts). Protesters shouted "Judas!" at such extras, who were required to bring their own leather outfits from home, and more than a dozen chose to quit, while others leaked the locations of future shootings to the activists, facilitating future protests.

The *Cruising* protests were effective in other ways. Every gay bar in the Village but one closed their doors to the filmmakers, and Friedkin added a brief disclaimer at the start of the film indicating that the characters in the film were not meant to be representative of the gay community as a whole. But the protesters were unable to halt the filming or distributing of *Cruising*—so they started another round of protests when the film was released in February 1980. Several hundred gay and lesbian activists picketed movie theaters in New York City and San Francisco, and there were smaller protests in other cities.

In the wake of the San Francisco protests, Mayor Dianne Feinstein threatened to send a bill totaling more than $100,000 to United Artists, which distributed the film, for the city's costs in policing the streets during the protests. When the American Civil Liberties Union objected that the mayor's threat represented a prior restraint against free expression, Feinstein backed off. On the other coast a New York City attorney proposed—also to no avail—that gays file a multimillion-dollar class-action lawsuit against Friedkin for libeling the gay community.

A minority in the gay community defended the film on First Amendment grounds, but almost no one defended the leather lifestyle. The gay and lesbian community of 1980 was greatly concerned that the American public not associate them with sadomasochism and dark, seedy bars—even to the point of assenting to attacks on the leather subculture. The closest thing to a defender of this aspect of the gay community came from pro-pornography author and novelist John Rechy, who penned "A Case for Cruising" in the *Village Voice*. But even Rechy relied mostly on support for the freedom of speech and wrote only vaguely about a more open "exploration of our problems."

Despite a strong opening weekend, the film bombed at the box office. Reviews were mediocre at best (*Time* magazine called it "hopelessly fouled up"), and the film—and the protests—quickly faded. Ironically, *Cruising* has enjoyed a revival in recent years. When the film played for a week at the Roxie in San Francisco in 1995, both of that city's major newspapers ran movie reviews that reevaluated the film and recommended it strongly.

87. How did Billie Jean King come out?

Women's tennis—like women's golf, men's ice skating, and other sports—has long been subject to rumors about the sexual orientation of many of its most prominent participants. Unlike Martina Navratilova, who spoke at the 1993 march on Washington and served as a plaintiff in the case that successfully overturned Colorado's antigay Amendment 2, 1970s tennis champion Billie Jean King has been much more private about her lesbian relationships. But a 1981 lawsuit brought her sexuality—and by extension that of women's tennis—into the public eye.

Billie Jean King had long been a pioneer in women's tennis, from breaking barriers by wearing shorts on the court instead of a skirt to helping found the Virginia Slims tennis tournament. Seven years after marrying Larry King (not the talk show host) in 1965, Billie Jean began a relationship with Marilyn Barnett, a Beverly Hills hairdresser. Barnett even moved into the Kings' Malibu house, and Barnett was at Billie Jean's side as her "secretary" when she defeated Bobby Riggs in the much-hyped Battle of the Sexes tennis match at the Houston Astrodome. The women were not public about their relationship, and the tennis star gained a reputation as a "women's libber"—but she was relatively safe from suspicion as a married woman.

But in 1979 the affair ended, and the Kings planned to sell the Malibu house, worth about three quarters of a million dollars. Barnett refused to leave and became distraught. She attempted suicide and ended up having to use a wheelchair because of a broken back suffered when she jumped off the balcony of the Malibu house. After a second suicide attempt (by drug overdose) failed, Barnett threatened to go public with more than 100 amorous letters Billie Jean had sent her. Despite receiving $25,000 in hush money from the Kings, Barnett was not satisfied and in April 1981 brought a palimony suit against the tennis star, alleging she had been promised financial support for life. Coming just two years after the celebrated palimony case brought by the former girlfriend of movie star Lee Marvin, the press gave considerable attention to the lawsuit against King—especially the tabloids, which described the affair as a "galimony" case.

Two days after the suit was filed, Billie Jean King called a press conference in which she declared, "I've decided to talk with you as I've always talked—from the heart." With her husband at her side, King conceded that she had been Barnett's lover and called the relationship "a mistake." Larry King publicly took the blame for the affair, saying he had neglected his wife through his frequent business trips. In subsequent interviews the tennis champion repeatedly denied being a lesbian, telling *People* magazine, "I hate being called a homosexual, because I don't feel that way. It really upsets me." Her 1982 autobiography rejected the very concept of labeling her sexuality.

A Los Angeles superior court judge threw out the case, calling Barnett's use of the letters "close to extortion," but the scandal nonetheless hurt King's career. She found herself heckled on the court during the summer of 1981, and she lost six endorsement contracts. In addition, Avon cosmetics threatened to withdraw its sponsorship of women's tennis as a whole.

At the time of the Barnett lawsuit, several publications ran stories exploring the extent of homosexuality in professional sports. Some of these stories were sensationalist, calling lesbianism "rampant" in women's tennis and questioning whether homosexuals were appropriate role models for children. But other news outlets were more pro-gay in their approach to the issue, notably *Sports Illustrated,* which declared, "The sex lives of individual athletes are strictly their own business." One *Newsweek* writer wrote, "Billie Jean managed to turn a tawdry legal blackmail attempt by an ex-girlfriend into a personal portrait in courage."

In the decade after the scandal, King was largely out of the public eye. But she did make a bold appearance at a tribute to Navratilova in the summer of 1993. At a fund-raising event for the 1994 Gay Games (for which Navratilova was the spokeswoman), King thanked her fellow athlete (and partner in victory in the 1979 Wimbledon women's doubles tournament) for helping her understand her own sexuality. She declared, "One thing I love about Martina is that she demands acceptance on equal terms for all of us. Not tolerance but acceptance. Because she is comfortable in her own skin, she helps all of us be more comfortable in ours."

88. What was the "Queen for a Day Clause"?

The Defense Department's policy in the Reagan and Bush years insisted that homosexuality is incompatible with military service for a host of reasons, from good order and discipline to security. But under what many gay military insiders jokingly called the Queen for a Day Clause, commanders who had evidence of a service member's having engaged in homosexual behavior were allowed to *not* discharge him or her as long as the behavior occurred only once and the individual regretted it. Needless to say, this policy gave the military the discretion to keep some gay and lesbian soldiers and discharge others (and to let "wayward straights" off with just a warning if they misbehaved only once).

This selective enforcement has been even more marked during wartime, when the military has often allowed gays and lesbians to serve, only to discharge them when the war ends. During World War II there were dozens of cases of the Army overlooking evidence of homosexuality among otherwise-wanted military personnel. In perhaps the most famous example, Gen. Dwight D. Eisenhower ordered Johnnie Phelps, a sergeant in the Women's Army Corps, to produce a list of lesbians in her battalion. When Phelps warned the general that the list would be quite long and begin with her name at the top, Ike replied, "Forget the order."

During the Vietnam War, increased acceptance of homosexuality within society led to what the armed forces saw as a new problem: straight recruits pretending to be gay to avoid the draft. The solution was to demand "proof" from potential inductees who insisted they were gay—a psychiatrist's note or sworn statements from sexual partners. Of course, since sodomy was a felony in nearly every state, both straight and gay malingerers looked for other ways to resist the draft.

Journalist Randy Shilts documented many instances of military personnel sent to the Middle East to fight in the Gulf War who returned to face discharge proceedings. Indeed, beginning in September 1990 the Department of Defense's "Stop/Loss" policy phased out nearly all discharges of personnel the army deemed useful, and lesbian and gay soldiers (some relatively out) fought and risked their lives in the Persian Gulf.

The Queen for a Day Clause and the fact that gays and lesbians have rarely been discharged when the army needs them point to a clear contradiction in the military's policy. If gay people are a threat to security, good order, and discipline, then wartime should be the time when gays are ferreted out most meticulously. Indeed, by the early 1990s most supporters of the military's ban on gays and lesbians admitted that homosexuals had the capability to be excellent soldiers. Even pro-ban Sen. Sam Nunn—who until 1995 was the chair of the Senate Armed Services Committee—indicated that it was only open homosexuality that was a threat to the military and that discreet lesbian soldiers and celibate gay sailors were all right by him.

The Clinton-era policy of "don't ask, don't tell" was supposed to have rectified the situation outlined above by allowing gays to serve as long as they did not engage in same-sex behavior or share their sexual orientation with anyone. But the new policy actually resulted in more witch-hunts and discharge proceedings against gays and lesbians rather than fewer. If history is any guide, such discharges are likely to continue until the United States goes to war again and gay and lesbian service members are needed to defend the country.

89. What was the early media coverage of AIDS?

In the early 1980s, as the AIDS epidemic began to devastate urban gay male communities across the United States, the American press was slow to report on the disease and its spread. With a few notable exceptions, AIDS was largely absent from America's front pages, nightly news broadcasts, and even many gay and lesbian publications until 1983. The articles and reports on AIDS that did reach the public in the first few years of the disease ranged from understated to prudent to hysterical.

The first article to appear anywhere on AIDS—by physician Lawrence Mass in the gay biweekly the *New York Native*—was far from an alarm bell. Rather, Mass responded to gossip about a gay cancer spreading in New York City with a May 18, 1981, article headlined, DISEASE RUMORS LARGELY UNFOUNDED. The article indicated that pneumocystis carinii was a "ubiquitous" organism that shows up in a handful of sick people every year. This piece was published even before reports of the first AIDS cases appeared in the nation's medical journals or newsletters.

Two weeks later a story went out on the Associated Press wire about the possibility of an epidemic affecting gay men, and American newspapers, including the *Los Angeles Times,* ran articles. But the disease did not appear in the nation's leading publication, *The New York Times,* until July 3, when a brief article headlined RARE CANCER SEEN IN 41 HOMOSEXUALS appeared on page 20. In spare prose that was nonetheless terrifying for many gay men who read it, the *Times* reported: "Doctors in

New York and California have diagnosed among homosexual men 41 cases of a rare and often rapidly fatal form of cancer. Eight of the victims died less than 24 months after the diagnosis was made."

Further reports in the gay and lesbian press soon followed. Mass wrote a second, much longer article in the *New York Native* in late July entitled "Cancer in the Gay Community." The article's 170 column inches (compared to seven in the *Times'* first article) included interviews with medical researchers and speculation as to the ways the disease might be spread. The paper also published close-up photos of Kaposi's sarcoma lesions.

The Advocate took a different approach. In a brief article the same month, the leading national gay and lesbian biweekly reassured its readers with this headline: 'GAY' PNEUMONIA? NOT REALLY, SAYS RESEARCHER. The article paraphrased an official of the Centers for Disease Control and Prevention who disputed the idea of a "new form of pneumonia that supposedly attacks gay men." Instead, the magazine wrote, "all of the gay men tested thus far have had impaired immunity and this fact—not their homosexuality—made them vulnerable to the disease."

Over the next two years, a distinctive pattern emerged. The *Native* continued in-depth medical and social coverage of the disease, winning praise from other publications even as it lost advertising for becoming an "AIDS paper." Particularly noteworthy were Larry Kramer's *Native* pieces, which called for more funds and activism from a complacent gay and lesbian community. Other gay and lesbian papers developed their own approaches to the disease, from *The Washington Blade* and its focused coverage of the political repercussions of the epidemic to the San Francisco gay newspapers that debated the implications of AIDS on the sexual lives of gays and lesbians.

But the mainstream media remained largely silent. In 1982 *The New York Times* ran a total of seven articles on AIDS, most of them quite short. By contrast the "Tylenol scare" merited more than 50 articles in October and November of that year alone, even though only seven people had died from cyanide-laced pain relievers. West Coast publications gave the epidemic slightly more attention. The *Los Angeles Times* described the epidemic in a front-page story in May 1982, the same month the first of what would eventually be hundreds of articles on AIDS by Randy Shilts appeared in the *San Francisco Chronicle*.

The nightly network news broadcasts were equally reticent. AIDS was totally ignored in 1981, and in 1982 just six stories lasting a total of 13 minutes appeared on the nightly ABC, CBS, and NBC broadcasts. NBC went first, on June 17, 1982. Introducing the story, Tom Brokaw indicated that scientists had released a study "that shows that the lifestyle of some male homosexuals has triggered an epidemic of a rare form of cancer." CBS ran its first story in August, and ABC waited until October to cover the rapidly spreading epidemic.

Beginning in 1983 media attention to AIDS became less sporadic although usually couched in terms of the danger to the "general population." As evidence mounted of tainted blood supplies and cases among famous "nongays" (the first of which was, ironically, Rock Hudson), newspapers and broadcast outlets gave increasing attention to the disease. But clearly the relative silence of the media during the first two years of an epidemic perceived as affecting "others" was a contributing factor both to the spread of the disease and the meager initial public response to it.

90. What were the lesbian sex wars?

The first battles in the lesbian sex wars occurred in the late 1970s, when cultural feminism began to dominate the movement. Cultural feminists talked about lesbianism not as a sexual orientation but as a political choice and the logical extension of living as a feminist. In theory, any woman could be a lesbian as long as she was "woman-identified" and rejected men and their patriarchal structures. This take on lesbianism resulted in a playing down of lesbian sexual experience. Though plenty of lesbians were having sex, they weren't talking about it publicly.

"Acceptable" lesbian sexuality took on a narrow definition that branded many sexual practices as "politically incorrect" and the lesbians who enjoyed them as outlaws. S/M dykes were turned away from music festivals, and the butch-femme heritage of the 1950s and early 1960s was denounced. For some lesbian-feminists, any kind of penetration or "dirty talk" in sex was taboo, a mimicking of aggressive male sexuality.

Pornography was at the top of many lesbian-feminists' hate list. Citing statistics connecting rape with the viewing of porn, groups like Women Against Pornography launched a campaign to ban porn as discrimination against women. Some lesbians were also staunch critics of gay male porn because of its S/M content. What these women were unwilling to accept, though, was that some lesbians *liked* pornography, both straight and gay, and found it sexually arousing. Lesbians were even creating their own porn, but cultural feminists viewed them as having bought into men's oppression of women.

Self-identified lesbian sex radicals began raising their voices in protest. Fierce battles raged in lesbian-feminist newspapers and magazines, most of which were controlled by cultural feminists. In 1981 the feminist art and literary magazine *Heresies* shook up the community when it devoted an entire issue to politically incorrect sex. In one article Amber Hollibaugh summed up 1970s feminism: "You didn't talk dirty and you didn't want dirty.... You couldn't talk about wanting a woman, except very loftily."

To pursue a frank discussion of sexuality and challenge the lesbian "sex police," academic and activist feminists came together to plan a conference, held under the auspices of Barnard College's annual Scholar and the Feminist conference. "Toward a Politics of Sexuality" opened on April 24, 1982, with 800 women in attendance. Speakers such as Dorothy Allison, Cherrie Moraga, Joan Nestle, Esther Newton, and Gayle Rubin explored how feminists had oppressed each other by instituting right and wrong ways to have sex. Ironically, organizers of the conference were accused of engaging in a "feminist fascism" similar to that which they had endured. They excluded from the planning process anyone who wasn't in their view "pro-sex," primarily antiporn feminists. But other lesbians also got left out of the process if they were perceived as "vanilla" and hence not rebels.

Battle lines were drawn, and some of the excluded antiporn feminists engaged in a series of mean-spirited tactics. Before the conference, for example, they called Barnard's women's center to protest the participation in the conference of "known sadomasochists." During the conference, antiporn groups picketed outside, handing out flyers targeting panelists by name.

The day after the conference, the newly formed Lesbian Sex Mafia held its first public speak-out. As 200 women listened, volunteers stood up to talk about their experiences. "I love sex rough," Dorothy Allison boldly admitted, "and I have many fetishes. If it's possible to do it, I'll try it three times." Pat Califia openly declared herself a sadist, "and that is not spelled *r-a-p-i-s-t*."

The Barnard conference divided lesbian-feminists into opposing camps that continued to skirmish throughout the '80s, mostly in print. Battles over "porn" (incorrect) versus "erotica" (correct) were the most heated. Lesbian sex magazines like *Bad Attitude* and *On Our Backs* (a sly play on the name of the more politically correct newspaper *Off Our Backs*) appeared on the landscape. Throughout the 1980s, however, many women's bookstores refused to carry these publications on the grounds that they were pornography. Lesbians purchased them instead at gay bookstores, thus forging an alliance with gay men that carried into the fight against AIDS.

By the early 1990s there was a new generation of lesbians, many of whom had never heard of the Barnard conference, who embraced the culture introduced by lesbian sex radicals without really understanding its history. Sex clubs for lesbians, complete with back rooms like those in gay men's clubs, replaced the tamer women-only dances of the 1970s. Strap-ons and butt plugs entered the lesbian lexicon, and Susie Bright (a.k.a. Susie Sexpert) packed auditoriums with lesbians anxious to hear her ruminations on latex and labia piercing. But for those who couldn't identify with Bright, there was also JoAnn Loulan, whose common-sense advice books guided many through the sexual ups and downs of lesbian relationships.

While they were volatile and polarizing, the lesbian sex

wars opened up a fuller discussion of sexuality within the lesbian community, freeing women to say what they had been socialized not to say. In that way the sex wars helped usher in a more diverse era of lesbian sexual expression.

91. Why aren't the Gay Games called the Gay Olympics?

In 1982, Olympic decathlete Dr. Tom Waddell organized what he hoped would be a "Gay Olympics" in San Francisco. More than a thousand athletes from around the world came to San Francisco for the August event but arrived to find out the event's name had been changed to the "Gay Games" because of a court order secured by the U.S. Olympic Committee.

Of course, the USOC had no objection to the Police Olympics, the Special Olympics, or even the Canine Olympics, but the Gay Olympics was unacceptable to them. Waddell's organization sued, and the case went all the way to the Supreme Court.

In one of the highest-profile gay or lesbian cases ever to come before the nation's top court, the justices ruled 7–2 that the USOC did have the right to stop the gay olympiad from using the word *Olympics.* The case, *San Francisco Arts and Athletic* vs. *U.S. Olympic Committee,* held in effect that the Amateur Sports Act had given the USOC broad rights to determine who could and could not use the term *Olympics.*

The initial reaction among Gay Olympics supporters was anger and protest. The city of San Francisco even defied the initial court order and declared August 28, 1982, Gay Olympics Day. But soon the squabble over the name was overshadowed by the sense of power, unity, and fun that came with the largest-ever gay athletic competition. At the opening ceremonies for the Gay Games in 1986, again in San Francisco, writer Armistead Maupin told the more than 2,000 athletes gathered there that the important word was *gay* not *Olympics.*

The Gay Games have grown exponentially since then, with the 1990 games in Vancouver, Canada; the 1994 games in New York City; and the 1998 games in Amsterdam drawing thousands. Many of the athletes and spectators are not even aware of the early squabble over the event's name.

92. What did gays and lesbians write to President Reagan about?

While many lesbian and gay Americans vilified President Ronald Reagan for his right-wing politics and inaction during the AIDS epidemic, Reagan received more than just hate mail from America's lesbian and gay citizens during his presidency.

A 1996 Freedom of Information Act request produced a variety of letters to President and Mrs. Reagan on lesbian and gay concerns, some of which were quite poignant. A Florida man wrote the president in 1988 about being fired for being gay, then finding that he had no legal recourse to get his job back. The White House's response was to pass the letter along to the Equal Employment Opportunity Commission (even though firing gay employees has never been against federal law). A young man dying of AIDS-related complications in 1983 wrote the president anonymously, and a note in the Reagan files indicates the letter was considered "extremely sensitive" and passed to the Secret Service—presumably because the young man was considered a threat to the president's safety in some way.

Other letters were much more friendly. One, from Houston's Gay Political Caucus, invited President Reagan or a representative of his administration to speak at the 1983 Gay Pride Week rally in Houston. In a similar vein a director of the International Gay Bowling Tournament, held in Washington, D.C., in May 1988, requested a letter of welcome from Reagan to be distributed to the 1,500 gay bowlers who came to the nation's capital from all over the world.

It is difficult to say whether these letter writers were aware of the irony of their requests to an administration that regular-ly vilified gays and lesbians. Clearly, the Reagan White House would never have considered allowing the president to address a gay pride event or to welcome gays of any persuasion to Washington. But perhaps such requests were a self-conscious political maneuver to remind Reagan that he was the president of a country that includes gay and lesbian Americans.

93. When did Rock Hudson's homosexuality become public knowledge?

Rock Hudson is an excellent example of the complex nature of the closet and of public awareness of a prominent figure's homosexuality. Hudson was rumored to be gay from the earliest years of his career, yet some people denied he was gay even after he died of AIDS-related complications in 1985. As Hudson was both an active lover of men and the movie star who throughout the 1950s and 1960s seemed to personify manliness, his case is a textbook study of American anxieties over masculinity, sexuality, and fame.

Born in 1925, Hudson made his first major splash as an actor in the 1954 film *Magnificent Obsession,* in which he played an unruly playboy who becomes a surgeon. As a 29-year-old bachelor, though, Hudson raised eyebrows throughout 1950s America, and articles with headlines such as TOO BUSY FOR LOVE appeared in the popular press. The scandal-happy tabloid *Confidential* wanted to do an expose on Hudson's homosexuality and even offered his lover $10,000 to discuss the subject, but no story appeared. Some say that Universal Studios offered *Confidential* dirt on another of its stars in order to keep Hudson's sexuality out of the publication.

To quash the rumors Hudson quickly married Phyllis Gates (who Hudson later claimed was bisexual, although she denied that). The three-year marriage temporarily boosted Hudson's heterosexual image. But in the following decades, as Hudson established himself as a leading man in feature films and on

TV's *McMillan and Wife*, rumors about him continued to spread, although it was never discussed explicitly in print. In 1971 someone sent fake invitations to the wedding of Hudson and Jim Nabors (TV's Gomer Pyle) to several gossip columnists. Although the pair had been good friends, they were not lovers and certainly never married—but the hoax hurt Nabors's career. In Hudson's case none of the rumors seemed to slow his fame as a masculine idol or his pursuit of handsome men.

In the 1970s, Hudson became friends with Armistead Maupin, whose serial novel *Tales of the City* about gay and straight San Franciscans appeared in the *San Francisco Chronicle.* Maupin (among others) urged Hudson to come out and break down stereotypes about gays and lesbians. Hudson consistently demurred, considering his sexuality to be private and objecting to the public spectacle of the gay liberationists with their parades (which he once described as marching with a jar of Vaseline). Nonetheless, Hudson threw parties for dozens of handsome men and joined Maupin in exploring the sexual playground of 1970s San Francisco.

Maupin later satirized Hudson by including him as a character in *Tales of the City*, albeit identified only as _____. In one extended plotline Maupin's gay character Michael Tolliver visits _____'s Los Angeles home, where he sleeps with _____. The movie star questions Michael's participation in the Gay Men's Chorus, contemplating why people make such a big deal out of being gay. Michael tells his host that gay organizations make it easier for gay people to be proud of their heritage—a heritage Michael informs _____ he's a part of.

Hudson was diagnosed with AIDS in mid 1984, although his disease remained a secret for more than a year. When he appeared increasingly gaunt in his role on the prime-time soap

Dynasty and in public appearances, his publicists insisted that he was simply dieting. He looked particularly ill in his last professional appearance, which ironically was a commercial promoting his old friend Doris Day's new show on the Christian Broadcasting Network.

In July 1985 news of Hudson's disease hit the newspapers, garnering far more public attention about the disease than any previous AIDS-related story. Several newspapers and TV stations initially treated the story as proof that AIDS affected more than just gays and drug users. Amazingly, some gay-run AIDS organizations cooperated with this farce. A representative of one such organization even told the press that Hudson's illness proves that "AIDS is not a gay white male disease."

Soon, however, the *Chronicle* and several other newspapers ran lengthy stories about Hudson's decades-long struggle with vastly different public and private lives. The media coverage of Hudson's illness was often ridiculous: Several news outlets raised the question of whether Linda Evans might now be infected because she had kissed Hudson, her costar on *Dynasty*, on TV. Tasteless jokes abounded (Why is everyone in Hollywood terrified of AIDS? Because they've all had a piece of the Rock), but the widespread attention brought public awareness of the ongoing AIDS crisis to a new level. Calls to AIDS hot lines soared, and private-sector fund-raising for AIDS research skyrocketed, boosted by a $250,000 contribution from Hudson to jump-start the American Foundation for AIDS Research.

94. What is the history of the AIDS quilt?

The Names Project AIDS Memorial Quilt is the brainchild of Cleve Jones, a longtime San Francisco politico who, as a college student in the 1970s, interned for openly gay city supervisor Harvey Milk. Jones was one of the organizers of San Francisco's annual candlelight march to commemorate Milk's assassination and to celebrate his contributions to that city's gay, lesbian, and bisexual community. As he prepared for the 1985 march, he learned that more than 1,000 San Franciscans had already died of AIDS-related complications.

Searching for a way to display such a large number, Jones invited marchers to write the names of a friend or loved one who had died on a piece of cardboard. When the march arrived at San Francisco's old Federal Building, the participants taped their pieces of cardboard to the wall, forming a mosaic of names that struck Jones as a quilt.

The next year Jones made what was to be the first panel of the Names Project AIDS Memorial Quilt, in memory of his friend Marvin Feldman. Jones began encouraging friends to make their own panels and, along with Names Project general manager Mike Smith, started raising money and organizing to bring as many panels as possible to the October 1987 march on Washington for a public display. As he prepared for the quilt display, Jones found out that he was HIV-positive himself.

The nearly 2,000 panels of the quilt were one of the most striking—and enduring—aspect of the 1987 march. Thousands and thousands of gay and lesbian Americans who were sorrowful, angry, and wearied from the toll of the epidemic were extremely moved by the sheer power of so many personalized panels. The next spring the quilt toured 20 American cities, raising a half million dollars for AIDS service organizations and collecting thousands of additional panels. When the quilt was shown in its entirety in Washington, D.C., in October 1988, it had more than quadrupled in size. The quilt continued to grow, with panels pouring in to the Names Project's San Francisco office from all over the country and the world. Portions of the quilt were displayed in hundreds of communities, and subsequent full displays in Washington in 1989, 1992, and 1996 attracted thousands of visitors, many of whom wept silently as a voice on a loudspeaker read name after name of people memorialized by a panel in the quilt.

The panels of the quilt commemorate the rich and famous as well as the poor and anonymous. Many quilt panels incorporate items that were important to the deceased, from wedding rings to love letters to Boy Scout uniforms. A few even include ashes from the deceased.

The quilt has become the most prominent symbol of the AIDS epidemic. The documentary *Common Threads: Stories From the Quilt* won an Academy Award in 1989, and that same year the Names Project is said to have been considered for a Nobel Peace Prize.

The quilt has attracted some criticism, from Christian right-wingers who called it a "gerbil blanket" and from AIDS activists who called it a "boo-hoo rag," feeling the quilt has drained energy away from the crucial political battles needed to provide health care to the sick and find a cure. But the quilt has also helped many Americans—straight people in particular—see AIDS as a disease they should care about. Quite a few panels have been sewn by parents who were estranged from their gay sons because of their religious beliefs, who never would have contributed to a gay organization or cause, but who saw the quilt as a way to express their feelings of loss. Visitors to quilt displays often come away with a better sense of the diversity of the people struck by the epidemic and the toll the disease has taken—not only on its gay and straight victims but on their family members, lovers, and friends.

This impact is no accident. The quilt's originators consciously drew on an old American tradition of quilt making, a form of art and craftsmanship that brought communities together. As Jones, a long-term survivor of HIV, wrote, "We chose the symbol of the quilt in a deliberate effort to evoke and recapture the traditional American values that had yet to be applied to this apparently 'nontraditional' situation—values of cooperation, mutual respect and individual freedom."

95. What were Liberace's legal victories?

Undoubtedly the most flamboyant entertainer of the century, Wladziu Valentino Liberace was also one of the most fiercely closeted. On three separate occasions the showman hired lawyers to help keep his homosexuality secret, each time defeating those who alleged that he was gay. The entertainer who absolutely reveled in gay stereotypes—from poodles to pink sequins—insisted on a heterosexual facade until the day he died of AIDS-related complications.

Liberace first went to court to swear to his status as a red-blooded American male in 1956, when a columnist for the *London Daily Mirror* called him, among other things, a "fruit-flavored, mincing, ice-covered heap of mother love." Liberace sued for damages and in the trial testified that his bachelor status was only temporary. "I am always looking around for a pretty girl to marry," he said under oath. "I have 12 proposals a month, and on Valentine's Day I got 27,000 Valentines."

This testimony came after more than a decade of sexual liaisons between Liberace and other men. But when Liberace was asked in court about his feelings toward homosexuality, he replied, "My feelings are the same as anyone else, sir. I am against this practice because it offends convention and it offends society."

William Connor, the columnist whose mockery of Liberace had occasioned the lawsuit, defended himself by denying that the column implied that Liberace was gay, even arguing that the words *fruit* and *fairy* have gay connotations only in America and not in Britain. The jury did not believe him, and his publication was forced to pay more than $20,000 in damages. Liberace later wrote that he felt his manhood had been vindicated by the verdict.

A year later the American scandalmongering publication *Confidential* ran a cover story entitled "Why Liberace's Theme Song Should Be 'Mad About the Boy.'" Liberace sued, and the parties settled out of court, this time enriching the entertainer and his attorneys by $40,000.

Thirty years later Liberace once again found himself in court defending himself against an accusation of homosexuality, this time in a palimony suit filed by his former chauffeur and lover, Scott Thorson. Thorson had met Liberace in 1977, when the younger man was 18 and the entertainer was more than three times his age. Liberace had invited a series of good-looking, young blond men into his many bedrooms in his many homes, but his relationship with Thorson was longer and by all accounts more devoted.

During their five-year relationship, Liberace showered Thorson with hundreds of gifts, investigated the possibility of legally adopting him, and paid for plastic surgery so the younger man could look more like his patron. Thorson's memoir describes Liberace as sexually ravenous, with a fondness for poppers, porno tapes, and multiple sex partners. Toward the end of their relationship, Thorson became increasingly dependent on cocaine, while Liberace increasingly had his eye on other young men.

In March 1982, Thorson was evicted from one of Liberace's apartments and given $75,000 in exchange for waiving future claims. But he soon argued he had agreed under duress and was entitled to $113 million in damages because Liberace had

promised to take care of all Thorson's financial needs in exchange for companionship and sex. Two years later a Nevada
judge threw Thorson's lawsuit out of court by holding that a
"money for sex" arrangement was prostitution, which even in
Nevada did not entitle Thorson to a permanent share of Liberace's income. Thorson's lawyers refused to drop the matter,
though, and in 1986, Liberace agreed to a final payment of
$95,000 to end the legal maneuvers.

By that time Liberace's health had begun to waver from
AIDS. Despite an increasingly gaunt appearance, the entertainer played to sold-out crowds in Radio City Music Hall, where
he made a grand entrance by flying above the audience on ca-
bles. When questioned about Liberace's weight loss, his manager told the press that Liberace was on a "watermelon diet"
and was in generally good health. Not until Liberace's coroner
held a nationally televised press conference were AIDS-related
complications revealed as the cause of death, and to this day
some of the devoted elderly women who conduct tours at the
Liberace Museum in Las Vegas insist that Liberace's so-called
homosexuality and AIDS are nothing but cruel rumors about a
talented bachelor.

Liberace's life was replete with contradictions about his
sexuality. His autobiography states that he lost his virginity to
a female singer in Milwaukee—yet he gives her the classically
drag-sounding name of "Miss Bea Haven." He would introduce
his lover to his audiences as his companion—yet he told the
press that gays were trying to "assassinate" him with Thorson's
lawsuit. With his extravagant costumes and flaming style, his
life can be seen as a befuddled attempt to argue that you don't
have to be gay to be campy.

96. What was Bowers v. Hardwick?

On June 30, 1986, the U.S. Supreme Court announced its devastating decision in the case of *Bowers* v. *Hardwick*, in which the court held that sodomy laws were constitutional.

Before the Hardwick case civil rights attorneys had spent nearly a decade looking for an ideal case with which to challenge the constitutionality of laws forbidding sodomy. In the last several decades, such laws have rarely been enforced, and arrests have almost never been made without complicating factors such as coercion or sex with a minor. So when Michael Hardwick was arrested for sodomy in Georgia in 1982, gay and lesbian activists latched onto the case even though the charges were soon dropped. Hardwick's case seemed tailor-made to show how sodomy laws violate a person's privacy: A police officer intent on serving a warrant entered Hardwick's bedroom and arrested him after observing him engaged in mutual oral sex with another man.

Influenced by the right to privacy established by previous cases, including *Roe* v. *Wade*, one court of appeals held that sexual activity in private between consenting adults was protected by the Constitution from government interference. The attorney general of Georgia, right-wing Republican Michael Bowers, appealed the case to the Supreme Court in order to defend his state's sodomy law.

Georgia's sodomy ban applies to same-sex and opposite-sex couples, including married heterosexuals, and Hardwick's attorneys found a married Georgia couple, "John and Mary Doe," who claimed that the sodomy law invaded their privacy as well. But the Supreme Court quickly rejected their claim and ruled on the narrower question of, in the words of the majority opinion, "whether the Federal Constitution confers a fundamental right upon homosexuals to engage in sodomy and hence invalidates the laws of the many States that still make such conduct illegal and have done so for a very long time."

Justice Byron White (succeeded in 1993 by Ruth Bader Ginsberg) penned the 5–4 majority opinion, which used sweeping, derisive language to mock the idea that gay Americans have a right to sexual privacy in their homes. Judge Harry Blackmun's dissent strongly disagreed, arguing that "depriving individuals of the right to choose for themselves how to conduct their intimate relationships poses a far greater threat to the values most deeply rooted in our Nation's history than tolerance of nonconformity could ever do."

But these two opinions don't tell the whole story of the ruling in *Bowers* v. *Hardwick*. When the case first came before the members of the court in April 1986, there were four justices who considered sodomy laws unconstitutional and four who thought them totally legitimate. In the middle was Lewis Powell Jr., a moderate jurist who in several previous cases had sought compromises between extreme positions. Powell initially indicated support for overturning the sodomy laws but was ultimately convinced by Chief Justice Warren Burger to switch his vote. In the meantime Powell received heavy pressure from both sides among his law clerks, including a conservative Mormon and a liberal, somewhat closeted gay man.

Powell's gay clerk on several occasions considered coming out to his boss but instead settled for an impassioned argument in favor of sexual freedom. In light of Powell's remark

after the decision that he didn't know any gay or lesbian people, some activists have suggested that the clerk's coming out
could have made the difference in Powell's vote. Indeed, in
1990, Powell indicated that upon further reflection he regretted his vote in the case.

The ruling in *Bowers* v. *Hardwick* was handed down on June
30, 1986, just one day after gay and lesbian pride celebrations
took place in major cities across America. The reaction among
the organized gay and lesbian community was one of outrage
and was one the major factors—along with the government's
sluggish response to the AIDS crisis—in the decision to call for
a march on Washington in October 1987.

97. Who was Terry Dolan?

On December 28, 1986, Terry Dolan, a key conservative activist of the 1980s, died of AIDS-related complications. Even as a child Dolan was active in Republican politics, volunteering for Richard Nixon's 1960 presidential campaign. When he was 25 he helped organize the National Conservative Political Action Committee, and he soon became that organization's director. Dolan was an extremely talented fund-raiser, and many credit him and the NCPAC with the stunning triumph of the New Right in 1980. Dolan worked hard for the nomination and election of Ronald Reagan as president, although his influence was equally significant in the defeat of liberal senators such as George McGovern, Frank Church, and Birch Bayh. The conservatives who replaced them (including Dan Quayle) gave the Republicans a majority in the Senate for the first time in a generation.

Dolan was also gay. He was a regular in the gay cocktail-party circuit of Washington, D.C., and often vacationed at gay resorts such as Northern California's Russian River. But Dolan's relationship to the gay rights movement was complex. Philosophically, Dolan was opposed to gay rights laws, insisting that the government shouldn't interfere in people's hiring practices. He balanced that view with a strong defense of privacy—which makes sense because a decade before "outing," he relied on the gay community's discretion to keep him from being discredited among his conservative peers.

In 1982 he granted an interview to *The Advocate* magazine

in which he repeated his support for privacy and criticized "some of the rhetoric that some of my friends in the Right have used on gay activism." Dolan later denied those comments and was not above using antigay rhetoric himself. NCPAC sent out a fund-raising letter that declared "the nation's moral fiber is being weakened by the growing homosexual movement and the fanatical ERA pushers (many of whom publicly brag that they are lesbians)." Some say Dolan approved the letter, although he apologized for it to *The New York Times,* calling it "totally inappropriate."

In the early 1980s, Dolan joined with former Republican congressman Robert Bauman, famed discharged gay Vietnam veteran Leonard Matlovich, and several other gay conservatives to found the Concerned Americans for Individual Rights. Unlike the gay group Log Cabin Republicans, CAIR found little success. Few members were willing to take leadership roles if it meant publicity, and while many gay conservatives offered words of encouragement and cash donations, few would write checks or allow their names to be associated with the group. At one point the group proposed to send out a fund-raising letter to find conservatives who would support gay rights, and several of the organizers are said to have requested the names and addresses of any antigay responses so they could target those individuals with homophobic fund-raising appeals. By the time of Dolan's death, CAIR had largely faded away.

When Dolan began to get sick with AIDS-related complications, he insisted publicly that he suffered from anemia and diabetes. When he died his family held a memorial service that excluded Dolan's gay friends. Instead, conservative mourners such as Pat Buchanan and Utah senator Orrin Hatch came to pay their respects to a key architect of the conservative revolution in American government. A separate service was held by Bauman and others who wanted to remember Dolan for all that he was. *The Washington Post* accurately reported Dolan's cause of death and later ran a long article about his homosexuality. The conservative activist's family and straight friends were furious. His brother Tony Dolan, a noted Reagan speech writer, even took out a two-page ad in the *Washington Times* insisting that Terry Dolan was not gay.

What can we make of a person whose personal and political lives seem so contradictory? Many would settle for a simple answer: Dolan was a self-hating homosexual who never became comfortable with his sexual orientation and expressed his discomfort by trying to hurt all gays and lesbians. But the truth is probably more complicated than that. There is no inherent "gay position" on issues such as military spending or taxes, and an individual, regardless of sexual orientation, who feels that conservatives are right on such issues may find himself or herself facing the same challenges Dolan did. The conflict between advancing causes an individual believes in and maintaining dignity as a gay person become almost insoluble. Given the slow response to the AIDS epidemic from the administration he helped put in place, Terry Dolan's death made for a final irony in a life full of paradox.

98. How was ACT UP founded?

In March 1987 the AIDS Coalition to Unleash Power was born, combining anger at the continuing epidemic with media savvy, artistic creativity, and street smarts to reshape the way AIDS was viewed in the United States and around the world.

ACT UP by no means invented direct-action techniques for bringing about changes in the government and social responses to the AIDS epidemic. San Francisco activists held AIDS-related demonstrations as early as 1984, and in the months prior to ACT UP's founding, a group of Manhattan-based gay activists called the Lavender Hill Mob staged a series of protests. But ACT UP was different, both for its ability to draw large numbers of activists and for its high media profile.

The idea for a new, widespread campaign to expand access to experimental AIDS drugs was generated by a remarkable evening at New York City's Lesbian and Gay Community Services Center on Tuesday, March 10, 1987. The scheduled speaker in the center's monthly writer's night, Nora Ephron, canceled at the last minute, to be replaced by author, playwright, and Gay Men's Health Crisis founder Larry Kramer. Kramer, who was the first person ever to call for funds to combat AIDS, had grown estranged from GMHC. But he remained committed to the idea that the gay and lesbian community needed to fight back against those he held most responsible for the spread of the disease: the government, the medical establishment, the media, and complacent gay leaders.

Kramer was expected to read from his works, and the audience was expected to listen politely and ask questions. That's not what happened. Instead, Kramer asked that the lights be turned up, and he reminded those assembled that at least 32,000 people had died of AIDS-related complications. He invited two thirds of the room to stand and told them, "At the rate we are going, you could be dead in five years." He went on to attack the slow rate of release of new AIDS drugs and implicated politicians like New York governor Mario Cuomo, publications like *The New York Times,* and organizations like GMHC in not pushing for more drugs to fight AIDS. Then he asked, "Do we want to start a new organization devoted solely to political action?"

During the question-and-answer period (which turned into a group discussion), the answer clearly became yes. Those assembled spread the word about Kramer's talk, and two nights later 300 people met and created ACT UP. The organization's mission was later expanded to other issues, but in 1987 it devoted itself to pushing for the early release of any experimental drug that could combat AIDS.

ACT UP's strategy of in-your-face activism had its public debut on March 24, 1987, when more than 200 activists descended on Wall Street to protest the high prices for AIDS drugs being charged by Burroughs Wellcome, the pharmaceutical company which the Food and Drug Administration approved to market AZT. ACT UP brought traffic to halt, burned the FDA commissioner in effigy, and had 17 of its members arrested for acts of civil disobedience.

The Wall Street action garnered considerable media attention, as did a protest at New York City's main post office on April 15. The post office was jam packed with New Yorkers filing last-minute tax returns and television cameras reporting on the rush to beat the deadline. The activists used the occasion to protest how few tax dollars were going to fight the epidemic. This protest also marked the first time ACT UP used placards with the slogan SILENCE=DEATH, usually printed next to a pink triangle. Throughout its history ACT UP used these placards and other artwork to portray their ideas and feelings about the politics of AIDS.

A flood of other demonstrations followed this first month of initial organizing as ACT UP chapters sprouted up around the country and attendance at meetings of the New York chapter reached 600 or more. The national headquarters of the FDA in Maryland were nearly shut down in October of 1988, and in September of 1989 half a dozen ACT UP members sneaked into the New York Stock Exchange, stopping trading for five minutes. Perhaps ACT UP's most controversial demonstration was known as "Stop the Church," when in December 1989 thousands of protesters picketed St. Patrick's Cathedral, and the media captured images of activists throwing condoms at priests and reported on a protester who deliberately dropped a communion wafer on the floor.

Although ACT UP has declined from its peak of more than 100 chapters worldwide, its members still push for more government action to fight AIDS. Its members have gained a reputation for in-depth knowledge of both the science and the politics of AIDS drugs, and it is no longer unusual for ACT UP members to be involved in high-level policy discussions.

99. Was Barney Frank the first gay congressman?

Barney Frank was the first congressman to come out as gay by his own choice, but there have been several other gay and probably gay members of Congress over the years. Some were exposed while in office (usually because of an arrest for public sex), and some came out after retirement.

Some examples of members of Congress who were exposed for pursuing gay sex while in office:

- New York Democrat Fred Richmond, who was charged in 1978 with paying a 16-year-old boy for sex.
- Right-wing Republican Jon Hinson, who pled not guilty in connection with his two arrests for public sex while in office, one in 1976 at the Iwo Jima Memorial and one five years later in a House of Representatives office building; the Mississippi representative later admitted, "I look back now and see that I was a gay man trying to lie to myself."
- Fellow right-winger Robert Bauman, a Republican from Maryland, who lost his bid for reelection in 1980 in the face of publicity about his arrest for soliciting sex with a 16-year-old boy; Bauman at first denied being gay, but a few years later he came out publicly, ultimately writing a book detailing his life as a closeted, conservative congressman.

Other members of Congress came out or were revealed as gay, lesbian, or bisexual after they retired. One example is Republican Stewart McKinney of Connecticut, who in 1987 be-

came the first former member of Congress to die of AIDS-related complications. Another was pioneering black congresswoman Barbara Jordan, a Democrat from Texas whose long-
term lesbian relationship was revealed after her death in 1997.

There have been five "out and proud" members of Congress
so far:

- Massachusetts Democrat Gerry Studds, who in 1983 was
  censured by the House for having sex with a 17-year-old
  male congressional page not long after he was first elected
  to in 1972; Studds responded to the censure by proudly affirming his homosexuality—and was reelected six times after
  coming out.
- Frank, also of Massachusetts, who came out in an interview
  with *The Boston Globe* in May 1987; Frank was involved in
  a scandal a few years later involving a former prostitute
  who worked for him and claimed he used Frank's Washington home as a base for prostitution. Frank was reprimanded
  by Congress in 1990 and has since been reelected three
  times. In 1995, Frank was in the news because House Majority Leader Dick Armey "accidentally" referred to him as
  "Barney Fag" while speaking to reporters.
- Steve Gunderson of Wisconsin, who was the first openly gay
  Republican member of Congress; in 1991 a gay activist confronted Gunderson in a suburban Washington bar, throwing
  a drink on his face when he refused to commit to coming
  out publicly. The incident was reported in the media both in
  the capital and in Wisconsin, and Gunderson slowly moved
  toward greater support for gay rights issues as well as increased openness about his own sexual orientation. By 1994
  he had come out publicly in *The Advocate* magazine and

was returned to office for a final term in the Republican
sweep that November.

- Jim Kolbe of Arizona, a Republican who came out in 1996
when he was threatened with being "outed" after he voted
for the antigay Defense of Marriage Act; since coming out,
Kolbe has supported gay causes in the House while maintaining his conservative credentials and winning reelection.
- Tammy Baldwin of Wisconsin, whose 1998 victory broke
two lavender ceilings: She is the first out lesbian in Congress
and the first gay person elected who was out before winning a seat in the House.

100. What was the custody battle over Sharon Kowalski?

The ongoing discussions and debates over the question of same-sex marriage have to be understood in the context of the decades-long struggle by same-sex couples for legal recognition of their relationships. In the 1980s no couple did more to raise awareness of the injustice of American family law than Karen Thompson and Sharon Kowalski.

In 1979, Thompson and Kowalski became lovers, exchanging rings and naming each other as life-insurance beneficiaries. Living in the town of St. Cloud, Minn., neither was public about her lesbian identity nor was the nature of their relationship clear to anyone but their closest friends. Thompson and Kowalski were anything but gay rights activists; Thompson even voted for Ronald Reagan for president in 1980.

A tragic accident on a Sunday night in November 1983 changed all that. Kowalski, then 28, was hit by a drunk driver while driving her car, and she suffered severe brain damage, losing the ability to walk, care for herself, or even speak more than a few words at a time. During the first several months of Kowalski's hospitalization, Thompson was at her side, providing love and support during her painstaking recovery. At first the Kowalski family thought Thompson was a good friend, and they appreciated her help. But eventually Sharon's parents began to ask questions about the nature of the pair's relationship, and with a psychologist's guidance Thompson explained that Sharon was her lover.

The Kowalskis did not take the news well. Calling Thompson "sick" and "crazy," they denied her further visitation rights and even accused her of sexually abusing their disabled daughter. They moved Sharon to another Minnesota facility several hours from Thompson's home—even though several doctors had noted that Sharon responded best to therapy when she was in Thompson's presence and even though Sharon repeatedly indicated her desire to be reunited with her lover.

An intense legal battle ensued. At first Thompson focused on the right to visit her lover. The Kowalskis and Minnesota courts denied her that right for almost four years. Thompson gave speeches and raised funds for her legal battle throughout the nation, even writing a book entitled *Why Can't Sharon Kowalski Come Home?* The couple's plight became a rallying point for lesbian activists throughout the country—but it also resonated with gay men, many of whom were dealing with similar legal issues as AIDS repeatedly pitted devoted lovers against antigay parents. In August 1988 more than a dozen cities around the country held "Free Sharon Kowalski Day" rallies to raise public awareness of the case.

In January 1989, Thompson finally won the right to visit her lover, although Sharon's father Donald remained Sharon's legal guardian. When the pair reunited, Sharon was moved to tears and typed "I love you" on her keyboard.

But Thompson's legal battle was not over. Donald Kowalski had recently petitioned the court to be released from his legal guardianship of his daughter due to his own health concerns. Despite the fact that Thompson was the only individual to petition for guardianship, a Minnesota court awarded custody of Sharon Kowalski to a woman it called a "neutral third party." A friend of the Kowalski family, Karen Tomberlin was anything but neutral. Tomberlin had shown little interest in Sharon other than to keep her away from her lesbian lover. In awarding guardianship to Tomberlin, the court criticized Thompson for invading Sharon's privacy by publicly revealing her as a lesbian and using her situation to raise money. Thompson, who had never before been a political activist or even openly lesbian, had a simple response: If she didn't reveal the nature of their relationship, how could she argue that she had a right to visitation? And if she didn't raise money for legal fees, how could she defend her position in court?

The case finally came to an end in 1991, when a Minnesota court of appeals reversed the lower court's decision and awarded guardianship to Thompson. The court's decision contained words of encouragement for lesbian and gay activists who hoped the government would move toward greater recognition of same-sex families:

> All the medical testimony established that Sharon has the capacity reliably to express a preference in this case, and she has clearly chosen to return home with Thompson if possible. This choice is further supported by the fact that Thompson and Sharon are a family of affinity, which ought to be accorded respect.

101. Was Bill Clinton the first presidential candidate to openly support gay and lesbian rights?

Gay and lesbian voters in the 1992 presidential election were energized by Arkansas governor Bill Clinton's campaign promises on a wide range of community issues, from AIDS to lesbians and gays in the military. Gays and lesbians provided Clinton's election campaign with crucial dollars, volunteers, and votes, helping provide the margin of victory in states such as Georgia and Ohio. But the gay and lesbian community has played an active role in many previous presidential campaigns, sometimes with significant support from the candidates.

In fact, the most important gay rights organization of the 1950s, the Mattachine Society, was originally conceived as a way for gay men to support a presidential candidate: progressive former vice president Henry Wallace. Gay rights pioneer Harry Hay attempted to organize among gay men he knew in Los Angeles, and some of them suggested he call their group Fruits for Wallace or Queers for Wallace. Hay instead proposed Bachelors for Wallace, but the group never really advanced past the idea stage.

Perhaps because of McCarthyism, perhaps because of the lack of an appealing candidate, gays and lesbians as a group largely stayed out of the presidential elections of the 1950s and 1960s. But in 1972 the Democrats nominated a candidate who had publicly supported gay rights as early as 1970: George McGovern. Many gays and lesbians had worked hard for Mc-Govern during the primaries, and in return McGovern allowed a convention debate about including a gay rights plank in the party's platform.

Thus, San Francisco gay activist Jim Foster and Buffalo lesbian activist Madeline Davis addressed the convention on national television in support of lesbian and gay rights. Twenty years later many newspapers reported Roberta Achtenberg's 1992 Democratic Convention speech as the first such address by an openly gay person, having apparently forgotten about the remarkable moment in 1972 when Foster told the convention and the nation:

> We do not come to you pleading your understanding or begging your tolerance…. We come to you affirming our pride in our lifestyle, affirming the validity of our right to seek and to maintain meaningful emotional relationships, and affirming our right to participate in the life of this country on an equal basis with every citizen.

Despite McGovern's earlier promises (he even ran ads in *The Advocate* magazine), the candidate later backed off his pro-gay stands under the pressure of a homophobic general public. Sound familiar?

Presidential candidate Jimmy Carter declared support for gay rights early in 1976 and even sent his handsome son Chip to campaign in the Castro during the California primary. A month before the convention, however, he withdrew his support for a gay rights plank, effectively dooming the measure. Though activists threatened that 10,000 gays and lesbians would protest at a rally outside the New York City convention, fewer than a thousand actually showed up. During the general election, incumbent president Gerald Ford fared no better with gay voters, unable to even comment when Michigan gay activists buttonholed him about America's restrictions on gay immigrants.

In 1980, Carter again refused to support a gay rights plank in the Democratic platform, and much of the gay and lesbian activist vote in the primaries went to Sen. Edward Kennedy. Of course, in the general election Ronald Reagan was the other choice, so most voters for whom gay rights was a main issue held their noses and voted for the defeat-bound incumbent.

Early in his campaign for the 1984 Democratic presidential nomination, former vice president Walter Mondale took the risky step of addressing over 1,000 gay activists at a human rights dinner at the Waldorf-Astoria in New York City. Mondale was received enthusiastically despite the fact that he never mentioned gay rights in his speech. A 100,000-strong gay rights march outside the Democratic National Convention that year helped ensure the passage of several gay rights planks, including one relating to AIDS research, in the Democratic platform.

Neither Gov. Michael Dukakis nor Vice President George Bush aroused much enthusiasm among gays and lesbians in the 1988 elections. In fact, the only candidate who elicited strong support within the organized gay and lesbian community was the Rev. Jesse Jackson, whose moving speech at the 1987 march on Washington and consistent inclusion of gays and lesbians in his Rainbow Coalition convinced many liberal gay Democrats that he was their best candidate in years.

In the 1992 election all the Democratic candidates (Clinton, Tom Harkin, Jerry Brown, Paul Tsongas, and Bob Kerrey) came out in support of gay and lesbian rights early in the primary season. In the general election, of course, Clinton stood out from George Bush and Ross Perot in his consistent promises on gay rights and AIDS issues.

Suggested Reading

Anderson, Jervis. *Bayard Rustin: Troubles I've Seen* (Harper-Collins, 1997).

Bayer, Ronald. *Homosexuality and American Psychiatry* (BasicBooks, 1981).

Beemyn, Brett, and Mickey Eliason, eds. *Queer Studies: A Lesbian, Gay, Bisexual, and Transgender Anthology* (New York University Press, 1996).

Bell, Arthur. *Dancing the Gay Lib Blues: A Year in the Homosexual Liberation Movement* (Simon & Schuster, 1971).

Benstock, Shari. *Women of the Left Bank* (University of Texas Press, 1986).

Bérubé, Allan. *Coming Out Under Fire: The History of Gay Men and Lesbians in World War II* (Plume, 1991).

Bérubé, Allan. "The History of Gay Bathhouses." *Coming Up!* vol. 6, no. 3 (December, 1984).

Bockris, Victor. *Warhol* (De Capo, 1997).

Caffrey, Margaret. *Ruth Benedict: Stranger in the Land* (University of Texas Press, 1989).

Cayleff, Susan E. *Babe: The Life and Legend of Babe Didrikson Zaharias* (University of Illinois Press, 1995).

Chauncey, George. *Gay New York: Gender, Urban Culture, and the Making of the Gay Male World, 1890–1940* (BasicBooks, 1994).

Cheney, Anne. *Lorraine Hansberry* (Twayne, 1984).

Cline, Sally. *Radclyffe Hall: A Woman Called John* (Overlook, 1998).

Cook, Blanche Wiesen. *Eleanor Roosevelt. Vol. 1, 1884–1933* (Viking, 1992).

Curtin, Kaier. *"We Can Always Call Them Bulgarians": The Emergence of Lesbians and Gay Men on the American Stage* (Alyson, 1987).

Davis, Angela Y. *Blues Legacies and Black Feminism: Gertrude "Ma" Rainey, Bessie Smith, and Billie Holiday* (Pantheon, 1998).

D'Emilio, John. *Sexual Politics, Sexual Communities: The Making of a Homosexual Minority in the United States, 1940–1970* (University of Chicago Press, 1983).

D'Emilio, John, and Estelle B. Freedman. *Intimate Matters: A History of Sexuality in America* (Harper & Row, 1988).

Duberman, Martin. *Stonewall* (Dutton, 1993).

Duberman, Martin, Martha Vicinus and George Chauncey Jr., eds. *Hidden From History: Reclaiming the Lesbian and Gay Past* (New American Library, 1989).

Creekmur, Corey, and Alexander Doty, eds. *Out in Culture: Gay, Lesbian, and Queer Essays on Popular Culture* (Duke University Press, 1995).

Ellmann, Richard. *Oscar Wilde* (Vintage, 1988).

Faderman, Lillian. *Odd Girls and Twilight Lovers: A History of Lesbian Life in Twentieth-Century America* (Columbia University Press, 1991).

Faderman, Lillian. *Surpassing the Love of Men: Romantic Friendship and Love Between Women From the Renaissance to the Present* (Morrow, 1981).

Feinberg, Leslie. *Transgender Warriors: Making History From Joan of Arc to Dennis Rodman* (Beacon, 1997).

Gerassi, John. *The Boys of Boise* (Macmillan, 1966).

Grahn, Judy. *Another Mother Tongue: Gay Words, Gay Worlds*, rev. ed. (Beacon, 1990).

Hippler, Mike. *Leonard Matlovich: The Good Soldier* (Alyson, 1989).

Hooven, F. Valentine, III. *Beefcake: The Muscle Magazines of America, 1950–1970* (Taschen, 1995).

Jay, Karla. *The Amazon and the Page* (Indiana University Press, 1988).

Jeffery-Poulter, Stephen. *Peers, Queers, and Commons* (Routledge, 1991).

Jones, James H. *Alfred C. Kinsey: A Public/Private Life* (W.W. Norton, 1997).

Jorgensen, Christine. *Christine Jorgensen: A Personal Autobiography* (Paul Eriksson, 1967).

Katz, Jonathan Ned. *Gay/Lesbian Almanac: A New Documentary* (Carroll & Graf, 1994).

Katz, Jonathan Ned. *Gay American History: Lesbians and Gay Men in the U.S.A., A Documentary History,* rev. ed. (Meridian, 1992).

Kennedy, Elizabeth Lapovsky, and Madeline D. Davis. *Boots of Leather, Slippers of Gold: The Making of a Lesbian Community* (Routledge, 1993).

Kennedy, Hubert. *Ulrichs: The Life and Works of Karl Heinrich Ulrichs, Pioneer of the Modern Gay Movement* (Alyson, 1988).

Kopay, David, and Perry Deane Young. *The David Kopay Story: An Extraordinary Self-revelation* (Arbor House, 1977).

Leeming, David. *James Baldwin* (Knopf, 1994).

Leverich, Lyle. *Tom: The Unknown Tennessee Williams* (Crown, 1995).

Madsen, Axel. *The Sewing Circle: Hollywood's Greatest Secret: Female Stars Who Loved Other Women* (Birch Lane, 1995).

Marcus, Eric. *Making History: The Struggle for Gay and Lesbian Equal Rights, 1945–1990* (HarperCollins, 1992).

Martin, Del, and Phyllis Lyon. *Lesbian/Woman* (Bantam, 1970).

Middlebrook, Diane Woods. *Suits Me: The Double Life of Billy Tipton* (Houghton Mifflin, 1998).

Myron, Nancy, and Charlotte Bunch, eds. *Lesbianism and the Women's Movement* (Diana Press, 1975).

Newton, Esther. *Cherry Grove, Fire Island: Sixty Years in America's First Gay and Lesbian Town* (Beacon, 1993).

O'Brien, Sharon. *Willa Cather: The Emerging Voice* (Oxford University Press, 1987).

Palmieri, Patricia Ann. *In Adamless Eden: The Community of Women Faculty at Wellesley* (Yale University Press, 1995).

Plant, Richard. *The Pink Triangle* (Holt, 1986).

Reynolds, David S. *Walt Whitman: A Cultural Biography* (Knopf, 1995).

Roscoe, Will., ed. *Living the Spirit: A Gay American Indian Anthology* (St. Martin's, 1988).

Rowbotham, Sheila, and Jeffrey Weeks. *Socialism and the New Life: The Personal and Sexual Politics of Edward Carpenter and Havelock Ellis* (Pluto, 1977).

Rule, Jane. *Lesbian Images* (Crossing Press, 1975).

Russo, Vito. *The Celluloid Closet: Homosexuality in the Movies*, rev. ed. (Harper & Row, 1987).

Scott-Stokes, Henry. *The Life and Death of Yukio Mishima* (Farrar, Straus, Giroux, 1974).

Shilts, Randy. *Conduct Unbecoming: Gay and Lesbians in the U.S. Military* (St. Martin's, 1993).

Shilts, Randy. *And the Band Played On* (St. Martin's, 1987).

Shilts, Randy. *The Mayor of Castro Street: The Life and Times of Harvey Milk* (St. Martin's, 1982).

Signorile, Michelangelo. *Queer in America* (Random House, 1993).

Souhami, Diana. *Gertrude and Alice* (Pandora Books, 1991).

Spoto, Donald. *The Kindness of Strangers: The Life of Tennessee Williams* (Ballantine, 1985).

Steakley, James D. *The Homosexual Emancipation Movement in Germany* (Arno, 1975).

Streitmatter, Rodger. *Unspeakable: The Rise of the Gay and Lesbian Press in America* (Faber & Faber, 1995).

Summers, Anthony. *Official and Confidential: The Secret Life of J. Edgar Hoover* (Victor Gollancz, 1993).

Summers, Claude J., ed. *The Gay and Lesbian Literary Heritage* (Holt, 1995).

Summers, Claude J. *E.M. Forster* (Ungar, 1983).

Teal, Donn. *The Gay Militants* (Stein & Day, 1971).

Thompson, Mark, ed. *The Long Road to Freedom: The Advocate History of the Gay and Lesbian Movement* (St. Martin's, 1994).

Timmons, Stuart. *The Trouble With Harry Hay: Founder of the Modern Gay Movement* (Alyson, 1990).

Vance, Carole S., ed. *Pleasure and Danger: Exploring Female Sexuality* (Routledge & Kegan Paul, 1984).

Watson, Steven. *The Harlem Renaissance: Hub of African-American Culture, 1920–1930* (Pantheon, 1995).

Wineapple, Brenda. *Genêt: A Biography of Janet Flanner* (University of Nebraska Press, 1989).

Young, Allen. *Gays Under the Cuban Revolution* (Grey Fox, 1981).

Young, Perry Deane. *Lesbians and Gays in Sports* (Chelsea House, 1995).

Zimmerman, Bonnie. *The Safe Sea of Women: Lesbian Fiction, 1969–1989* (Beacon, 1990).